D0152355

PROFESSIONAL ETHICS IN EDUCATION SERIES

Kenneth A. Strike, Editor

The Ethics of School Administration
Kenneth A. Strike, Emil J. Haller, and Jonas F. Soltis

Classroom Life as Civic Education: Individual
Achievement and Student Cooperation in Schools
David C. Bricker

The Ethics of Special Education
Kenneth R. Howe and Ofelia B. Miramontes

The Ethics of Multicultural and Bilingual Education
Barry L. Bull, Royal T. Fruehling, and Virgie Chattergy

Ethics for Professionals in Education:
Perspectives for Education and Practice
Kenneth A. Strike and P. Lance Ternasky, Editors

The Moral Base for Teacher Professionalism
Hugh Sockett

THE
MORAL
BASE
FOR TEACHER
PROFESSIONALISM

Hugh Sockett

Teachers College, Columbia University
New York and London

Published by Teachers College Press, 1234 Amsterdam Avenue, New York, NY 10027

Copyright © 1993 by Teachers College, Columbia University

All rights reserved. No part of this publication may be reproduced
or transmitted in any form or by any means, electronic or mechanical,
including photocopy, or any information storage and retrieval system,
without permission from the publisher.

Library of Congress Cataloging-in-Publication Data

Sockett, Hugh.
   The moral base for teacher professionalism / Hugh Sockett.
     p.   cm.–(Professional ethics in education series)
   Includes bibliographical references (p.) and index.
   ISBN 0-8077-3238-9 (alk. paper) : $29.00
   1. Teachers–Professional ethics–United States.   I. Title.
II. Series.
LB1779.S58   1993
174'.93711–dc20   92-34913

ISBN 0-8077-3238-9

Printed on acid-free paper

Manufactured in the United States of America

98 97 96 95 94 93   8 7 6 5 4 3 2 1

OLSON LIBRARY
NORTHERN MICHIGAN UNIVERSITY
MARQUETTE, MICHIGAN 49855

Contents

Introduction

The central objective of this book is to provide a broad vision of the moral foundations of teacher professionalism by linking the professional role of the teacher, the men and women who occupy it, the moral demands it makes, and the practical arts of teaching to the institution of education and its contemporary problems.

Underpinning this vision are four main elements. (1) I follow Hoyle's (1980) important distinction between *professionalism*, where the focus is on the quality of a person's professional practice, and *professionalization*, which is concerned with the status of the occupation. (2) I also use the term *teacher* in a generic sense, referring to all those who engage on an occupational basis in the activities of getting others to learn with a primarily educational end in view, that is, with a sense of concern for the development of the individual learner as a person, as well as for his or her mastery of whatever is being taught. (3) But I locate the professional in a role. Unlike many other analyses of teaching—which see it as an activity, an act, or a performance—my concern is the constellation of (moral) rights and duties constituting a role. (4) Finally, I take feminism and feminist theory very seriously. We have to consider men and women as having differing perspectives and aspirations and see those differences as important for children to experience in their education. The implications are profound for the character of institutions, what counts as the quality of practice, and the structure of the relationships between individuals and institutions.

However, in the structure of the book, the moral foundations of teaching are expressed in four dimensions of professionalism—community, knowledge, accountability, and ideals. The teacher is a member of a professional *community* that provides a framework of relationships and understandings within which a career can be developed and a life composed. The teacher's knowledge or *expertise* is moral, but with technique subservient to moral criteria. I thus reject the possibility of a science of teaching and try to find an alternative to the empiricist approach by sketching the development of a moral epistemology of practice. This epistemology has a moral language, based in the virtues, that describes the professional's expertise and entrenches the significance of the person and the role. Additionally, the individual teacher and the professional community have to face professional moral *accountability* to individuals and to the public. Finally, a professional cannot comprehend his or her moral role without seeing the interplay between practice and *ideals* (of service) and ultimate purposes.

Chapter 1 sets the stage through introducing three classroom teachers who serve as examples throughout the book. In particular, the chapter makes the distinction between professionalism and professionalization, introduces the notion of the "generic" teacher as the professional, and assesses in a preliminary way the professionalism of the teachers described. It also outlines briefly the four dimensions of that professionalism—the community, expertise, accountability, and the ideal of service—which constitute the basic framework for the book. Each teacher is given a pseudonym; one "teacher" is a composite of two teachers I have known.

In Chapter 2, I explain some of the difficulties for a single profession split three ways, against which the very idea of a unified professional community looks somewhat ragged. Not only do we lack a single profession, but we have no clear conception of what the development of a professional career, even in classroom teaching, would look like. We are thereby unable to determine a path of professional development. Professional development is linked to the professional community, on the basis of which an outline of a career in teaching with implications for professional development at all levels can be understood. For a single profession, basic principles of partnership in professional development are needed, particularly in the education of novices to the profession.

In Chapter 3, the discussion of the professional community moves to the continuing professional development of teachers and the place of research. Master's degree programs provide a major opportunity to pursue change and development, and I believe these degrees require serious reappraisal to meet the needs of the professional community, so that they become a precious experience for practitioners and academics. *Action research*, which is a generic term for a type of research carried out in contexts other than education, is the historical base for teacher-research. As a partnership research model, it is seen as particularly appropriate for a unified professional community. Within it, each individual professional has to be seen as a person in a role with a life and a career who needs emancipation, not empowerment.

Chapter 4 is the first of two on the topic of professional expertise. I start from the moral character of teacher professionalism and try to illustrate how five major virtues are central to an understanding of the practice of teaching—honesty, courage, care, fairness, and practical wisdom. These five are not intended to exclude other virtues, but they are primary. Each has a necessary place at the heart of the teaching enterprise. Teachers trade in truth, so they must avoid *deceit*; learning is difficult and demands *courage*; teachers are responsible for the development of persons, a process demanding infinite *care*; *fairness* is necessary to the operation of rules in democratic institutions; and *practical wisdom* is essential to the complex process teaching is.

This is the basis for a different epistemology from that which presently dominates educational theory. Professional expertise is described primarily through professional virtues (as the social practices that constitute teaching) rather than through a knowledge base. In Chapter 5, I explain why I am treating professional expertise as a matter of professional virtue, and begin the defense of these claims by outlining four views of the theory–practice relationship against which the account of expertise as virtue would have to stand in the study of education. I point out three apparently insuperable difficulties for the applied-science view of educational theory into which accounts of the knowledge base of teaching are intended to fit. I take the risk of defining conditions for an epistemology of practice, particularly for a moral practice. From that basis knowledge and knowing-in-action are characterized as an epistemology of practice applied to teaching. This chapter is insufficient for its ambitions, because although we have a discredited epistemology in education, this attempt to sketch an alternative, although traveling in the right direction, requires a much fuller account.

I turn in Chapter 6 to accountability, the third dimension of professionalism. Here I articulate a new approach to the question of professional accountability that is consonant with teaching as a moral endeavor. This proposal relaxes the administrative demands on teachers but heightens their moral obligations. I argue for four main positions: (1) that accountability may sensibly mean something akin to moral obligation; (2) that *trust* is a primary condition for the development of professional accountability; (3) that a professional code of practical guidance provides a potential vehicle for accountability that can be congruent with the public's claims; and (4) that a moral stance toward professional accountability is central in professional development at all levels.

All major professions have at the heart of their raison d'être a commitment to human betterment in a fundamental sense; for example, health, justice, education. These are ideals that govern what different professionals do. In Chapter 7, I argue that teaching is an ideal of service to developing persons that demands constant change and improvement if that service is to be properly pursued; but, although it can function as a guide and a sustenance, an ideal is unrealizable as a picture of a desirable good. Ideals also vary considerably in definition, and human beings enrich one another's understandings of what they might be as they pursue them, learning ideals as they learn different roles. In the second part of the chapter, I focus on the ideal role of *in loco parentis*, with its interesting implications for gender issues. I examine an imaginary, but difficult, dilemma that demonstrates the problems of this ideal. I also view *in loco parentis* in the context of what parental choice of school might mean, and I look at it from the viewpoint of an individual teacher's personal integrity. The purpose is to show that moral discussion, particularly about ultimate purposes, is at the very core of teaching.

Finally, in Chapter 8, I place this account of teacher professionalism in the contemporary context. That context, I argue, is one of educational transformation, not reform. I suggest what we could build with the tools and materials of conceptual transformation, reflective teacher research, new conceptions of teams and partnerships, new relationships between the professional and the institution, transformative educational leadership, and transformation in teacher education, the last specifically in terms of its moral and intellectual climates, caring quality, and concern with gender and race as critical to the development of moral professionals.

I am a white, male, British citizen, resident in the United States and likely to remain here for the remainder of my career and life. I am conscious of that status when I criticize American institutions or make proposals for change, but I am not thereby saying that institutions in my country of origin are perfect. Far from it. Most of what I have said in this book by way of criticism would apply in Britain. America is very important to me, and my criticism springs from a sense of concern and shared responsibility, not from a spectatorial superiority. However, I do believe that educators, whatever their status or location, should be concerned with children, wherever they are, and do their utmost to promote their welfare. For me, that concern overrides everything. I therefore see the issues of a teacher's professionalism raised in this book as transcending national boundaries, even though this nation's system is the context for these issues.

This book has not been an academic exercise—in the traditional sense—for me. I believe that all educators should look at the central problems of education, work out what those problems mean for them, and match what they believe to that context. I am presently working on the creation of two different institutions, and for me institutions are no more than the embodiment of ideas. The first, The Center for Applied Research and Development in Education, is directed at teacher collegiality, emancipation, and teacher knowledge (Sockett, 1989b). The second, The Institute for Educational Transformation, is promoting through an extensive partnership the kind of transformation I describe in Chapter 8. As I am also a member of a graduate school of education that contains these two institutions, I have a university context on which to draw. I see myself as engaged, with others, in continuous experiment to improve teacher professionalism for all of us by seeking to develop new roles, new products, new systems, new approaches, and new experiences.

I am acutely conscious of the many things I have been unable to do in this book. For example, I have paid no attention here to the work of critical theorists. My primary concern is with the description of the moral foundations of teaching through teacher professionalism and if those foundations can provide the framework for adequately addressing the new conceptions of community, expertise, accountability, and ideals. In short, irrespective of whether I have the details right, is the approach itself valuable? If it is, then, while I don't expect to have the right answers, am I asking the right questions within that framework?

My thinking about these subjects has been enhanced by my practice in different countries and with countless teachers. Since coming to George Mason University in 1987, I have had the opportunity to promote professionalism and partnership, both of which seem to me essential to the task of improving public education. I have been immensely privileged by being paid to do things I find of consuming interest. Over more than 30 years of my career, I have also been very fortunate to have worked with particular educators. Richard Peters, who almost singlehandedly transformed philosophy of education in Britain, was an exhilarating teacher. Paul Hirst, Lawrence Stenhouse, and Philip W. Jackson have been very different but important influences on my work, and I have been privileged by their friendship.

Many other friends have contributed to my thinking—Larry Bowen, Bill Cockcroft, Marilyn Dimock, John Elliott, Todd Endo, Jim Finkelstein, Ken Green, Sam Hellier, Sandra Hollingsworth, Barry Macdonald, Richard Pring, Bill Purple, Paul Regnier, Ann Sevcik, Kenneth A. Strike, and Wendy Atwell-Vasey, among others. I am grateful to the University of East Anglia for granting me study leave in 1986, and to the Benton Center at the University of Chicago for making me so welcome as a Visiting Scholar and allowing me to try out some of these ideas in seminars of various kinds. I am grateful to Kathy Easton, David Evelyn, and Francoise Alberola for allowing me to use their experiences as examples.

Early versions of some of this work have appeared in the *Journal of Curriculum Studies*, in the *Cambridge Journal of Education*, and in the

Harvard Educational Review, the details of which are in the References. Chapter 6 is a substantial rewriting of my chapter "Accountability, Trust and Ethical Codes of Practice" in *The Moral Dimensions of Teaching*, edited by John Goodlad, Ken Sirotnik, and Roger Soder, and I am most grateful to Jossey-Bass for allowing me to use some of the material printed there. Susan Liddicoat and Neil Stillman of Teachers College Press have been indefatigable editors, for which I am most grateful.

None of this work would have been possible without the constant support of my dear wife, Ann. If it has a certain missionary zeal to it, that will have been inherited, like much else, from my father, Benjamin Sockett. To his treasured memory and to my mother, Dorothy Sockett, this book is dedicated.

CHAPTER 1

The Moral Core
of Professionalism in Teaching

From our childhood in school we can usually recall good and bad teachers. The bad teacher was lazy, spiteful, ineffective, and inefficient and often actually made us dislike the subject matter so much that we believe we can trace our mathematical incompetence or our hatred of poetry to the disastrous influence of one individual. A good teacher was efficient, enthusiastic, or passionate about the subject, as well as fair and concerned for us as individuals. These qualities were often expressed in kindness and friendship—or even in quite eccentric ways. In good teaching there seem to be elements of art, craft, vocation, and technique (Gowin, 1981; Greene, 1986). But however teaching is conceived, we must try to make the standards of professionalism clear so as to offer a guide to novices, to develop appropriate ways of evaluation, to find ways for improvement, and to inform the public of what we stand for.

CATEGORIES OF PROFESSIONALISM

The continuing search for standards and for best practice is at the heart of professionalism in teaching. Most teachers, and indeed most people, are unable to research or record teaching. They learn about good teaching as witnesses—sometimes as students, sometimes as visitors, and sometimes as professional learners in classrooms (Elliott & Adelman, 1974; Mohr & MacLean, 1987). I was a witness to the following three teachers, whose work, for different reasons, has left me in awe. Taken together, their work adds up to a provisional account of the categories of professional teaching and gives us a common base for discussion of professional issues throughout this book.

Mrs. Simpson and Moral Education

Some 30 five-year-old children were clustered around Gabrielle Johnson in a carpeted corner of a classroom in a school built in 1932. Gabrielle,

1

a student teacher, had started the day nervously, telling her class a tale Bernard Shaw would have recognized as *Androcles and the Lion*. Questions and comments poured out after the drama had been unfolded. Outside the room the class's regular teacher, Mrs. Simpson, was talking to a middle-aged man in dungarees who was painting a new door that would give access to the large grass plot around which the school had been built. As the story ended and the children bustled about the classroom to begin their writing or drawing about Androcles and his escapade, Mrs. Simpson came into the classroom, had a brief word with Gabrielle, and asked the class to listen. As a witness, this is how I remember her remarks.

"Mr. Thomas has come to paint the new door this morning," she said in a very quiet voice, "and I think we ought not to go near it until the paint's dry. Can anyone tell me why?"

One or two murmurs and then several hands were raised:

"Because we might get paint on our clothes, miss."

"That's right, Sheila, but does that matter?"

"Because it would look all messy on my skirt, and my mum would have to clean it off."

"Yes," said the teacher, "Shiela's right. Mum will have to clean your clothes if you get paint on them, won't she?" Various voices added comments on their mother's washing habits, and one small aspiring painter said, "The painter's clothes get very mucky."

"But they are really overalls," Mrs. Simpson immediately pointed out, "like the overalls you wear when you paint, aren't they, Wayne? Why else do you think we mustn't go near the paint?"

"Because Mrs. Higgins [the school principal] wouldn't like it," said another child.

"Because the door would get all messed up," said Yvonne, a diffident little girl standing near the teacher with her arm cocked around her ear as if to protect herself from the surprise of her interjection.

"Does that matter?" said the teacher, "It's bound to get dirty sometime."

"Oh yes," replied Yvonne, more confident now, "but the painter's work would get all spoilt."

"And Mrs. Higgins wants us to keep the hallway neat and tidy," added Kevin.

"That's right," said Mrs. Simpson, "So we want to keep clear of the door today, don't we? Or we'll get painty clothes and Mum will have to wash them, the painter's work will be spoilt, and the hallway will look untidy and spoilt so we won't enjoy it as much. Do you understand that, Paul? Is that right, Lesley? Does anybody not understand that?" A general murmur of acknowledgment. "Thank you, Miss Johnson," she ended as she slipped out into the corridor, leaving the space for blue lions and red Androcleses to make their way from the children's imaginations onto paper.

This was a brilliant cameo of moral or social education in four or five minutes. Simple and immediate to the children; comprehensive in its attention to the interests of all who might be concerned—mother, painter, the school, everybody; the use of "we" not simply as a heuristic but as a way of stressing the notion of community; building on the children's answers, not dismissing the rogue who would be a painter but using his answer to make a point. No question of rules and orders. Apparently so easy. Confident, stylish, elegant, unplanned questioning of young children bringing out the fundamental feature of moral agency and democratic citizenship, namely, concern for the interests of others and ourselves; obviously a pattern built into the fabric of her everyday work as a professional.

Mrs. Simpson shows a clear understanding of what becoming moral is and an acute pedagogical sensitivity to the teaching opportunity. She demonstrates how the "foundations of any subject can be taught to anybody at any age in some form" (Bruner, 1974, p. 12). I was indeed a privileged witness, seeing this example of highly professional practice in teaching as I was sitting at the back of the room ready to observe Gabrielle's student teaching. When I asked Gabrielle what she thought of what Mrs. Simpson had said and done, she could not recall it, except to say that Mrs. Simpson had told them not to mess with the paint. As a student teacher she had not the experience to know what best practice is; more likely she was preoccupied with my presence as an assessor, as a "hostile" witness. Gabrielle taught competently, but she had not got to the point of seeing other people teach through the eyes of a learner.

Mrs. Simpson was an expert. She provides a stunning riposte and example to those who think there is nothing much to being a teacher, or that teachers need neither training nor the opportunity to reflect constantly on their practice. The expert professionalism lay in the ability to construct a learning experience based on carefully chosen questions, to take each child's answer seriously and make something of it, to define the problem as a community responsibility rather than a matter of discipline, and to develop the children's minds through the use of reason rather than authority. It encapsulated excellent technique with moral concern.

Tom Stevenson and the Teaching of History

My colleague Tom has been in the profession some time. In his laconic way he seemed always able to get students enthralled and excited with anything on the history curriculum. He could get good work out of them, apparently without much effort, whatever their future ambitions.

Yet Tom was always at ease. He was the teacher who would begin a series of lessons on the Greeks by walking into class and saying, "Does anyone here speak Greek?" Students would look at him quizzically, thinking he should be locked up—if they didn't know something was up his sleeve. Then he'd ask them conversational questions, and every time an English word with Greek etymology cropped up, he'd write it on the board: *cinema, camera, photograph, politics,* and so on. "You speak Greek," he'd conclude, "if you speak English."

The history of the Elizabethan age was his forte, though he had been a Japanese specialist. I arranged with him to attend a lesson on the Spanish Armada, the huge sea-borne army that King Philip II of Spain used in an abortive attempt to invade England in 1588. The class was a typical group of alienated 14-year-olds. As we walked to the classroom, I asked how he would approach the subject. "Not sure," he said, "I've got some detailed plans, but I think I'm going to trash them today. Somehow they have to *experience* it." So I expected some histrionics about the naval battle, the swish of sabers, the blast of cannon, and the howls of the wounded—the usual stuff when you want students of this age and ability to enjoy history.

"Een zee hills behind Cadith," Tom began, "leeved Antonio Manana, zee 17-year-old son of Maria and José Manana." In the first 20 minutes he held the class spellbound as he told the basic story of the Armada, in his dreadful mock-Spanish accent, from the point of view of a poor Spanish farming kid. We heard how Antonio was recruited by force, was quickly trained on board a Spanish galleon, was blessed by the priests, and prayed regularly to Santa Maria Compostella. We heard how Antonio saw the leading general (the Duke of Medina Sidonia) being sick and how he had to clean it up; how he drank more wine than he should have; how peaceful the sea was; and how, drunk like the other sailors, he watched in horror the approach of the English fireships in the night (the first major assault on the Armada by the English fleet). The class erupted with glee at Antonio's sudden grasp through the haze of "madeera vine" that he was seeing "vireships" and how the sheer terror made him leap over the side and swim to the French shore.

This was the Armada of the counterhero, not a story of wise or foolish admirals. It was a brilliant way to get youngsters to identify, not merely with a story, but with someone who had had a part in history to which they could relate. How much more easily they could then grapple, in cooperative learning groups of either Spanish or English sailors, with a construction of their story that had to contain the accurate facts—numbers of men on the ships, their tonnage, the command structure, the conditions, and the details of the voyage.

But it also led them gently into the issues of bias in history—of what stories look like from different sides and what cultures make of their histories. His pedagogic device of dividing them into groups of English and Spaniards was a brilliant elision of subject and pedagogy. Tom was courteously translating (Bruner, 1974) a set of major political events for children of barely mediocre attainment, slight motivation, and no academic expectations. Where Mrs. Simpson used questions to get the children into morality as a fundamental mode of human thought, Tom used his histrionic talent, his knowledge, and his overwhelming enthusiasm to illustrate the most significant feature of understanding ourselves through our history—that we tell stories as *we* see them. Yet what still strikes me about him was his courage, his preparedness to take *risks*, notwithstanding his exceptional confidence and maturity for a young teacher. He was always searching for innovations—and sometimes they failed—because the risks were worth taking if history could live for his classes.

Elizabeth Beck and Learning Not to Shout

To my mind, Mrs. Simpson and Tom Stevenson were mature teachers of perspicuous talent. Elizabeth Beck was a student teacher working in a classroom for the third period of field experience. She showed immense determination in wrestling with a major difficulty. She demonstrated an intense commitment to improving her practice.

She had a fifth-grade class whose teacher was Mrs. Old. From Elizabeth's observation notes of Mrs. Old and the class, it was clear that she believed that all the children were underachieving: They had poor reading levels, produced sloppy writing, and were uninspired in their artwork; moreover, they were working in a dismal and unattractive classroom atmosphere devastated by a constant earthquake of noise. Mrs. Old, as Elizabeth recorded, shouted all the time, raising the decibels to command attention; the class outshouted her. On the basis of her observation notes, she constructed a strategy that was an attack on all fronts. Elizabeth did not know how she was going to cope with the problem of noise if it persisted. It did. She tried ignoring it. She tried pleading with the class by inventing headaches. She was determined not to resort to traditional disciplinary methods, which, for her, just meant defeat. She tried playing music quietly to distract attention. She attacked the classwork with gusto, indeed with brilliance, but nothing seemed to alter the noise. For two weeks her evaluation notes on each day returned to new strategies for noise reduction, each latest attempt being subjected to fierce critical scrutiny. Finally she told herself, "I have fallen into the trap. I am shouting. Tomorrow I will not raise my voice for a whole day."

Her notes for that Monday recorded that, just before lunchtime, Mrs. Old (who had been asked not to be in the room when Elizabeth was teaching) came into the class because she heard the students' noise but had not heard Elizabeth's usual loud response. So Mrs. Old shouted at them and left. But, as Elizabeth noted in her journal on Tuesday evening, during the day children had to come close to her to ask her questions (since she was using only her usual speaking voice), and they gradually began to ask one another to keep quiet so that they could hear what Miss Beck was saying. On Wednesday, first thing, she brought the whole class around her and said very quietly that she was never going to raise her voice again and that she wanted them all to try to work more quietly. She had tried this before without success. But this time, after each change of subject, after each break, she did the same and then began a "noise report." By Friday afternoon, the noise level had dropped. She had only to say "shhh!" and there was instant silence. I spent several hours with her three weeks later and read her journal. I also watched her teach a bustling group of contented, hard-working children. She had excellent qualities as a teacher, and it was a privilege to watch such a professional. But for me the heart of her excellence, at this stage in her career, lay in her unassailable commitment to improvement, to self-criticism, and to changing her strategies without sacrificing her principles. Methodologically, she was exceptionally rigorous.

Character, Commitment, Subject, Pedagogy, and Beyond

I was a happenstance observer of Mrs. Simpson, a colleague of Tom's, and an evaluator-supervisor in Elizabeth's classroom, a witness of different kinds to the quality of their work. Any education professional will respond to the quality I have tried to record. Each teacher manifested immense care and commitment—dedication, if you like. Each was a teaching occasion that I felt privileged to see, and from which I learned.

Watching others teach seems almost a natural process from which we can learn as teachers. We may pick out something we can use; we may emulate a person's style. We certainly are refreshed by watching a real teacher, but we can also learn at second hand. The movie *Stand and Deliver*, for example, teaches and inspires us through the work of Jaime Escalante, even when he is splendidly portrayed by an actor (for further comment on this movie, see Chapter 4). Journalists can watch teaching and convey acute perceptions of a teacher to us, as Freedman's (1990) record of Jessica Seigel reveals. Sadly, many professional teachers never watch their colleagues teach. The "cellular" character of teaching seems to prevent opportunities for learning through witness that would enhance this very natural process (Kottkampf, Provenzo, & Cohn, 1986; Lortie, 1975). Moreover, watching others or working with them is a part of the collegiality necessary in professionalism (see Chapter 2).

Mrs. Simpson, Tom, and Elizabeth offer us a picture of the teacher as a professional in which four major categories of professionalism stand out: character, commitment, subject knowledge, and pedagogical (or methodological) knowledge.

First, the individual *character* of each teacher is a critical component in professionalism. Each teacher displays different sorts of virtues, for example, patience, courage, determination, or respect for children. In our obsession with performance, we ignore character in teachers, perhaps because we believe that all such judgments would be subjective and nonscientific. But we miss so much of teaching quality when we ignore character. In fact, as Reeves' (1990) study of the relationship between John F. Kennedy's performance and character demonstrates, coming to grips with a person's character is critical to understanding human action and its motives. It is, I think, impossible to give a comprehensive account of what a teacher does without describing the person within the teaching act.

Second, Elizabeth and Tom see themselves as *committed to change and to continuous improvement.* For them, a teacher never reaches a plateau of achievement. The enterprise is too complex, and individuals change too much. Striving to adjust to change seems inevitable for a professional if teaching is to be good, since children in classrooms are never replicas of those who have gone before. They are individuals, each with their own particular history, personality, perspective, and problems. Striving to do better is a constant. Striving therefore becomes a necessary habit and a condition for teaching excellence. That need not be a source of discomfort, for the only things worth doing in life, as Lawrence Stenhouse (1983) put it, are the things worth falling short of. Every context is a potential challenge.

Third, Mrs. Simpson and Tom demonstrate the depth of *knowledge and understanding* teachers have to have of what they teach. There is no substitute for this, and without it a teacher is something of a charlatan. Tom is so confident of his historical knowledge that he can translate it with such vigor (and justified license) to ensure that the subject is alive for his students. Mrs. Simpson is morally highly educated. She has not simply "learned" that you have to teach community responsibility or concern for others because the school board says so. It is part of her knowledge and her understanding of the world. The moral knowledge she has is different from historical, scientific, mathematical, or any other type of knowledge. But moral knowledge and understanding is as much required by every professional teacher as is knowledge of other "subjects" in an appropriate "courteously translated" form.

Finally, each teacher described has immense *pedagogic strengths*. They are actually good at the "hows" of teaching—questioning, dramatization, class control, the strategies and tactics about which modern teaching seems so obsessive at the expense of other vital categories. Most difficult to capture in the work of teachers is "why they do what they do when," those seemingly inexplicable tacit understandings and insights that people like Tom and Mrs. Simpson manifest.

Much more needs to be said about each of these central categories of practice and of teacher professionalism: character, commitment, subject knowledge, and pedagogical (or methodological) knowledge. These are the stuff of classroom actions. Yet they are not the whole story. Professionalism in teaching goes further. For outside the classroom a teacher has wider obligations and working relationships with colleagues and with parents in the exercise of his or her role as a teacher. Professionalism requires that we go beyond classroom performance or classroom activity as descriptors of teaching acts to the complete and complex role a teacher fulfills. Public education needs teachers who are able not only to shine in the four categories mentioned within the classroom but also to undertake the demands of partnership with other professionals, of collaborative leadership, and of a wider role within a school. Teachers can also contribute to emerging visions of education and seek, as citizens and professionals, to resolve some of the complexities of political disagreements and to be public ambassadors for education. This wide role, reaching beyond classroom to school and public, is particularly important for a democratic society, for the teacher is a main purveyor of democratic civilization.

However, this more comprehensive notion of excellence and teacher professionalism is not one that calls for teachers to be social workers, priests, and counselors as well. It is not to advocate a supraprofessional role for teachers by demanding that they provide an amalgam of other professional skills. It is simply to urge teachers to reach out beyond classroom performance to commitments to colleagues with whom one works and parents whose children are in one's care and, beyond that, to the social enterprise of education. This broad conception of the arena for professionalism underpins the arguments in this book.

PROFESSIONALISM AND PROFESSIONALIZATION

As a witness of these teachers, I saw examples of *professionalism*, of excellence in professional practice (Downie, 1990). I believe it is accurate to say that these teachers were professionals. But such a claim says nothing about their status, that is, whether the community values them, how much they are paid, whether they have secretarial support, whether they have paid annual leave, fringe benefits, entitlement to study leave, whether their profession governs itself, and so on. To say they are professional in the contexts I have outlined is a description of their practice, not their status.

Professionalism describes the quality of practice. It describes the manner of conduct within an occupation, how members integrate their obligations with their knowledge and skill in a context of collegiality and of contractual and ethical relations with clients. Every action within the role is to be judged by standards specific to the profession. The collection of those constantly changing standards is the corpus of understandings, values, insights, and knowledge we call our professionalism. Hoyle (1980) sensibly distinguishes this conception of professionalism from *professionalization*, which is the process whereby an occupation (rather than an individual) gains the status of a profession. When we professionalize teaching we change its status; but a teacher's professionalism is apparent in his or her practice.

This distinction is embedded in our language and our understanding. For example, Tom Stevenson was highly paid, a departmental chair, a professional (in practice and status terms) if ever there was one. At times he may have uttered chauvinist remarks about his female colleagues that were—well, what word do we naturally use?—simply "not professional" or "unprofessional." Our description of his remarks as unprofessional has to do not with his status (which remains as it is), but with his practice. When we use "professional" in this sense, we are using it as the adjective of professionalism. Another example: Suppose Mr. Simpson was a computer scientist who had never been trained as a teacher or even taught anyone. His wife invited him to come to teach some of her class about the computers that had just arrived. He taught brilliantly, doing what we would call a "really professional" job. Again, it is his practice to which we are referring, not his status. He does not have any professional status, though we correctly call his performance "really professional." Any general search for excellence in teaching, as indicated by the National Board for Professional Teaching Standards (1989), is not a direct concern with professionalization, that is, with teacher *status*, but with professionalism, the quality of the *practice*.

Professional practice has many implications for professional status and its accompanying politics. A profession—*as an organization*, whether it be teaching, law, or dentistry—must consider *both* problems of its practice *and* problems of its status, as well as how status can be protected through standards of membership. Sometimes members of an occupation that has the status of a profession become corrupt and inefficient, thus demeaning the very idea of their profession in their practice. Attorneys are disbarred; priests are defrocked; accountants have their licenses revoked. Sadly, as a group we teachers seem to have no sanction to impose on someone whose actions run totally counter to anything we might regard as professional, like a former Virginia school principal convicted of drug dealing to children in 1989. He can still claim to be a teacher. As with individuals, so with organizations. Professions as organizations may also atrophy, fail to police themselves, or be blind to the social context of their work.

Professionals presumably believe in the purpose of their profession, be it health (medicine), justice (law), or education (teaching), and they will want the public to commit to these values. Improving their practice will support claims to improved status, provided the basic values of the profession command public support and appropriate financial remuneration. The most obvious common danger is that status (better salary, for example) will become a goal to which practical improvement is subservient, rather than the other way around, and that leads to a poor public image of a profession (Sockett, 1988). Indeed, some argue that professions are in such disrepute that talk of profession and professionalism is outmoded and that professions have become simple monopolies (Friedman, 1972; Gouldner, 1978; Illich, 1977; Sockett, 1989c; Steifels, 1979). From this perspective, teaching should avoid being described as a profession altogether. Yet the important distinction remains. Even if we do not like the way in which professions now are, and/or even if we do not like to use the word *profession*, some word or phrase will still be needed to distinguish those occupations whose members see themselves committed primarily to quality of practice or to an ideal of service of some kind *from* other occupations whose purposes are simply utilitarian and seen by their members as such. Whether we choose to use the word *profession* or not, teaching has some moral purpose and an ideal of service in the minds of many who profess it.

This distinction between practice (and professionalism) and status (and professionalization) seems important to capture to provide a conceptual framework enabling us to discern the relation between status and practice more clearly. Issues of status are very important to members of a profession, but my focus in this book is on practice, its standards, and the professionalism implicit in that practice.

THE TEACHER: A GENERIC VIEW

John Houseman, acting the well-known part of the crusty senior law professor in the TV series "The Paper Chase," once exclaimed robustly to a junior member of faculty: "I would never have become a judge or a diplomat. First and foremost I am a teacher—*teacher*, do you understand?—someone who imparts wisdom to the young." Houseman's character was picking out the generic sense of teacher as opposed to the specific sense in which we would talk of a mathematics teacher, a classroom teacher, or a university teacher.

But who counts as a teacher? *Teacher* is taken in this book to be a generic term, and Griffin (1986) paints an excellent portrait of such an ideal. It covers all those who engage on an occupational basis (full time or part time) in the activities of getting others to learn with a primarily *educational* end in view. This is the intent of a teacher's practice, although it does not exclude the possibility that he or she may do research, administer institutions, or whatever. The teacher as educator has a primary concern for the development of the individual learner as a person as well as for his or her mastery of whatever is being taught. In this view, university and college professors of education, school principals and educational administrators, as well as classroom teachers, are teachers and thereby putative members of the teaching profession (see Chapter 2). (Many other people teach: clergy, parents, nurses, for example. But teaching is not the rationale for their occupation, as it is for professors and principals.)

Fenstermacher (1986) also regards teaching as a "generic" term, but he is looking at it as a verb describing a person's *actions*, performances, and activities. My use of *teaching* in this book complements that analysis by focusing on the social role and the professional occupation of teaching, within which actions, performances, and activities are played out. Clearly this usage is stipulative and needs some justification.

Tom Stevenson was not just a classroom teacher of history; he also had a role as department chair (which meant having responsibilities for young teachers like me, for advising colleagues, and so forth). He played an active role in the government of the school, for example, at department chairs' meetings. He set up a United Nations Association, taking on a role as the teacher who wanted to get the institution to give serious thought to international issues. He mentored students and young teachers. He ran drama productions, drawing in parents to the school. Such roles multiply for all teachers; to one child, Tom was "like a father."

Typically his career might have developed another way. He might have become a principal after several years as an assistant, perhaps even finishing his doctorate early and going into teacher education. With a specialization in administration, he might have taken up a superintendent's role, finally returning to open a new large high school in his late 40s. Yet his profession is teaching, although his career has carried him into different professional jobs outside the classroom but within the profession.

It will be objected that "teacher" is not a role played by university professors and school superintendents; even principals are not usually called teachers. Yet any profession has its researchers, its specialists, and its administrators. The attorney general is a lawyer, not a *former* lawyer. The surgeon general is a doctor, not a *former* doctor. But if either of these appointees had been teachers, particularly classroom teachers, they would be called *former* teachers. Doctors and lawyers become administrators and researchers in the health or legal systems without ceasing thereby to be doctors and lawyers. Unfortunately, teachers and teaching do not seem to have grown up like these other professions, perhaps because of the lowly status of the profession. Career progression is still seen only in terms of getting out of classrooms, of getting out of the role of *schoolteacher*. The result is that we only know what careers look like for those who want to move into satellite occupations of our profession (research, administration, teacher education). We seem to have no generally recognized core conception of what a teaching career looks like, particularly one spent in the classroom with the obligations I have described (see Chapter 2). Indeed, the dominance of satellite occupations prevents the emergence of a single generic conception of teaching.

The emergence of public education, K–Ph.D., has included the development of teacher education and its shift from normal schools into universities. With the hard pressure for research—as a satellite to the occupation— the idea of research and teaching being naturally bound together by a single purpose has become much harder to achieve. That split has also contributed to the problems of quality at all levels on which there is now so much national attention. For Goodlad (1990), the answer is to bring the university and school cultures together to enhance both teaching and teacher education. I agree, but go further. We can begin to see ourselves as one single profession devoted to the purposes of education.

This book therefore focuses on the practice of all those who teach, the generic view as I have called it. I seek to discover qualities and standards, as well as ways of looking at teaching, which articulate teacher professionalism. I refer consistently to the practical situations of the classroom teacher's work, but the book does not attempt to describe ideal features of pedagogical practice in any systematic way. The work of each individual teacher is part of a particular context. That is a context bound by socioeconomic conditions of children's parents, by a school's history, by the character of the principal, by the individual teacher's autobiography, and by much else. But every educational and teaching context remains a moral context.

THE MORAL CORE OF PROFESSIONALISM

Mrs. Simpson, Tom, and Elizabeth help us to develop a perspective on teaching that includes the character of an individual person in a complex role that goes beyond classroom and school to public education itself.

Anything within the role is open to judgment in terms of the qualities of professionalism the individual displays. Professionals must also judge themselves on the quality of their professionalism. The generic teacher does not just get people to learn within an educational endeavor, for teaching is an interpersonal activity directed at shaping and influencing (not molding), by means of a range of pedagogical skills, what people become as persons through whatever it is that is taught—high school calculus, motor skills to autistic children, or singing and dancing for a dramatic production in a college. As a teacher is one who helps to shape what a person becomes, so the moral good of every learner is of fundamental importance in every teaching situation (Peters, 1966; Tom, 1984). The character and the commitment of the teacher is part of each context. It is necessarily a part of professionalism.

I am describing a view of teaching as primarily moral (i.e., dedicated to an individual's welfare) rather than instrumental (e.g., for economic reasons) or noneducational (e.g., for custodial reasons). From this view, three things follow:

1. Our discourse and our vocabulary in teaching will become very different as we use a moral language in teaching and education.
2. We will need to see technique(s) as subservient to moral considerations.
3. The present system of public education will have to be transformed if education is to be authentically moral.

Professionalism and Moral Language

Teaching in an educational context is strongly connected to the betterment of individuals. It is therefore impossible to talk extensively about teachers and teaching without a language of morality, but that seems an unfamiliar form of discourse when we discuss teaching. For example, in a discussion I held with a group of teachers in 1991, one teacher found himself unable to use moral language. He used a medical metaphor to get across what he wanted to say about children becoming good or bad, talking of metaphorical lobotomies as a task for the school in moral education. It was as if he had never used moral language in his professional situation. This is not necessarily unusual. Bellah and his associates (1985) demonstrate the inability of many people to examine their moral predicaments because they simply do not have the vocabulary. They have not been taught it and are embarrassed to use it. Straightforward *moral* words—*courage, honesty, kindness, carefulness, patience, compassion,* and so forth—are among those we need to recover if we are to describe with any proper depth aspects of what a professional is and what a professional does. Tom's courage, Mrs. Simpson's patience and carefulness, Elizabeth's determination and courage—these are all descriptions we have stopped using to describe or evaluate what teachers do in classrooms.

Discussions of professionalism, then, are moral discussions. Recall Tom's mild chauvinism. Who cares? Does it matter? Surely it only *matters* if it is seen as morally reprehensible; it is only on *moral* grounds that we care one way or the other how Tom behaves toward women. We would care much less if "treatment of women" were just a matter of etiquette, like "never eat peas with your knife," or a matter of superstition, like walking under ladders. Or take Elizabeth's approach to her own self-improvement; why do we think that's so wonderful? Because of its clear relation to her concern for children. We would be less impressed, morally speaking, if her *only reason* for self-improvement was, "Oh, I just want to get good grades." That egoistic answer is rather different from the concern for others expressed in "I ought to get these children learning to their full potential."

Moral character matters in teaching. We cannot understand Mrs. Simpson, Tom, and Elizabeth without it. If we play down the importance of the moral by taking little account of the significance of character, we face the real danger of losing our capacity to see teachers as people, people who are beset with all the problems of living in a complex society that continuously influences the way in which they work in their chosen role. Character can be shown in altruism. The task of shaping what people become morally attracts many whose motive is idealistic (Goodlad, 1990) and altruistic (Lortie, 1975). Many teachers have a moral vision, a moral sense, and a moral motive (however mixed up it may be in any individual person). Psychologists may describe this as *intrinsic motivation*, but this is a somewhat mechanistic term blurring the nuances of a moral vocabulary that allows us to describe teachers as people. Attention to character as a part of moral language invites teachers to help children use and understand that vocabulary and will allow us to develop much stronger rationales for the education we deliver.

Teaching Technique Governed by the Moral

Following this line of argument, there can be no such thing as a *purely* empirical or technical judgment about a teacher or a teaching act. Much of what we read in the literature of education and much of what we are told is "good" in the process of schooling is morally totally unexamined. Our conversation is dominated by mechanistic language: strategies, skills, time on task, and so forth.

As we look at the work of Mrs. Simpson, Tom Stevenson, and Elizabeth Beck, we can see that teaching is not a technical operation, like the work of the dental hygienist. Nor is it like servicing a car, programming a computer, policing a district, leaping from a trapeze, or baking a cake. We have come to see teaching as a set of mechanical performances judged by the quality of the product, almost as if the person of the teacher was a ghost in a machine that "produced" learning from raw material, called learners. For example, Skinner (1975) made various recommendations for social engineering, yet he seemed oblivious to the fact that his technical schemes for human improvement had underpinning values that are highly contestable; or maybe he saw them as so obvious as to be beyond argument. But technique in teaching itself implies a view about what a human being is, what a person is, and that is at the very least evaluative and certainly moral.

A technique in teaching is always subservient to a moral end, but it can also be evaluated morally as a means to that end. Effective questioning is different from interrogation under torture. Lecturing is different from the harangues of the propagandist. Rewarding and punishing children is different from changing the behavior of rats or pigeons to "produce the desired effects." An effective school is not simply a smoothly running organization (like a concentration camp) but one in which individual autonomy is respected and promoted. Behavior modification techniques are on a moral not a technical borderline, witness the treatment of Alex in A Clockwork Orange. Lovass (1967) experimented in constantly shouting orders at children with schizophrenia, a morally uncertain practice whatever its results. The differences are moral.

Moral Professionalism and a Transformed System

We should note at this stage that, from the moral point of view, certain features of our system are profoundly disturbing. First, we do not take the needs of each child seriously; rather we have built systems to accommodate children who fall into categories. Second, we abuse our professionals. Superintendents have a short shelf life. Teachers are overregulated and controlled (Kean, 1986). Universities rarely protect their teacher educators, and as institutions they seem uninterested in education in schools (Goodlad, 1990). Third, our professional language, both in school and in research, largely ignores significant moral issues. If we are to take the claims for moral professionalism seriously, our ways of working will need to be drastically transformed. For example, if we look at ways of working in modern business practice, especially in the process of continuous improvement and total quality management principles, we will find considerable stress on the ethical character of working relationships. Such ideas are important for educators to examine in depth as we search for organizational frameworks that can assist the installation of professionalism in educational, as opposed to commercial, institutions (Sockett, 1989c).

THE FOUR DIMENSIONS OF PROFESSIONALISM

There are four primary dimensions in teacher professionalism:
(1) the professional community, (2) professional expertise, (3) professional
accountability, and (4) the profession's ideal of service.

The professional community. Teachers most often work in institutions,
and within those institutions in formal communities such as departments
and informal communities such as a club. They are members of educational
institutions and subinstitutions, departments, committees, grade levels,
schools, and unions. They work in universities, colleges, and schools and
are members of all kinds of associations and groups. Each of these creates
sets of professional relationships that call, in different ways, for levels of
trust and collegiality—in other words, for moral relationships. Different
though these groupings are, professional teachers have a common identity
as members of an occupation getting people to learn with an educational
end in view and seeking for standards of best practice to pursue that end.
Whatever the actual situation, it makes sense to describe that group as
potentially a professional community. Such a professional community is
not an assemblage of utopian purity. It provides a focus for those who wish
to maintain certain standards and to tell the public they serve about those
standards and commitments.

Professional expertise. Teachers are concerned with knowledge, understanding, or insight in two ways. They hand on a heritage of expertise and
experience, frequently construed as the disciplined study of a subject or
the acquisition of skills that are necessary to, or a part of, those disciplines.
That defines in major part what the profession seeks to do. It necessarily
involves matters of truth. However, as we have seen with Mrs. Simpson,
Tom, and Elizabeth, there are also matters of pedagogical knowledge, the
"hows" of teaching, that can also be described as knowledge. These two
are interrelated and may be described as the professional expertise that is
contained in a professional's practice.

Professional accountability. The professional teacher is morally responsive to the client's needs (whether the client be defined as the child, the
parent or caretaker, or the public through the mechanism of the state). The
teacher has moral obligations to these individuals or groups, which can be
expressed through relationships of professional accountability. These moral
obligations may be interpreted in specific or general ways. A specific performance standard could be viewed by a community as morally important
to reach. Others may judge both efficiency and moral commitment through

the successes or failures of students. Accountability in moral terms could be more generally seen as keeping to ethical standards appropriate in a professional teacher.

The professional ideal of service.   Finally, professions work within some moral vision of human betterment, some set of professional ideals which describe the moral purpose of the enterprise and to which altruists and others are attracted. Obviously we see this in the Hippocratic oath, in lawyers' commitments to justice, and in teachers' commitments to education. An ideal in teaching would have to be seen as an ideal of service of some kind, no doubt with constituent pieces. In every case, ideals are likely to be a consistent source of disagreement and debate, examination and reinterpretation. Ideals require constant inquiry.

These four dimensions of teacher professionalism—the professional community, professional expertise, professional accountability, and professional ideals—provide a structure for moral debate focused on practice. Each is a massive topic that cannot be fully explored within the confines of this book. My intent is to present a broad vision, not a fully detailed account of each, for it is my overall approach to the topic that first needs to be articulated and examined. If the insistence on moral language and the approach through these four dimensions makes sense, more detailed exploration of each dimension will later be necessary. For the moment my focus is on the larger picture. That is a risk, for it is likely to leave moral philosophers dissatisfied with the abbreviated arguments, while others will find the philosophical basis getting in the way of more elaborated implications for the development of the profession. I think the risk is worth taking.

CHAPTER 2

Professional Development and the Professional Community

If we use the generic view of teachers, we can discern three different professional groups—academics, practitioners and administrators. Together they clearly do not form a single well-established professional community. Each group seems to have a different primary identity even though their common reference point and rationale lies in the social practice of education and the occupation of teaching. Partnership between these groups is still relatively rare, and collegiality is non-existent.

In the 1990s various interinstitutional challenges are being mounted to this split profession by the development of partnerships and collaboratives (of universities, schools, and administrations) that implicitly or explicitly aim at constructing a single professional community (Graham, 1983; Lieberman, 1988; Sirotnik & Goodlad, 1988). These partnerships attempt to forge a unified community recognizable by the common values, ideals, and commitments already shared by many individuals professionally committed to education and teaching. Yet too often the work of creating partnerships is left to independent individuals with the result that new institutional models of collegiality and mutual responsibility are not developed or installed.

Building partnerships across communities and within communities is an endeavor that faces numerous challenges, such as creating trust and collegiality (Nias, 1975), building organizational health and a moral ethos (Cusick & Wheeler, 1988), finding out how to mix the values of the community with individual values (Little, 1990), addressing the differences in the relationships between the three parties to the profession, and discerning how professional education contributes to the development of a professional community. My attention in this chapter and the next is limited to this latter challenge, the development of a community through the activity of professional education as an example of ways in which a community can be built. Professional development is a keystone to development of the profession, but it is by no means the whole story. "Successful reform of our educational enterprise," Goodlad (1990) argues, "requires the coordination of three related agendas. The first pertains to the performance of the school system as a whole; the second, to that of the individual schools that make up that system. Clearly success with the second virtually assures success with the first. The third, the agenda of reform in teacher education, arises out of the other two" (p. 17).

In this chapter, a brief account of the background to the split profession is presented first. I suggest that academics keep their distance from practitioners and administrators, and that they also face a problem of dual identity. Practitioners are not well served by academics or administrators. Administrators face complex political challenges and are frequently tempted to manipulate the professionals for whom they are responsible. Teachers (in the generic sense, including these three groups) need to see themselves as a single profession.

In the second section, I first indicate the weaknesses in school-university relationships, and argue the case for strong collaboration between them. Second, I suggest that professional autonomy and academic freedom are as significant in schools as they are in universities, which is a primary reason for promoting these relationships and for rejecting the hierarchialism that presently characterizes them. Third, to give this argument some weight, I outline such a conception of the intellectual and moral structure of a career in teaching, and the chapter ends with a discussion of the basic principles that interprofessional partnership offers in professional development, with primary reference to the education of novices to the profession.

In Chapter 3, the discussion shifts to the continuing professional development of teachers and the place of research within the professional community. In neither this nor the following chapter will I deal in any depth with administrator participation in this professional community because, whether principal or superintendent, this role must be discussed in the context of the political control of education, which would take us too far from the central themes of this book.

THE SPLIT PROFESSION: ACADEMIC, SCHOOL-BASED PRACTITIONER, AND ADMINISTRATOR

Education has come under increasingly fierce political attack in recent years. A sense of crisis developed across the system for many reasons—as varied as the recession, disparity suits in many states, the failings of teacher education, and international comparisons of children's mathematics scores. Higher education has not escaped criticism, much of it self-inflicted. In 1991, the scandal of research overheads at Stanford University and the antitrust suit against private colleges were public symptoms of what critics claimed to be a much deeper malaise (A. Bloom, 1987; Smith, 1990; Sykes, 1988). Without a unified profession, coordinated responses to such a diversity of issues are impossible, since there are no built-in loyalties across the sectors of education.

The Identity of the Academic in Education

Academic educational researchers and teacher-educators are frequently far removed from practitioners in schools. This distance is not hard to explain. In part, it is a symptom of the fact that education as a field of study sees itself as part of an applied (social) science model (Fox, 1990), although that view has been challenged for a long time (Bracey, 1989; Walker, 1990). Academics teach practitioners to respect that model and its hierarchical implications. In part, the gap may be explained by the fact that, for many university faculty, their position represents a career climb out of the classroom, thus reinforcing for them the hierarchical relationship between the two groups. In addition, the gap is preserved because universities, as research institutions, are subject to a funding agenda and research activities that are seen by practitioners as hostile or irrelevant to their occupation. The gap becomes even more difficult to bridge because these factors are sustained by a teacher–student relation (e.g., in in-service courses or master's degree programs).

Partnerships thereby become both difficult and resistible. Collegial teaching/learning relationships are rare. Academics do not seem concerned with their image and the attitudes they convey to practitioners, even though Goodlad's (1990) data show that many of them still seem committed to teacher education and teaching. Too frequently classroom teachers are treated as mere subjects in discussion and in writing, and schools are regarded as subsidiary in importance and stature. Some researchers feel able to ignore the basic etiquette of collegiality, perhaps because they feel no sense of common educational purpose deriving from a single professional community. Such people often do not see that their chosen role, whatever its value, often means that they earn their living by scrutinizing the failings of others. In sum, the gap is preserved and can even be widened by the behavior of academics.

Yet education academics have more intense problems than are generally realized by practitioners. They have a dual identity: to the practitioner with whom their work is closely bound in theory *and* to peers in other disciplines in the academy. These days higher education and education academics are being held solely responsible and publicly accountable for what are seen as the weaknesses of teacher education. "Developments of profound significance to the schools," Goodlad (1990) claims, ". . . are somewhat remote to the central concerns of universities" (pp. 106–107). For universities with initial training responsibilities in teaching, accreditation procedures demand that their (initial training) work be subject to a more or less strict accountability. Unlike other professional degrees that are accredited, the content can also be determined by agencies and by nonprofessionals (e.g., state politicians). That is unthinkable, for example, in engineering (for which all who ever cross a bridge should be profoundly grateful). Teaching has been increasingly subject to regional and national governmental whim or plan (usually to both), unlike those professions that are coherent single professional communities with their own governing professional associations.

But noneducation academics see such vagaries as indicative of suspect professional status. Indeed, their suspicions are confirmed about education's low status as a university subject and the quality of its research. In the academy, education academics and refugees in education from cognate disciplines (e.g., psychology, sociology) have struggled to establish themselves as a proper part of the academy by pursuing government- and foundation-sponsored research, particularly since 1950. Unfortunately, the academy does not prize them and education, as Choppin (1982) lamented, has not become any better. But to establish themselves, many education academics have been pursuing more and more research, while others develop instructional strategies for publication, write textbooks, or try to keep up with the demands of teaching pedagogy for classrooms of which they often have had little or no recent experience. Some academics do create mutually productive relations with practitioners, but for them there is little reward in the arcane promotion and tenure criteria of the modern American university (Boyer, 1990; Pincoffs, 1975).

Sustaining the university identity is not necessarily the best strategy for academics. Practitioners can reject them, a fact dramatically illustrated at the founding of the National Board of Professional Teaching Standards in 1989. This board initially refused to recognize accredited teacher education qualifications as a *sine qua non* for being granted its certificate. As a cooperative venture between the teaching unions, it appeared to eschew cooperation with the collegiate establishment, specifically with the American Association of Colleges for Teacher Education, which was reported to be particularly critical of the board's proposals and its initial intention to ignore teacher education. The implication was clear. For the board, initial teacher qualifications were of little importance in the certification of the "real" professional.

The School-Based Practitioner

The practitioner is differently placed. Halberstam (1990) sympatheti-
cally identifies classroom teachers' frustrations. In his essay on *The Next
Century,* he sees these teachers faced with an American middle class that is
apparently content to ignore the significance that the nation's economic com-
petitors give to education and the impact of education on a country's economic success or failure. Global difficulties apart, the "cellular" character
of the teaching context, with its constraints on teachers' ability to witness
one another, restrains the development of a sharing community of practical knowledge schoolwide and professionwide. Practitioners often seem
threatened by openness, by interclassroom partnership, and by the demands
of self-evaluation. Occupationally, classroom teachers are loners, and schools
are not, by and large, places where *they* learn (Feiman-Nemser & Floden,
1986; Lortie, 1975; Zahorik, 1987). Perhaps, as currently constructed,
schools cannot be.

Practitioners do not see academics as sources of support for their task,
even if they are "hungry for technique." The resources of research and
development do not seem to be able to deliver what teachers can use. New
research-based ideas get tried, but they often live a short classroom life
because practitioners are seen as technicians executing the ideas of an
expert. Rarely are classroom teachers given a sustained opportunity to master
practice and simultaneously to investigate critically the ideological or
empirical assumptions in the rationale. A practitioner may want to implement "what the research says," since it is an obvious source for technique,
but research cannot say much that is loud and clear. Where there are
research conclusions on matters of pedagogy, they are not often perceived
by practitioners as relevant to the teaching situation, because teaching
is viewed in the research as a context-free *activity.* So a practitioner may
be left feeling that "the research may say that, but I can't do that here
because . . ." Researchers often use methodologies that focus on the con-
trollable detail of performances, whereas teachers see themselves in an
occupation filled with constraints on context and role. Finally, where a practitioner actually comes into contact with researchers, it is more usual, as
the saying goes, for a teacher to be worked *on* rather than worked *with.* In
sum, neither within many schools nor in the professional community at
large does the practitioner encounter an obvious atmosphere of cooperation, particularly not for the development of teaching knowledge.

This academic–practitioner relationship is embodied in most educational writing. *What Works,* which was published by the U.S. Department
of Education in 1986, is a living testament to the hegemony of the applied
science view of the theory–practice relationship (Richardson-Koehler, 1988;

U.S. Department of Education [USDE], 1986). It presents to classroom teachers the conclusions of research by academics on a range of matters of classroom practice. It claims that great strides have been made in understanding the activity of teaching in the past 15 years by researchers outside the schools. The implicit notion is that once the academics discover the truth, it can be passed on "down" to the practitioners, who can then be told what to do. So the title, naturally, is *What Works*; not what challenges, intrigues, invites criticism, but *works*. *What Works* is typical in that it characterizes the practitioner as a mere technician implementing research conclusions. Here, once again, is the applied science model of the relationship between practice and theory that reinforces the academic–practitioner divide and with it the split profession. The split is at root epistemological, from which flow its institutional embodiment and the intensive socialization patterns on each side of the gap.

The Educational Administrator

However, this is a three-way, not just a two-way split. The broadly hierarchical management of schools makes the educational purposes of a school or a school district difficult to frame within the perspective of a professional community, for many administrators do not see themselves as instructional leaders. Hierarchical management by administrators drives workers into protectionism. So teachers in the classroom are imbued with a mutually protective notion of community such that they are frequently reluctant to acknowledge the reality that Mrs. Old is incompetent or Mrs. Simpson is outstanding, even though they know it to be true. Bureaucracies even seem to go along with that notion, rarely finding the courage to dismiss the incompetent. Teaching excellence is seldom recognized, except in the cutesy "teacher of the year" awards. It is left to such mixed union-business enterprises as the National Foundation for the Improvement of Education to develop a Christa McAuliffe Institute of educators who are top-notch classroom teachers.

Fairfax County, Virginia, offers an example of the intransigent problems administrators face. Superintendent Robert "Bud" Spillane promoted the introduction of merit pay in 1986 on the recommendation of a blue ribbon commission to enhance the professionalism and status of practitioners. After three years of hard work, 2,000 outstanding career teachers were identified; but the school board decided that these individuals should not be publicly identified for fear of breaching the myth of equal competence sustained by teacher unions. In 1991 the school board, acting against the advice of the superintendent, voted to abolish the bonus pay as a money-saving device. Spillane is able to please neither the board, the unions, nor the bulk of the practitioner employees as he seeks to find ways to enhance professionalism, however controversial.

Often the tasks that principals and central office administrators are set and/or that they are expected to fulfill in their schools seem to militate against the development of honest and mutually constructive professional relationships. Administrators, we should remember, are part of a bureaucratic system that they may or may not choose, with politicians on school boards who may have political ambitions that have little to do with education (Chubb & Moe, 1990; Kirst, 1984). Administrations are frequently extremely cavalier in their patterns of in-service education, picking up the latest from the research on a random basis, but not providing teachers with space or time to learn the rationale and the practice and to assess and evaluate the results—a phenomenon first remarked upon by William James and more recently aggressively criticized by Herbert Kleibard (1988).

Nor do attempts at collaboration necessarily change the relationship. Collaborative partnerships can be undermined by administrators. Hargreaves and Dawe (1989) argue that they may recognize that "collaborative professional development . . . is a tool of teacher empowerment and professional enhancement, bringing colleagues and their expertise to generate critical yet also practically-grounded reflection on what they do as a basis for wiser, more skilled action" (p. 7). Yet administrative attempts to break down teacher isolation can also be a "mechanism designed to facilitate the smooth and uncritical adoption of preferred forms of action (new teaching styles) introduced and imposed by experts from elsewhere" (p. 7).

I believe that this three-way split in our profession is of profound importance to public education. It is a major structural weakness in our education system, which, like a smokestack industry, is trapped in a gridlock of distinctions and differences that bear little relationship to the tasks it faces. Although there is a common reference point and rationale in the occupation of teaching for individuals in these three groups, one sometimes wonders how often that fact influences their behavior and how often we really see our jobs as one of a common cause. It is difficult to see how a society can expect radical improvement in public education when the primary participants are so much at loggerheads.

DEVELOPMENT OF THE PROFESSIONAL COMMUNITY

Although this has been a critical account of the relationship of academics, practitioners, and administrators, I think it is both fair and recognizable in a context of national concern about education quality. It indicates that no one should underestimate the considerable problems of developing an inclusive professional community, even if there are partnerships being promoted. Nor should we assume that creating a single professional community will do more than remove an obstacle to educational improvement.

Arguments for Collaboration

Two possible strategies can be used to promote improvement in public education—increasing control over the system and its agents or increasing the autonomy of those agents. Those who value increased control believe in bureaucratic accountability, strengthened curriculum mandates, extensive testing, hierarchical management, and teachers as technicians. Alternatively, those who value autonomy believe in accountability to consumers, curriculum independence within broad goals, testing as sampling, democratic forms of management, and teachers as artists and professionals. Universities have rhetorically supported autonomy. Academics have in fact been agents of control, primarily because they define themselves as knowers, not seekers. The fact is that, over the century of public education, the drive for improvement through control has proved to be a failure. There is no alternative to taking autonomy seriously, if we wish to improve education. That must mean a mutual respect among education professionals, not a split community.

The development of a professional community must begin with the struggle to define professional standards and teacher professionalism on moral, realistic, and political grounds. First, collaboration and an implicit move toward a common professional community is justified morally because of its power in strengthening professional development and increasing professional dignity (Griffin, 1986); as a basis for wiser, more skilled action (Shulman, 1988); and, indeed, as a central condition of teaching excellence (Holmes Group, 1989). A profession must be a community where issues of quality of practice bind individuals in their common cause. That cannot be done when the profession's dominant epistemology leads to a hierarchical system.

Second, such a community is becoming a reality, even though it is not yet *conceptualized as such*. It appears in the introduction of the professional development school (where academic, practitioner, and administrator work together on the initial education of new entrants to the profession), although the writers of *Tomorrow's Teachers* (Holmes Group, 1986) retained a strong patronizing tone. Teacher-research, too, represents in many of its manifestations a partnership between academic and practitioner (Hollingsworth & Sockett, in press). The work of the National Board for

OLSON LIBRARY
NORTHERN MICHIGAN UNIVERSITY
MARQUETTE, MICHIGAN 49855

Professional Teaching Standards (1989) has great potential for supporting a unified profession.

Third, public education is also facing a harsh political challenge to its very existence and to its ability to deliver achievement, assuming, as Graham (1991) does, that it has delivered attendance and access in the twentieth century. Educational institutions, in my view, should accept the challenge and go out of their way to work effectively *with* the national demand for educational improvement (Boyer, 1983; College Board, 1983; Education Commission of the States, 1983; Goodlad, 1984; National Governors Association, 1986; T. R. Sizer, 1984; USDE, 1991). That does not mean acquiescence in all aspects of policy, but professionals in education have a responsibility for contributing to and shaping such a crusade for improvement rather than being obstacles to it. To do that, they need an internal cohesiveness they presently lack. For example, some claim that the teacher's role is easy enough for any intelligent person to undertake. That claim seems to me to be false; but it requires a sophisticated, not a protectionist, response. Professional standards and professional knowledge can be consistently displayed without making them esoteric and inaccessible, and deep mutual understanding between academic and practitioner is necessary to produce such a result. Right now, academics are risking great political and public dissatisfaction, to say the least, by suggesting that we are on the verge of discovering some elixir called the "knowledge base of teaching" (Sockett, 1987; see also Chapter 4). There is real danger in making an implicit promise to improve teaching dramatically that cannot be delivered.

School–University Collaboration

Must such collaborative partnership include the academic and the university? Might the profession not be conceived simply as classroom teachers and administrators? Might the university not be ignored in future professional development and left to concentrate on "research," but without a teacher education function at all? The link with the university, which has been historically significant, is now in disarray but is ideologically important if academic freedom itself is thought valuable.

Historically, education became broadly accepted as a university discipline precisely because it distanced itself from practice, even though the education and socialization of recruits went on in the university. Educational theory identified closely with the dominant positivist epistemology within universities (with such notable exceptions as John Dewey, who was a professor of philosophy, not education), and it conformed to norms of research and publication. The undergraduate degree and the quest by normal schools and colleges to become "real" universities offered the education academic a place in the intellectual sun because education became thereby a "proper" university subject. However, U.S. university courses in education for undergraduate education majors came under such harsh criticism for lack of rigor and weakness of methodology that the degree has been virtually abandoned. In Britain the undergraduate major was only developed in the late 1960s, and the emergence of the undergraduate degree coincided with a vigorous concern with the constitutive disciplines of educational theory (philosophy, psychology, sociology, history); thus whatever it may have initially lacked in practical application, it gained in conceptions of rigor (Dearden, Hirst, & Peters, 1973; Tibble, 1966). This was also matched by a unity of international research purpose reflected in a range of outstanding interchanges and publications (Haydon, 1987; Mischel, 1969, 1971, 1974; N. F. Sizer & Sizer, 1970).

But the present disarray among those who would improve education is all too apparent. The development to university status has led to problems in the study of education and in teacher education identified by Goodlad (1990), and the academic–practitioner gap is exposed by Clifford and Guthrie (1990) in their classic analysis of *Ed School*, where they plead with academics to orient themselves toward the profession. But while historically the ambition seemed sensible, the situation to which it has led is far from encouraging, and these generally sympathetic critics may be too late. The academic teacher-educator seems to be in the process of losing control of the professional-entry qualification. The closing of a school of education in Oregon in 1991 invites the question of whether this is the beginning of a trend, one that might be facilitated by the financial restrictions bound to dominate higher education in the 1990s. The Holmes Group (1986) of universities pledged to the reform of teacher education has led the way to innovations such as the four-year liberal arts degree abandoning education majors as the basis for teaching. The post-baccalaureate programs, usually involving a different school-university partnership will not improve the teacher-educators' position unless it is very carefully planned and executed with a strong eye on the character and quality of that partnership.

Those academics who see research as more practically oriented, perhaps more qualitative, and who are more sensitive to Schön's (1983, 1989) notion of the reflective practitioner are likely to welcome the trend toward professional development and lead a collaborative academic participation in the professional community. For instance, Lytle and Cochran-Smith (1990a) at the University of Pennsylvania work in schools with novice teachers within a teacher-research perspective, seeking to support students in teaching "against the grain" of traditional professional socialization and thereby providing a much better grounding in professionalism. On such individuals rests the task of assuring the practitioners that there is value and point to the university's participation in education. To promote that, there will have to be a dramatic increase in the quality of the partnership and newly defined modes of collaboration among academic, practitioner, and novice, as well as a radical change in university expectations (Lieberman, 1988; Sirotnik & Goodlad, 1988).

Whatever the problems in existing relationships, it remains socially and intellectually important to the single profession for the study of education to continue as a university study for ideological reasons, notwithstanding the historical background and the unfortunate contemporary situation. The university as an institution is sometimes limited by financial or political influences and notions of "political correctness." Yet it continues to offer a base of ideological neutrality for the development of ideas about education and teaching. Derek Bok's (1982) account of the social responsibilities of the modern university includes the notion that the institution continues to offer protection for challenging social, political, and philosophical ideas.

But the principle of academic freedom (Pincoffs, 1975) is important for *all* teachers—teachers in the generic sense. It is not just a privilege granted by natural right to the inhabitants of the ivory tower. The development of such freedom and the inherent autonomy is needed if teaching as a profession is to be more assertive about the moral character of its mission and of the roles teachers occupy. The university can be a constant watchdog for the widespread development of the academic freedom of all teachers, and it can seek to extend privileges to more and more professionals in teaching, a matter of great importance in a public education system. Universities as institutions can support practitioners in school classrooms who are improperly subjected to censorship or political control and can assist teachers in contexts where autonomy is threatened. For academic freedom by itself can become a dissolute sort of right if it is not balanced by individual and institutional social responsibility, and a sense of responsibility for all who teach would seem a paradigmatically important function for a university.

Tragically, the university study of education, as of many other subjects, is dominated by its own version of political correctness. I refer not to long-haired, left-wing sociologists to whom this weakness is usually attributed, but to adherents of positivist epistemology. It is almost a "political tyranny" that obliges faculty to publish in the "right" journals and to avoid work with practitioners or on teacher research if they want to get tenure (Smith, 1990). That weakness is manifest in the hierarchical attitudes the epistemology engenders. Not only do academics fail to be deeply and collegially involved in issues of practice, but they also seem to find the writings of teachers only worth reading if the teachers are their students. Both these characteristics are part of an epistemological dominance. The education academy is liberal enough to allow alternative theoretical perspectives, but its institutional structure has not yet caught up with its principles. The clarification of alternative epistemological perspectives and moral purposes *that are directly linked to practitioners and practice* seems to me the central mission of the study of education in a university and from it arises naturally the value of an integrated teaching profession. This mission would take professional autonomy seriously.

Against an account of the splits and fissures in the education community, I have suggested that a single professional community focusing particularly on professional development is important for moral, pragmatic, and political reasons. I have argued that the link with the university has been historically significant, is in contemporary disarray, but is ideologically important if academic freedom is valuable. That freedom should be extended to all who teach. As my comments reveal, however, I am not sanguine that the study of education and its academic high priests are intellectually grown up enough to welcome innovative ideas at every level and to constantly rattle institutional assumptions. The principles and practices of the single professional community should be most apparent, however, in the arrangements it makes for initial training and professional development. How might we build from where we are to a professional community? To try to answer that question I take professional development as the context for the argument.

THE CAREER OF THE PROFESSIONAL TEACHER:
COMPOSING A LIFE

A view of a professional community, integrated or not, is dependent on a view of what a career in that profession comprises. We have no clear conception of a career in teaching. Indeed, teaching is the only profession that institutionally denigrates the art and craft that lies at its heart. If a practitioner is excellent in a school classroom, he or she will become a principal or advisory administrator. Unions have been content to support this attitude by claiming salary differentials on the basis of longevity of service or of administrative tasks, not on the basis of teaching quality. The attitude is reflected in the university (even in faculties of education), where there is still a constant struggle to make the quality of teaching itself properly valued.

Apart from a sketch offered by a United Kingdom national report in 1972 (James, 1972), there is no generally recognized, full-blooded conception of what a career in *classroom* teaching looks like, even though that is how the majority of professional (generic) teachers spend their lives. So when a novice asks a career counselor about teaching prospects, he or she will learn only of opportunities *outside* the actual context of the activity of teaching—becoming a principal, a curriculum adviser, or a teacher-educator. This absence of career perspective may explain why some do not enter teaching, and it may also be a reason for Lortie's (1975) claim that the profession attracts a conservative type of person with traditional expectations of the role and those with a family history in teaching, although this account has to be balanced with understanding teaching as a "woman's profession" (Laird, 1988).

Because we have no idea what a "career in the classroom" could look like in the future, our patterns of in-service education are not matched to professional growth. Many school district in-service courses are geared to the needs of a particular crisis or moment. Teachers undertake master's programs while in service, but whether they do so at the right time, what they gain from them, or whether their design fits professional needs and profiles is not clear. Doctoral programs in education seem irrelevant to the practitioner. Take the example of Kathy Easton, a high school history teacher with whom I work. She has been teaching for 15 years, has developed a profound understanding of cooperative learning, and runs in-school and other programs to induct teachers into cooperative learning that enable them to integrate their classroom practice with rigorous examination of the theory. She decided to pursue a master's program, parts of which she acknowledges as relevant to her classroom. But she would like to pursue the development of her classroom practice in a depth appropriate to a doctorate. Not only is that difficult because there are few if any precedents for doctorates *in teaching*, but most teachers (and certainly university professors) would think it absurd to pursue a doctorate and stay in the classroom. So concerned have we become to ape the social science disciplines, where Ph.D.s are training degrees for research, that we have failed to develop doctoral degrees appropriate to the professional task. But my guess is that we do not really understand the career significance of graduate degree work, except in terms of added remuneration. We lack a conception of a career, of growth in teaching. Sometimes it almost seems as if we lack self-respect, as if the activity of the profession is not fundamentally important. To combat that, we need to develop a model for a career.

A Model for a Teaching Career

In Chapter 1, I suggested that we need to view the teaching profession as a moral commitment to complex roles and abandon the preoccupation with performance. Of course, during a career, a professional's classroom work will be sophisticated and continuously improved. However, teachers must also play a variety of highly complicated roles in the social reality of the school, all of which should be reflected in any notion of a career (Boyer, 1991). This is *not* to say that teachers should be social workers, counselors, caregivers, or priests. A teaching career demands that an individual grow as he or she assumes a more complex role and deepens in understanding and experience. The examples of Mrs. Simpson, Tom, and Elizabeth in Chapter 1 showed the four constituent elements: character and commitment, which suggest a moral dimension, and subject knowledge and pedagogy, which suggest an intellectual dimension. Bearing in mind also the argument that the teacher's role extends beyond the classroom to the school and to the public, it is possible to conceive a career in teaching as consisting of an eight-point base, divided into two main parts—the intellectual and the moral. The *intellectual* career involves the growth of wisdom, and the *moral* career involves development of virtue. At the center is the individual person striving to compose his or her own life and career.

The *intellectual* career has four main elements, each with its own illustrative components:

1. *Content and method renewal:* Consistent opportunity for study of subjects being taught, for critical examination of new methodologies and technologies, and time to absorb and to work on classroom implementations
2. *Leadership opportunities:* Mentorships for novice teachers, leadership in curriculum and/or instruction, working with external or parents' committees; particularly the chance to develop a policy and implement it, external representation (e.g., as an ambassador for public education)
3. *In-service teaching of colleagues:* Opportunities to share classroom expertise with others, to lead classroom-based innovations, to develop skills of teaching adults
4. *Reflective practice and research:* The development of sophisticated classroom observation techniques, critical examination of one's own practice, collegial research

The *moral* career demands the development of understanding, skill, and expertise in four areas of interpersonal and personal behavior, again with illustrative components.

1. *With students:* The development of increasing sophistication in handling students in groups and as individuals inside and outside the classroom and gaining moral insight into the issues they confront
2. *With parents and the public:* The development of increasing sophistication in working with parents in groups and as individuals in the promotion of the school's mission and in the individual concern for their children; with the public as ambassador for public education

3. *With colleagues*: The complex tasks of working in diverse roles—as team leader, team member, support group, member, evaluator and critic, in-service teacher
4. *With one's self*: In understanding one's duties to one's self and family and the balance of commitment between chosen profession and personal responsibilities

The Advantages of the Model

This framework does not rule out technical specificity—of skills, knowledge, or expertise. For example, as teachers turn to teaching their colleagues, they will need to master technique for teaching adults. As they become ambassadors for public education, they may need coaching in public speaking. This framework serves primarily as an antidote to skill-based conceptions of professional development that ignore both the complexity of the individual's life and the complex relationships between an individual's personal life and his or her role as a teacher.

Nor is the framework linear. Indeed, it assumes that individuals construct or compose their careers rather than having it done for them. We do not have to "advance" from one to another stage. A career in teaching can involve growth, in depth and breadth, changes of focus, and, sometimes, wrong directions. For our lives and our careers are in part what we make of them. Catherine Mary Bateson (1989) has suggested that we can and do *compose a life*. She writes of women's careers and life experiences being asymmetrical. Composing does not necessarily mean picking out the rungs above you on the linear ladder at the age of 22, but it does mean seeing the range of areas for one's development at that age. This eight-point conception of a career can help people who enter teaching see how their careers will mesh with their lives. They know they will have moral relationships with students, parents and the public, and colleagues, as well as duties to themselves. They will have careers in which content and method renewal, leadership opportunities, the teaching of colleagues, and reflective practice and research will be an integral part.

Our lives outside the classroom influence and are of great value for our work. For instance, Mrs. Simpson had young children of her own at the time I saw her. She thus brought to her classroom life experiences that gave her a different (note—different, not better) understanding of children from that of teachers who have not been parents. Yet there appears to be no avenue for the systematic exploration of the complex interrelationship between teaching children and being a parent to one's own children. Teachers are not encouraged to address the interaction of their personal lives with their professional understandings and commitments. We ignore this huge resource of understanding, comparison, *and* mutual support for school and home. We fail to use it as a way of developing our thinking and practice.

The nonlinearity of the career and its integration with our own lives may well mean that some aspects of our professional development are left in abeyance for some years. As she brings up her young children, Mrs. Simpson is unlikely to spend much time working on curriculum committees, which meet after school. Indeed, if she is to fulfill her family commitments (which as moral beings we must all want for her), she could not (and should not) be paying great attention to much else. We cannot deplore the absence of the caring mother or father for our students in schools but then create expectations for professional teachers which demand such absence from their children. It would make sense for Mrs. Simpson, at that time and in appropriate ways, to focus on the interrelationships between her bringing up her own and other people's children. That would mean her giving attention to the *moral* aspects of her relationships with children and how she is growing, professionally and personally, in her dealings with them and *their* parents. I need hardly say that this would be true for Mr. Simpson too, if he were a teacher.

Such a conception of a career puts great emphasis on the individual within the occupational framework of teaching (see Chapter 3). What is appropriate for Mrs. Simpson at any one time may not be appropriate for others. In the life of a school, as Roland Barth (1988) has argued, a community of learners can be created that also gives opportunities for leadership, and the points at which an individual is ready to take such leadership are immensely varied (Little, 1987; Schlechty & Whitford, 1988). Equally, Kathy Easton was able to assume an in-service responsibility at a time in her life when she had the space inside and outside the classroom to have developed a deep understanding of cooperative learning. Composing a career without a linear order of professional growth but in line with other commitments needs to be made explicit for all of us so that we can understand its elements and its possibilities. With these elements necessary to a teaching career, an autonomous and emancipated teacher can be as creative as he or she wishes.

There is much room for discussion and analysis about each of the eight elements in terms of their location in career and life growth and at what points, for most people, they might best be attended to. For instance, reflective practice leading to the development of teacher-research (one of the four "intellectual" elements) is usually treated as something to become acquainted with after five years in the classroom. Elizabeth Beck, however, was extraordinarily sophisticated at both classroom analysis (her original diagnosis of Mrs. Old) and reflecting rigorously on her own practice. She was a student for an undergraduate degree in education at an institution of higher education in England; at that time, some institutions emphasized the development of such a research stance toward teaching from the outset of a four-year degree. A different example: A young teacher of my acquaintance, Francoise Alberola, is now in her third year in the classroom. Leadership is thrust upon her: She gets much more opportunity to deal with parents than many other teachers in her school because she speaks two languages other than English and is therefore able to communicate with many parents much more effectively. Her work is not framed by her as a professional learning experience, conducted within a framework of reflective study from which she could profit and develop. Her employers, I suspect, simply congratulate themselves on their good luck in having her on staff. But Francoise's case indicates that individual perspectives have to be developed to mesh with institutional provision.

Right now, as a profession, we seem stuck with an emphasis on method and content renewal—and not much else. That will not provide young teachers like Elizabeth or Francoise with much opportunity to compose a career, and maybe it hems Kathy in, too. Interestingly, when I have tentatively set out this eight-point framework to my older colleagues who work in classrooms, their invariable reaction is one of pride, because they recognize in themselves, as they look over their shoulders at their careers, the value of their increasing maturity within their moral career. As David Evelyn, a teacher and colleague put it, much of what he had done as a teacher "seemed all worthless in the eyes of the bureaucracy." Classroom teachers seem to find in the conception a statement of their full professionalism. Unfortunately, they have been socialized into rejecting the moral career as governing anything in schooling or their work (Strike, 1991). This framework thus recognizes the central elements in the role of the generic teacher, though it is worked out here in terms of the classroom teacher. Each element is present in the generic conception of the teacher and will thus apply, more or less, in satellite occupations of academic and administrator, although of course those satellite occupations will need to add their own specifics, for example, the management of organizations as related to moral leadership. However, it should be understood that this eight-point framework is not the result of an empirical survey and is not intended to address the chronological patterns of actual teachers' experience.

Breaking The Mold: Thinking Differently About a Career

This set of elements (or something like it) constitutes the breadth of a life's work. Practitioners particularly do not have the opportunity to frame their careers and compose what they want to do. What then are the general implications of such a framework for the profession, for institutions, and for individuals?

Professional development opportunities.   All professional development opportunities, from master's degrees to one-shot afternoon programs, could be perceived within this conception of composing one's professional career growth. From the beginning we would be taught to see our careers as integral to our lives and to discuss our development with our superiors and our colleagues. A radical shift in the way personnel departments, colleges of education, staff developers, principals, and teachers themselves look at all professional development patterns would be implied. How are the moral demands of leadership being addressed? Are teachers taught how to work with adults, such as colleagues or parents? How can the university degree system become relevant to a real career, rather than to one relatively insignificant part of it? How are these elements to be built into the emerging structure of the National Board for Professional Teaching Standards? How do institutions such as the Association for Supervision and Curriculum Development plan their programs to fit with a conception of teacher development? How do we exercise our professional responsibilities for those entering the profession?

If we paid more attention to the demands of the role, rather than the mechanics of teaching, effective internal coherence could be built into teachers' lives. Career development support systems are urgently needed. Individuals need to have access to advice and support as they look forward and sideways at what they do. That means transforming our present atomic cultures into a common framework of professional development responsibilities covering all relevant institutions, employers, universities, and associations.

Coordination, particularly in assessment.   Such a framework could link these professional development institutions within a coherent professional pattern, particularly in assessing such things as graduate credit, recertification, performance evaluation, and national board certification, which implies different assessment patterns. We would then look at our own performance and that of others within the subtle constraints of a person within a role, which is critical to a cogent account of professionalism. The widespread use of profiling and journals as well as the acceptance of subjective generalizability in autobiographical self-reports provide a start on this mammoth task, for it does mean breaking down a solid institutional structure and institutional habits. The perspectives that individuals bring to the assessment of themselves and their professionalism should be fostered in a profession in pursuit of excellence.

Career growth and individual growth.   Congruence must be established between the activities necessary at different career stages and patterns of personal growth; thus some attention probably must be paid to notions of adult development. A career must be set within some conception of the variously defined stages of adult development (Oja & Smulyan, 1989; Patterson, 1979; Sockett, 1980). Adult developmental theories offer an avenue for linking the moral career and issues of character (e.g., in ego development and in moral development) with the intellectual aspects (e.g., the development of the cognitive), although we must constantly bear in mind feminist perspectives on stages of moral development (Gilligan, 1979, 1982). A career path then becomes linked to a broad range of understandings of adult development, defining the character of professional development needs (Huberman, 1988, 1989; McLaughlin & Lee, 1988) although the very notion of their being stages of development may founder on the fact that adulthood is a social status; we may just have to talk of personal growth.

The hypothesis is important: How do we conceive professional development in teaching if we take seriously the various aspects of personal development? The provision of all professional programs would need to be governed logically by criteria of development, as well as by clear understandings of the relation between role and personhood. For example, the traditional Foundations of Education courses rarely pays any attention at all to where the learner is (Goodlad, 1990). In grappling with this problem I have experimented for two summers as a university teacher with a course I called "Foundations: Origins and Horizons." I give "teachers who study with me" (to use Hollingsworth's nice phrase) a self-analysis instrument of perspectives drawn from philosophers or educators. They are invited to work out their ideological stance against quotations from Froebel, Dewey, Pestalozzi, Plato, Skinner, Neill, Peters, or whomever. In subsequently reading the texts of the course, they can begin to establish their origins as a teacher and further their self-understanding. In the second half of the course, using the eight-point framework, they can begin to examine their career and life horizons, armed with the principles and commitments they have uncovered in themselves. "Foundations," in this course, refers to the foundations of one's life and one's career. It is a first attempt to provide an integration of the individual professional's work or life with educational thought, not just to present those ideas as free-floating and unconnected to the life and work of professional teachers.

The career and the professional community. The framework of a career could apply to all who teach, although there are specific additions for those who become specialists. As we think about any career in an educational workplace, the intellectual and moral requirements are very similar. However, this is not just a matter for the individual teacher, for we have here, differently stated, an extension of the fourfold characterization of teaching excellence built from the stories of Mrs. Simpson, Tom, and Elizabeth.

Character, commitment, subject knowledge, and pedagogy divide into intellectual and moral elements, into wisdom and virtue. This eight-point framework expands them into significant dimensions of professionalism within each of which will be criteria of excellence. But the emphasis on the notion of career is needed for us to understand the significance of the profession as a community. The career pattern adumbrated illustrates the role of the professional teacher, and *ipso facto* stresses the breadth of those rights and duties a professional has as a member of a workplace and a professional community. It is the interweaving of professional development, career, and role that distributes responsibilities within the professional community. Contemporary politics puts the pressure on content and method renewal. This framework gives us a panorama for personal and professional growth through which we can fundamentally reappraise how we initiate the young into our work.

THE EDUCATION OF THE NOVICE
IN THE PROFESSIONAL COMMUNITY

So far I have argued in this chapter that collaborative professional development is the key to a coherent single professional community, without which, I have suggested, the prospects for educational improvement nationwide look dim. I have suggested that the profession needs a conception of a career, seen as a framework of eight elements within which we as individuals compose our lives and our careers as befits autonomous moral individuals. From this perspective the education of the novice offers both an essential place to model professional partnership across institutions and to initiate novices into a conception of a career. The professional development school is still in its infancy. It is being developed against the background of strong criticism of initial teacher education, to which brief reference has already been made.

The Contemporary Scene

Initial teacher education has been debated in the public and professional arena for some years (Carnegie Forum on Education and the Economy, 1986; Clifford & Guthrie, 1990; Governors, 1991; Holmes Group, 1986; Lanier & Little, 1986; National Committee on Excellence in Teacher Education, 1985). Thomas Kean (1986), now chairman of the New American Schools Development Corporation and a former governor of New Jersey, suggested a five-point agenda which defined the initial teacher education issues, here summarized:

- that teachers have to have high standards and a machinery for ensuring them
- that colleges and universities must rebuild teacher education: intellectual rigor based on solid practice is needed
- that schools must be redesigned to make them productive places to learn and work, for which collaborative arrangements are needed
- that a different kind of regulatory system is needed, one that is very clear about the expected results, but leaves the methods up to the people on the scene; there is no excuse for the "tangle of directives that has grown up at every level of the system"
- that thoughtful teacher recruitment and retention programs are needed

This is a commonly agreed-upon diagnosis that emphasizes the weakness of initial and induction phases of teacher education. All these matters are interrelated. For instance, regulatory systems are the responsibility of the states, which do not necessarily take heed of professionals, although school districts can take their own initiatives, for example, in school-based management as in Edmonton, Alberta, and Prince William County, Virginia (Hill & Bonan, 1991). Teacher recruitment and retention problems, too, are always likely to be critical, although increasing entry-level standards could raise quality of entry rather than diminish it (Silber, 1989); but whether brighter recruits will stay in teaching without a coherent picture of a career before them, irrespective of considerations of status and financial reward, is not certain. Kean's analysis indicates the failure of the systems of accountability that have been installed. Whether the alternative "machinery for ensuring high standards" will materialize through the National Board for Professional Teaching Standards remains to be seen. "Intellectual rigor" has been espoused by Shulman's (1986b) work on the articulation of the knowledge base in teaching (Reynolds, 1989), in Goodlad's (1990) publication of 19 postulates for teacher education, in the Holmes Group's (1989) proposals for professional development schools (Lieberman & Miller, 1990), and by the growing numbers of partnerships between academics and practitioners that are responses to Kean's agenda on "collaborative arrangements" in initial education. The reconstruction of teacher education proceeds, particularly in the professional development school.

The Professional Development School

A professional development school is an elementary or secondary school where university and school-based faculty work in full partnership with novice students. It differs from earlier forms of initial teacher education in the following ways: The curriculum of learning to teach is developed jointly by university and school faculty; this curriculum is driven by the practical experiences students encounter in specific environments; the assessment of students performance is formally a joint responsibility; since most, if not all, of the curriculum is taught within the school, the student's experience corresponds much more closely to the postqualification experience. The professional development school also provides a context for research and development partnerships. This rudimentary description takes different forms in different parts of the country (Levine, 1992). The professional development school offers the novice four things:

1. A chance to learn to teach
2. A chance to learn how to work with others and to see that partnership modeled
3. Engagement in intellectually rigorous debate on classroom practice
4. A start as a teacher–researcher.

It should prompt the rethinking of professional induction courses within the four-year degree program.

Novices will not be alone in reaping the benefits of this innovation. The professional development school can be a building block in the development of a unified professional community, a model of inter-institutional partnership, provide a research focus within its practical orientation, and facilitate learning from other professions.

First, the professional development school can be the major building block in the development of a unified professional community. Novices will see modeled the single profession taking responsibility for training. This improves mutual understanding. It presupposes a recognition of different expertise between the functions of teacher-educator and teacher. It can lead to professional and institutional restructuring to close the breach between the academic and the practitioner. It can shape the novice's expectations of future professional relationships between school and university. Fortunately, the range of ideas and practical possibilities for the professional development school is growing fast and away from the notion of "clinical teacher education," a concept misleading in the analogies it uses between medicine and teaching.

Second, the professional development school then provides a demonstrable working model of interinstitutional professional partnership. One of the real difficulties in the old models of supervision of novices by teacher-educators has been the reluctance to discuss classroom practice with the host practitioner. Ideas about best practice were left hanging for the student, hoist between what the school (or teacher) and the university (or

supervisor) thinks "best." There was no real conversation about best practice. However, a properly established partnership should remove the barriers of etiquette and obliterate that nonconversation. Indeed, it should
replace that appalling advice "forget everything they told you in college"
with wide-ranging discussion of effective teaching. The student's experience
in a professional development school can be *intellectually* rigorous if practice becomes a central point of debate. In particular, a professional development school offers, through its very structure, opportunities to ensure
that real ethical problems are faced (Strike & Soltis, 1985).

Third, professional development schools can develop a research focus
within the practical orientation. It is possible to promote serious reflective
research partnership among academic, practitioner, and novice and to
develop detailed case studies of children, of programs, of individual teachers in a collaborative framework with novices. This new community need
not delegate its research to university academics, as old models presume.
As the teacher-research movement has demonstrated, classroom teachers can
get hold of research and own it, because it is they who face the social and
political factors in what they do and because, in the course of reflective
research study, they can become better equipped to deal with those factors. That induction into the political world of schools and teaching
becomes a significant piece of the education of the novice.

Finally, the professional community of teachers can embrace insights
from other forms of professional education without being overtaken by
them. There is a major need for the establishment of centers of cross-
professional studies concentrating primarily on professional education.
As a start, professional education courses in ethics could be made available within liberal arts degrees as part of professional induction, whether
students are headed for law, medicine, teaching, accountancy, or other professions. Professional education in universities tends to be locked within
specific schools of study, and continuing education in other professions
is usually within departments of adult education. Schön's (1989) case studies of different types of professional competence are highly suggestive for
teacher education, not simply because of the pedagogic strategies some of
them employ but because of the ways in which insights from one activity
are transferred to a quite different setting.

Provided these horizons for professional education remain wide and
are continuously expanded, the quality of the recruits to the profession
through the professional development school may also be dramatically
improved. The ideals of the professional development school mesh with a
coherent career path as part of a novice's vision of what he or she might
do. Ensuring that entrants to the profession perceive the significance of
intellectual freedom, too, is a joint task for academics and practitioners

within the profession. Ensuring that initial professional education is methodologically crisp will enable new teachers to begin their professional lives with maximum potential for effective career growth. Ensuring sophisticated exposure to the social and political issues through examining the context of their work is equally essential if initial preparation is to embody the full range of career dimensions.

The quality of the profession as a single community is therefore to be judged in part by developments in initial teacher education. In the profession and in the rest of the academy, now that the initial education pattern is in the process of profound change, interest must inevitably shift to advanced studies. The question is whether the whole area of postqualification professional development can be constructed as a partnership within the professional community.

Building a single professional community around individual teachers can be achieved in part through a cogent perspective on professional and career development. I have pointed to some of the historical and contemporary obstacles to that enterprise, outlined a conception of a career with a major stress on the individual composing it, and suggested some criteria for the work of professional development schools that are building new partnerships and with it a single community. This overall theme of the relation between the community and professional development is now pursued in Chapter 3, with a focus on in-service and on teacher-research work.

CHAPTER 3

A Professional Community of Reflective Practitioners

"Teaching," writes Hollingsworth (1990), "is the best form of educational research. The art of teaching represents not only critical thought about practice, but continuous change as a result of that thought" (p. 3). This echoes Lawrence Stenhouse's (1983) comment that "the really important thing about curriculum research is that . . . it invites the teacher to improve his art by the exercise of his art" (p. 157). In the previous chapter, we have seen that bridges between the "purity" of research and the "harsh reality" of practice are difficult to build, and we have noted the need for the novice to begin to think critically and reflectively about practice.

In recent years two notions of the teacher have gained ground—that of the teacher as reflective practitioner and/or the teacher as researcher. Stenhouse (1975) first articulated a notion of the teacher as researcher. I take Schön's (1983) phrase "reflective practice," however, to be a generic term that allows for a variety of *practices*, of which teacher-research, action research, and applied research in their various forms would be examples. He also uses the phrase "knowing-in-action" to describe what the professional does, which is a very different account of the theory–practice relationship from that given in the traditional model (see Chapter 5). In this model a professional knows a theory and then applies it to practice, which is not only the traditional way of conceiving the theory–practice relationship, but also embodies the positivist view of knowledge and rationality. Against that model Schön not only offers "reflective practice" as a term characterizing various types of research but he also offers us a nonpositivist account of knowledge-in-action, an idea that will be explored as an epistemology of practice in Chapters 4 and 5.

Different views of epistemology yield different views of research. It is surprising, therefore, given the absence of any *a priori* justification, how many empirical researchers today think that they have some kind of privileged access to the concept and that only empirical research is "real" research, with everything else being a "think piece." At worst, holders of this view are simply foolish to exclude Plato's, Descartes', or John Dewey's work as research because it was not empirical. At best, they ignore significant intellectual changes that have occurred since the time of their intellectual ancestors, Auguste Comte and John Stuart Mill. A formal definition of *research* is needed, one that leaves the field open for intellectually differing views of what it might substantively be. For instance, "research is systematic inquiry made public" is a good basic definition because it does not determine a methodology (Stenhouse, 1983) but picks out the three essentials of any definition of research—system, inquiry, and publicity. Within that definition of research, reflective practitioners (as I have characterized them above) might or might not do research, though teacher–researchers would. Both reflective practice and teacher-research, as a species of that kind of practice, are significant to the career professional development I described in Chapter 2.

This chapter continues the theme of professional development in the professional community, particularly for teachers already in service, but it picks up specifically "reflective practice and research" from the intellectual part of the career framework. Four primary principles governing the provision of master's-degree levels of professional development are critical. Master's degrees are the primary meeting place and teaching–learning vehicle of academics and practitioners. They require serious reappraisal if they are to meet the needs of the professional community and become a valuable experience for practitioners and academics. But we also need, as I explain in the second section of this chapter, a research model appropriate for a unified professional community. This is found in action research, a generic term for a type of research carried out in a variety of social science disciplines, which provides the intellectual base for the development of teacher-research in the professional community. In the final section, I indicate that if the research model used is to enhance the community of teaching, it must both support the individual professional as a person with a life and a career and enhance the collaborative enterprise between institutions and individuals. This complements my discussion of the individual composing a career in Chapter 2.

PROFESSIONAL DEVELOPMENT FOR REFLECTIVE PRACTITIONERS

Master's-degree programs are the core of professional development for teachers. Purportedly they respond to a professional's need. Yet the apparatus of unit structure and electives turns out frequently to be a prescribed set of credits determined by what academics can teach rather than on what teachers might want to learn. Programs are usually framed by academics, with the professional insights of the teacher-student relegated to a marginal place in the intellectual experience. Rarely are programs negotiated and developed within a local community of professionals. Courses on "research methods" (reflecting the dominance of empirical research) or "foundations" (reflecting an uneasy conscience about philosophy) are often mandatory. The degree becomes merely a device for getting credentialed, that is, possessed of only an instrumental purpose; and as long as receiving a master's degree brings a cash reward, the university is in a seller's market.

Too harsh a criticism? Perhaps. But as we entertain these criticisms, we can discern guidelines for the reconstruction needed in degrees which will support a professional community:

1. Practitioners must frame and set the problems.
2. The focus must be on the predicament of the unique case and its susceptibility to change.
3. Tacit knowledge and understanding must be acknowledged and described if possible.
4. Academic-practitioner relationships (and perhaps many other teacher-learner relations) should be defined as coach-practitioner relationships.

Such principles will facilitate the development of the "systematic inquiry" called research in the career of the teacher and in the professional community. Manifestly, relations between academic and practitioner will change in consequence. Each principle deserves separate examination.

Framing the Problems

The agenda (where academic and practitioner are gathered together) can consist of problems that the practitioners frame and set or that are jointly set. Academics could bring to the partnership guidance on how to frame these problems as hypotheses. There are many examples in educational research and in some course programs. Hollingsworth's (1989) important series of papers on collaborative research and on developing an epistemology of learning how to teach teachers describe the establishment of a framework in which teachers come to share her perspective as a researcher and through that, to develop their own. The course Hollingsworth develops is in an antiphonal relationship with the work of the teachers. Clandinin and Hogan (1991) have been jointly defining collaboration (in teacher education) as an improvisational art guided by an ethic of caring. In 1973 a project on teaching race relations provided a group of teachers, each of whom was concerned about promoting racial understanding, with a framework for articulating and sharing alternative pedagogies (Stenhouse, 1982). Elliott's

(1991) excellent recent publication, *Action Research and Educational Change*, describes both his political and intellectual development before and after he, with Adelman, drew together teachers interested in exploring and developing their skills as practitioners within an inquiry/discovery pedagogy in *The Ford Teaching Project* (Elliott & Adelman, 1983). Throughout his work, Elliott has placed major importance on the definition of problems for research by the teachers with whom he has studied and worked.

Such links may also be institutionalized. There already exist many different examples of school–university partnerships and collaborative enterprises (Clark, 1988). Such creations as the Puget Sound Consortium (Keating & Clark, 1988), the Center for Applied Research and Development in Education at George Mason University, the Center for Applied Research and Innovation at the University of Minnesota, and the Stanford Collaborative (Calfee, 1987) work through different structures to bring academics and practitioners together to define problems and devise strategies to tackle them. Interinstitutional partnerships can provide an opportunity for professionals to contribute differing expertise, to speak with distinctive voices (Davies & Aquino, 1975; J. P. Macdonald, 1988), and to develop ownership of a new institution. A structural issue common to all such collaboratives is whether this is really an institutional partnership or whether a partnership of professionals for collegiality can turn out to be cooptation. Griffin (1986) warns, that practitioners may be co-opted to a school district's political agenda containing problems that the practitioners would not, as professionals, themselves frame and set.

The Predicament of the Unique Case

The focus could therefore be on the predicament of the unique case or cases which is/are susceptible to change. This is a familiar starting point in the general literature of action research, as it was in the experimental foundations course I described in Chapter 2. It is also a principle for effective procedure in professional development. The word *predicament* is important: It is not specifically a dilemma or merely a problem; it describes the many facets of a context and a situation and allows for a very wide range of factors to be included. Specific cases are the occasion for features of the predicament to come together. Elizabeth Beck does not just have a problem to be solved: Her unique case is a predicament. It would be trivial to say it was a dilemma (i.e., she could choose *a* or *b*). Rather the complex of relationships with children, supervisors, Mrs. Old, the parents, and her emerging commitments and understandings all define the predicament of her unique case. In principle, any professional partner can then share in that predicament, research it, and learn from it.

Indeed, improvement in educational practice may come primarily not from theory's search for generalizations but from intellectual attention to this predicament of the unique case. We have become accustomed to looking only for objective generalizability, although feminist pedagogy is developing a notion of subjective generalizability (Hollingsworth, 1991). (This idea is close, I think, to the idea in idealist metaphysics where the particular could be an instantiation of the universal, the particular being a concrete universal [Murdoch, 1970]). Searching for generalizations obscures the contextuality of practice; to some degree it presupposes its insignificance. Goodlad (1984) drew to our attention the fact that the verisimilitude of context that researchers see in "the place called school" is not matched by the perspectives of the practitioner. Practitioners have access to perceptions of difference denied to the external researcher, who usually enters the school with a set of myopic lenses through which to view practice. Practitioners constantly undermine "validity" and "reliability" thereby. The academic researcher can, however, support and articulate the description of unique cases and help to make the process more sophisticated. That transition will arise from enhancing the practitioner's reflective capability and building on the descriptive language already in use, already implicit in the incorporation of the techniques of others. This principle must, I believe, inform every aspect of professional development.

I learned a great deal from Elizabeth Beck on this. I had been for some time puzzled, even dismayed, by student teachers of young children who regularly described their problems with "silly" children. I regarded such a description as trite and meaningless and took her to task for her description of a particularly "silly" child in her notes. She argued that it is an adjective that is understood by teachers and children. "Silliness," she insisted, stands on the edge of the norm of acceptable behavior; that is, it invites attention but does not court discipline, (a jester in a teacher's court—a Fool to the Lear pedagogue). Moreover, as she explained it to me, it is usually a "trying-out of expression through action"—rolling eyes, strange noises, funny walks, and so on. It is, as she put it, often an original comment, not a protest. "Silliness" thus began for me to take on a richness of meaning *explanatory of a child's classroom behavior* that I, with my academic hat on, had simply not seen or bothered to try to understand. Rejecting the language and with it the classroom problem as I saw it, I was incapable of assisting the teacher in a matter of her practice that was susceptible to change. I was also an academic fool, but not, I also now understand, silly. Practitioners need technical assistance, not intellectual browbeating.

Describing Tacit Knowing

The task of describing tacit knowing must be a matter for mutual enquiry between practitioner and academic. Tacit knowing, to amend Polanyi's (1960) term, picks out that which someone knows how to do when—not merely spontaneously. Many teaching acts by individuals appear to have this quality. Recall Tom Stevenson. As we walked along the hallway that day, he clearly had no idea (in the kind of detail that any objectives-based instructional leader would understand) of what on earth he was going to do. He had had some such plan but had rejected it as inadequate to the task. Yet out of his experience, his judgment, his autobiography, his sense of who those children were, his love of history, perhaps the fact that I was an audience (and much else) came this inspirational teaching. It was a sort of improvisation of the practical mind, building as he designed. He built what he did as he went along, moving at great speed from idea to idea as his mind led him. Can we put that in a textbook and pass that knowledge and understanding, intuition and insight on to other teachers? I am not sure that we can. I think I hope not. But while we can describe the events, we cannot describe what he knew, in part because the speed of his improvisational art outpaces the witness's pen and, I am sure, the videocamera as well. What we can do, as I did, was to learn through witness and reflection.

We tend to leave this extraordinary human power and other areas of teachers' actions in the limbo of tacit knowing, ineffable, elusive by definition. Even how far we can effectively describe it remains to be seen. (Clearly novelists manage to describe it; witness Emily Brontë's sublime portrayal of Heathcliff's malevolence in *Wuthering Heights*.) Its importance for teacher professionalism is that our understanding of tacit knowing can provide a reservoir for understanding excellence: perhaps it can only be emulated, but teaching skill may actually be as much caught as taught. To ignore tacit knowing as irrelevant to the description of something called the "knowledge base of teaching" is as neglectful as ignoring counterevidence to a theory.

The Academic–Practitioner Relationship

Finally, a major implication of Schön's (1983) perceptions about reflective practice as an epistemology is that it must change the relationship between academic and practitioner. Schön's suggestion that the academic take on the relationship of a "coach" is a handy analogy. In the movie *Chariots of Fire* where the story of British athletes in the 1924 Olympics is told, Montebeeni the coach is as involved in getting Abrahams to win the 100-meter dash as Abrahams is himself. The coach is as much locked onto the detailed goals of the practitioner as is the practitioner. A coach does not ignore the individual's or the team's goals. His or her aim is not to help a team win: His or her aim *is* to WIN by having the team win. The (teaching) coach is thus no (classroom) voyeur.

The term *coach* is interesting for another reason. The coach is rarely capable of doing what the person being coached can do. The coach provides technical assistance. Montebeeni could no more have competed in an Olympic final than fly to the moon. Navratilova's coach would not get through the first round at Wimbledon. For the academic to be a coach does not imply that he or she could do the practical job of teaching children better than the practitioner, for this is not a master-apprentice relationship. The coach usually brings experiences, ideas, and insights into a cooperating relationship. In the education of novices there is room for both academic and expert practitioner as joint coaches.

In professional continuing education, the notion of an academic-practitioner relation being that of coach-practitioner utterly changes the relationship. If the problems are the practitioner's, the academic teacher who has no idea of those problems cannot function as a coach, since he or she does not share the learner's goals. It will also change our view of the theory-practice relationship, for on this account theory can no longer be handed down to practitioners, who then follow the rules. For there has to be constant interplay between coach and teacher, which we can only understand in general terms as working at knowing-in-action. That suggests the need for a more appropriate epistemology in education, an epistemology of practice that will run against the traditional theory-practice view of technical rationality.

A Program Possibility

For the development of a community of reflective practitioners, then, four guidelines should govern professional development programs: that practitioners frame the problems, that the focus be on the predicament of the unique case that is susceptible to change, that consistent attempts be made to describe the tacit, and that the academic be seen as a coach to the practitioner. These principles are in marked contrast to teacher education classes at all levels that focus on students "learning" skills, arguments, or facts, rather than engaging in debate about ideas and practices and sophisticated reflection on their own experience. This is a problem inherent in the behaviorist dogmas as applied to teaching, and it results in dreary teaching techniques. The dogma is too easily accepted that we need to set out objectives that describe what the students are to do, for reasons that are obviously not educational but rather driven by assessment. This rules out such intellectual objectives as "realizing the depth of one's own confusion and ignorance." Taxonomies of educational objectives also seem to mesmerize educators with their gross epistemological confusions that treat knowledge as given rather than problematic (Pring, 1972; Sockett, 1971). We should realize that the nature of our knowledge is reflected in our teaching, as we saw in Tom Stevenson and as the Stanford case studies are portraying in such excellent detail (Grant, 1991; Gudmundsdottir, 1991; Hall & Clark, 1991; Hall & Grant, 1991).

These four principles are the basis for the planning of a new track in a Masters Degree at the George Mason University Graduate School of Education. We began by offering places only to teams (not fewer than three) from eight schools. The demand was such that we enrolled 143 teachers from 34 schools. The development of the ideas from the four principles proceeded quickly, especially as we developed them in concert with teachers and officials in school divisions. The result has been a new model for any M.Ed structure that has *six distinct differences* from the traditional Masters Degree track: recruitment in teams; workplace-centered, product-driven inquiry; integrated learning experiences; consultancy teaching in partnership; and assessment through quality. The epistemology of reflective practice underpins the whole conception (see Chapters 4 and 5).

The recruitment of teams, from schools, rather than individuals, provides a supportive context, a chance to affect the culture of the school, and the opportunity for additional leadership and educative roles. It is a statement that the degree is a partnership *contract* between individual, teams, school divisions, schools, and university.

The focus of the program is on products in the teacher's workplace, not on theory-driven syllabuses. This values the teachers' practical wisdom, but challenges them to establish an appropriate understanding of the theory-practice relationship, while placing maximum emphasis on products (not tests) of intellectual rigor, and relevance to the workplace.

The program is an integrated learning experience that replaces the part-time evening three credit course-by-course structure. Beginning with a common four-week workshop in the summer, members pursue some "foundation" questions about their ideological origins as teachers and the horizons they search for (see Chapter 2); an introduction to major content areas to be pursued throughout the program (e.g., in humanities, language arts); some basic diagnoses of school-based problems that they share with others; and some developing techniques of teacher research, which they will practice. Throughout the program coaching is necessary. After the initial summer workshop, members of the program go through four semesters (two academic years) and two additional summer workshops.

During semester 1 (fall, year 1), there are three to five intensive days in which preparations are made for semester 2 (spring, year 1), which constitutes the first team-teacher research project in the schools. The pattern continues through semester 3 (fall, year 2) and 4 (spring, year 2), either with a different project each semester or an extension of the original. Intensive days are provided for detailed discussions of projects or of new relevant material. In the final semester, practitioner members of the course plan and implement the four-week summer workshop for incoming teams. Thus, with overlapping segments of work and study, the learning experience promotes the opportunity for seeing connections and developing broad-based understanding. This will, we think, remedy ineffective structures presently in place for organization of learning for professionals. We believe that traditional programs treat the teacher audience as either would-be researchers or technicians, not professionals.

In the new track, teachers are taught by coaches. University teachers work regularly in partnership with business people and practicing teachers to support those enrolled on the program. Teachers on the program work in partnership teams themselves (from university, business etc.) as the program develops. Rather than thinking in terms of 24 students to a class, we consider the enrollees as 8 on-site teams of 3 people each.

Assessment—as judgement of quality—is driven by criteria of continuous improvement. The intellectual and moral task for the teacher ceases to be one of "reaching the grade," and becomes that of building a professional lifestyle of continuous improvement to meet the new challenges children present. That principle is incorporated in this model through the development, not of objectives, but of criteria of quality which are used as the basis for common judgement by teacher and teacher-student alike.

We are therefore building with the teachers who study with us a strong sense of collegiality and professional community, aspects resulting primarily from adherence to the four principles I have outlined. Practitioners must frame and set the problems by submitting team proposals to us on entry and working throughout the program in teams. The focus is on the predicament of each unique problem and its susceptibility to change through the commitment to the workplace issues established by the teams. Tacit knowledge and understanding is explored through our commitment to teachers writing reflective journals from the outset, and through the work we seek to develop in the "foundations" element. Academic-practitioner relationships (and perhaps many other teacher-learner relations) are becoming differently defined as coach-practitioner, and we expect to interpret the term "coach" in increasingly broader ways as we work in partnership in the program.

ACTION RESEARCH: A MODEL
IN THE UNIFIED PROFESSIONAL COMMUNITY

We could therefore begin the creation of a professional community in part by recasting the relationship between academic and practitioner in the comprehensive redesign of master's programs to recognize the different elements in a teaching career. Research on teaching becomes a shared collegial goal. But this is impossible under the domination of the contemporary epistemological paradigm and the way it is embodied in human professional relationships. Why is this so?

The goal of the university is research and teaching. As *What Works* (USDE, 1986) demonstrates, the model of research in universities is still that of the natural sciences, where the pursuit of truth involves the development of description, explanation, and generalization in an effort to construct hypotheses and, hopefully, laws governing the natural world. The methodology is experiment; the rubric governing progress is the attempt to falsify existing hypotheses or laws. While differing paradigms of scientific methodology have been made familiar by Kuhn and they take different shapes in education (Shulman, 1986a), this brief outline is what captures the dominant institutional norm (see also Chapter 5).

In the past hundred years, many education academics have tried to emulate this model and its by-products, for example, by writing and publishing for other academics rather than for practitioners and by regarding the job of the university as something akin to the "production of knowledge." Apart from the internal weaknesses of positivism (Harre & Secord, 1972) and its variants, in this view of educational research the teacher is an object of study, as are students, parents, or overhead projectors. It is absurd to suppose that one could get objectivity on oneself; indeed, this was one of the main reasons for the victory of behaviorism over nineteenth-century introspectionism. *So a teacher cannot be a researcher in this epistemology, for one cannot get scientific objectivity in studying one's self.* The idea of academic–practitioner partnership is therefore very circumscribed. It can only be that of the researcher and a researched subject. Of course, a teacher could assist a researcher, or do studies of his or her own students and their performances, although even that might be tainted. In this model, therefore, the notion of partnership in a research community is not simply impossible, it is faintly absurd; hence the refrain that researchers do research and teachers teach.

While it is not logically inconceivable that a coherent profession could emerge based on that model of research, there are other more promising models to explore that fit the reality of the practice of teaching and are not derived from a theoretical conception that tries to fit the practice within it. Action research is the generic form usable in many disciplinary contexts; the species is teacher research. Action research has a different focus. Its "primary goal . . . is not to write research reports and other publications," McKernan (1988) writes. "Action research aims at feeding the practical judgments of actors in problematic situations" (p. 179), and that does not rule out the publicity of the systematic enquiry.

One important caveat. In developing arguments for action research and teacher-research, I am not suggesting that there is some kind of final choice to be made between traditional empirical research and action research. My objections to the traditional model lie in its overbearing claims to intellectual dominance, the failure of its advocates to bring realistic judgments to bear on its limitations, the ways in which some of those advocates use its institutional form to prevent intellectual innovation, and the serious internal difficulties the theory itself faces, which are insufficiently examined with students. That it has come up with useful methodologies for certain areas of inquiry and has established knowledge in certain areas cannot be denied (for further comment, see Chapter 5).

Action research, however, looks more appropriate to a professional community in education. Practitioners are experts; research on teaching without them is simply lopsided. The perspective of the expert practitioner is critical to getting the research problem correctly diagnosed. Additionally, if practitioners are to be users as well as generators of research, the language they use must be embedded in the research. The problems of jargon need to be dispelled, and the implications of such problems of language as that illustrated in the example of "silliness" in the previous section deserve reexamination. The profession also urgently needs effective practice-based research, that is, research that is close enough to the context to consistently influence change. Practitioners can also develop ownership of it by seeing research as part of a career expectation (Lytle & Cochran-Smith, 1990b). Finally, beginning teachers can then be inducted into a sociopolitical and professional climate where research and its use are commonplace.

Indeed, in the professional development of the eight aspects of the moral and intellectual career (see Chapter 2), I have suggested that teacher research has a special place, beyond these particular attractions of action research in general. It was characterized there as "intellectual" in that the capacity for sustained self-evaluation, analysis, and understanding is critical for developing an understanding of one's own career growth. It provides an active and reflective basis for interrelating the eight elements in an appropriate pattern of growth for one's self. Teacher research thus promotes and sustains professional autonomy, for it provides the teacher with the opportunity to *originate* teaching knowledge as the basis for action in classrooms (see Chapter 4).

Action research is therefore attractive as a generic research form for a practically oriented professional community. Teacher-research is simply a specific example of it, for it can be conducted in nursing, policing, soldiering, or elsewhere. Historically its roots are in participation. Conceptually it provides a research model for participatory work across the split profession with a strong emphasis on practice. Professionally it can also provide for individual emancipation of teachers, allowing them to perceive themselves as creative individuals composing careers as well as lives.

Historical Development

But what is action research? McKernan's (1988) loose-limbed definition I have quoted is sufficient for my purposes. It can include action research methodologies used in evaluation, curriculum development, and research, as well as the sophisticated distinctions made by Elliott (1991) between "teachers-as-researchers" and "teachers-as-action-researchers," but it also describes a movement that seeks to close the gap between research and practice through close collaboration or partnership. It is a particular but not the only mode of reflective practice.

It differs in outline from the applied science view of theory–practice in the following ways:

1. Its scientific model does not seek for generalizations or laws applicable in all contexts, but emphasizes the predicament of the unique case.
2. It is not methodologically severe about the replicability of evidence, using methodologies drawn from anthropology, sociology, or ethnomethodology somewhat eclectically.
3. Unlike the natural sciences, where the research agenda can be defined in theory at any time, action research agendas are rooted in practice and problem solving.

Historically and practically, three different levels of "collaborative" action research can be distinguished: the traditional, the "weak" collaborative, and the "strong" collaborative. These collaborative features demand exploration.

Traditional action research.   The 1950s, the core period of the *traditional* conception of action research, are described by McKernan (1988) as an era of cooperative action research because teachers and schools cooperated with outside researchers by becoming clients in making their pupils and teachers available for research. It was a top-down strategy still insulating professional researchers from the teaching ranks (Corey, 1953). McKernan calls the conception *traditional* in that the political organization of educational systems remained the same. Neither researchers nor teachers conceived it as being different. In universities researchers did research, and in classrooms practitioners taught.

But we must assume that Corey and his contemporaries who promoted this conception were engaged in something that they, following Kurt Lewin, saw as radical in *theoretical* terms, even though they were traditional enough about institutions not to see the logic of the inclusion of practitioners as research partners, which Lewin had indeed proposed. The radical character of the idea had yet to reach organizational form. It was a radical idea in a traditional political framework of operation, and was therefore marginal to "real" institutional purposes.

"Weak" collaboration in action research. In the second, "weak" collaborative phase in action research, teachers, researchers, and others worked as partners in teams. This phase grew out of the failure of the traditional conception to take hold. Interactive research and development became a growing feature of the mid-1960s and 1970s. This was the period in the United States and Britain in which the development of case studies using naturalistic and/or qualitative methodologies proceeded apace, drawing on sociology, anthropology, and their constituent methodological camps. This was also the period in which the term *teacher-research* began to be used as a species of action research. On the institutional front, the gradual, hesitant construction of links between universities and schools and the development of small-scale alternative structures also proceeded, albeit slowly.

However, the larger educational context in the United States changed quickly, in the 1970s moving toward the installation of tough-minded accountability systems (Darling-Hammond & Berry, 1988; B. Macdonald, 1977), and then in the 1980s moving toward professionalization (Darling-Hammond, 1988). Institutional collaboration was rejected as a general solution to the problem of educational improvement, nor fortunately was it perceived as one of those quick-fix solutions to which American education had become accustomed. Rather it was something that many experimented with and a few—John Goodlad, for example—perceived as a worthwhile idea whose time would come.

The traditional version of collaboration left institutions as they were, with some individual collaboration at the margins. The weak version of collaboration extends institutional partnership but does not change those institutions. Practicing teachers may be invited to teach undergraduate or graduate courses (usually ones for which no academic can be found); there will be liaison committees, the development of some degree program electives in action research, researchers negotiating for work in classrooms, and occasional meetings between the leaders of schools and university departments or their representatives. Committed participants will form the residue of the relationship after an initial burst of interinstitutional enthusiasm. This kind of weak collaborative partnership we have seen in pre-service teacher education.

"Strong" collaborative action research.   Yet the notion of collaboration within and outside action research per se has progressed conceptually from the *weak* version of collaboration as "interactive" to a *strong* version that heralds a "fusion" of collaborating institutions—of schools and universities.

The professional development school implies one kind of strong collaboration or fusion. But in action research, strong versions of collaboration are attempts to develop an institutional structure for a university and a school (or for a profession) that matches the epistemology of action research *in the same way* that existing university structures match the dominant applied-science epistemology. Indeed, that must be the target, for the kind of collaborative institutional relationship we have, as we work together within our professional community, must reflect our view of what constitutes professional knowledge and understanding.

Sirotnik (1988) exemplifies the strong version when he connects research and evaluation under the rubric of collaborative inquiry. He describes the inadequacies of the positivist tradition of evaluation and shows how action-oriented formative inquiry is especially important for internal program improvement. He pushes the collaborative research paradigm "to its logical conclusion by making explicit the inevitable evaluative nature of research in action in social settings" (p. 174). This epistemological logic he connects to the notion of mere collaboration (of a weak kind) giving way to institutional fusion (of a rather stronger kind). Whatever counts as fusion, it is clearly a political agenda for institutions and for the profession as a community (Goodlad & Sirotnik, 1988; Pine & Keane, 1990).

Implications for the Professional Community

Whereas the traditional conception of action research left everything institutionally much as it was, the epistemological evolution taking place as collaborative activities grow has radical implications for the professional community.

First, it suggests new institutional forms. The political (i.e., the character of the professional community and the interaction of institutions) and the epistemological (the theory of knowledge used in the profession) constantly interact. At the *weak* end are forms of partnership, usually for specifically limited purposes, between existing institutions. At the *strong* end lies an unspecified ideal of integration or fusion. The professional community, on this account, is looking at new "fused" institutions to install the collaboration demanded by the new epistemology and to meet the challenges of educational improvement, notably for the conduct of research. Strong collaborative action research implies new institutional forms going well beyond the first steps of the professional development school, although none of these are, to my knowledge, fully in place because many university-teacher consortia are marginal to both school and university.

Second, it raises the question of whether the institution or individual should be the conceptual and practical focus of collaboration. This discussion of collaboration in action research has focused on institutions (universities and schools) rather than on the individuals in roles (academics and practitioners) who make up the single professional community. In moving toward professionalism—with its focus on the individual in a role—it may be that the *individual* rather than the *institution* should be the target of change, whether that individual be a teacher, administrator, or academic. On the one hand there is a small-scale conception of collaboration whose focus is on individuals; on the other there is the large-scale conception of institutional renewal and reform. Curriculum action research seems to have been strong on individuals, but weak on institutions, in its collaborative mode. That requires detailed explanation in the context of a rationale for teacher-research in the unified professional community.

INSTITUTIONAL AND INDIVIDUAL COLLABORATION IN THE PROFESSION

In the traditional model, institutions remained as they were, with researchers crossing the divide into the schools. In the weak collaborative model, some researchers began to see teachers as partners, most often in cases where teachers were also students for higher degrees. Along the continuum were a range of different institutions, that is, collaboratives set up to promote an interinstitutional agenda. These different sorts of collaboratives formed the context for action research.

Role Empowerment and Person Emancipation

Throughout this literature, there is an important difference of emphasis in conceptions of collaborative action research. Crudely, one emphasis seems to be on the teacher as the occupant of a *role*, within an institutional system, whereas the other emphasis is on the individual person finding the way to interpret his or her role. The former talks of *empowerment*, the latter of *emancipation*. Role issues are critical in the discussion of teaching as a professional community because of the primary significance accorded to individuals both in moral terms and in terms of effective practical professionalism. Yet what is the relation between a person and a role he or she occupies? If there is no significant difference in the ways we look at the relationship, the distinction between empowerment and emancipation would be insignificant.

By way of an interlude, we can clarify some of these matters by exploring a philosophical metaphor within an educational analogy. Principal Jones operates totally within the set of bureaucratic regulations that *define* him as a principal. He cannot conceive, quite literally, of doing anything outside what the role stipulates. The notion of creative interpretation of the rules, of even bending the rules, is outside his comprehension. When he returns home to his wife and family, he dons another role, that of husband and father. Or rather another role simply takes over: there is no "he" to enable us to say that he (non-role Principal Jones) *does* anything. There is an individual "he" (that is this physical body we call Thomas Jones) who acts within his role as what he perceives the "rules" demand. It does not make sense for him to say that he likes this role or finds that role oppressive. He is just a collection of roles. No individual chooser/liker/or disgruntled person exists beneath the skin.

Principal Smith, on the other hand, sees the rules as a set of guidelines for the exercise of her authority but is a continuing critic of them. She brings her own individuality to bear on how the rules are interpreted and whether they serve educational purposes (as she sees them). She spends a great deal of her working day figuring out how to "work the system" and prevent the rules enslaving her in her role, or for that matter, tyrannizing her and the teachers and students in her school. It is she who defines the roles she plays (wife, mother, principal), and she regards the conventional rules of the role as barriers or obstacles to what she wants. But does she *really* make choices? In principle, yes. The public character of the role, however, still bears down heavily upon her; that is, the margin of room for choice is, in the day-to-day experience, somewhat marginal.

Principal Smith appears to be a more compelling account of a human being, for it is difficult to understand what a person like Principal Jones would *in real life* look like. So we need, following Hollis (1975), to construe the relation between a person and his or her roles as that of a "free social individual [who] creates his own social identity by acting rationally within a consistent role-set of his own choosing and becomes what he has chosen by accepting his duties as his duties" (p. 212). By implication, however much individuals may get socialized by institutions, conceptually and morally the individual is primary.

Put more theoretically, Hollis (1977) distinguishes two conceptions of human nature that influence how we see the relation between the individual and his or her role, which he calls Plastic Man and Autonomous Man. Plastic Man (Principal Jones) is basically molded by cause and effect: he emerges as an individual with an identity thrust upon him by a central value system, inducted into socioeconomic relations and with drives and dispositions that are the legacy of the mechanics of genetic programming. Roughly, those who operate with Plastic Man see him as constituted by his roles. There is no individual (except in that he is a bunch of matter), just a bundle of roles. Autonomous Man (Principal Smith), on the other hand, is the self of common sense, with privacy, self-consciousness, identity, and rationality, who selects and chooses the roles he will play. These conceptions are too stark, but the passivity of Plastic Man may be found in those whose perspectives are dominated by institutions and the constitutive roles within which individuals find themselves. Yet the notion within Autonomous Man, that is, that we can always choose the roles we play, does not quite ring true either in our understanding of human conduct (see also Chapter 5).

Human beings are properly seen as individual persons, not just bundles of roles. Principal Smith, as a rational human being, shows us that we can interpret, evaluate, criticize, and reconstruct any role we may be in rather than simply accept what particular authorities define as the legitimate duties. We thus can distance ourselves from our roles, though we are certainly creatures of them, but only that distance provides the space for self-criticism. This is the conception of a person underpinning Bateson's (1989) account of how we can compose our lives, how we can shift in and out of roles as we work out the frames of our existence and its modes.

Individuals and Institutions

In education we tend to focus strongly on institutions. That has meant that we have paid less attention to the significance of individual moral autonomy. Institutionalized teachers could be regarded simply as pawns in someone else's game plan, regulated in their roles by all manner of rule books and standards. Institutions are very powerful; they develop a particular kind of arrogance unless there is consistent individual assertion of freedom *and* professional responsibility. To combat this institutional arrogance, from which we all suffer in different ways, we need to change the conception of the roles so that they *empower* individuals because, among other things, institutional power can undermine the notion of professional

responsibility. For example, we could set up procedures for collaborative decision making or, more broadly, institute school-based management. Another way to combat this arrogance (Gitlin, 1990) is to develop a sense of profession as community in which individual autonomy is exercised within a comprehensive and commonly shared perspective on professional standards.

Sirotnik and Goodlad (1988) seem to me to be radical and imaginative in their conception of strong collaboration, but they lack a robust sense of the individual teacher and thereby give insufficient weight to the fact that, within the professional role, lies a moral individual. True, the person-in-the-role needs empowerment; but the individual person needs emancipation. This tension between empowerment and emancipation is central to understanding different approaches to the teacher as professional. McKernan (1988) seems primarily concerned with changes in individual teachers and lacks the sense of institutional power. Stenhouse (1975) in his advocacy of teacher research is concerned with concepts of authority and emancipation and also with an adequate epistemology of practice. For him, a teacher–researcher is an individual person wrestling with the moral problems of role occupancy, and his commitment is to emancipation from bureaucracies (whether managed by school administrations or by universities). In his discussion of professional education, Schön is looking at the institution of professional education, at the reflective practitioner as a role concentrating on role performance, not role interpretation. Elliott (1991) suggests that the major hypotheses that emerged from the Ford Teaching Project tended to focus on the problems of personal change in teachers, particularly self-esteem, that is, the extent to which they became different persons within their roles (see also Elliott, Bridges, Ebbutt, Gibson, & Nias, 1975; Rudduck, 1991). Sirotnik (1988), by comparison, sketches the individual as the enfranchised participant in a group process. Collaborative inquiry is about "rigorous and sustained discourse" in which individuals "say how they feel and what their own beliefs, values and interests are and . . . participate in controlling the discussion" (p. 77). The individual here is learning what is needed within a role redefined *for*, but not *by* him or her. He or she is not a self-conscious critic of that role. For Stenhouse, group process was a tool of individual emancipation in the context of a struggle for power. For Sirotnik it is a tool of role enfranchisement, a matter of communicative competence.

These examples, with their difference of emphasis, no doubt reflect the individual researcher's focus of interest, itself reflected in political infrastructures. British teachers have until recently had much more classroom and curriculum autonomy, and British action researchers have operated with that assumption. The American concern may be more with systems than with individuals, for, as the system has moved from working with a con-

ception of *due process* and away from a conception of *in loco parentis*, so the teacher's individual exercise of his or her role has been circumscribed. Mandated curricula describe content and severely circumscribe the teacher's classroom actions. However, action research or teacher-research needs a primary but not exclusive focus on individuals. That will encourage us to place less importance on the public requirements of our duties and obligations and enable us to focus on the way we as individuals can contribute to those institutions. For example, an individual teacher-research piece of work might lead to political conflict over an educational practice between teachers and a school board.

Constraints on Professional Growth

I have tried here to outline the complex relation between a person and a role and also to indicate how the notions of empowerment and emancipation, as part of the task of professional improvement and the creation of a single community, differ in their relationship to the person as professional. Both the institutional and individual perspectives are important. A comprehensive attempt at professionalism demands an attention to the emancipation of the person and his or her enfranchisement in new institutional organization. If we have, for example, *institutional* changes like the restructured school or site-based management, then we must provide for the *individual* changes, for example, the emancipation of the teacher. This gives the role the breadth of consideration needed.

Yet this stress on the individual is not to celebrate the "cellular." Indeed, it is critical for the development of professionalism within workplaces that isolation be broken down and that individuals work in groups or teams. They come together as volunteers, drawn by a focus on common problems, learning from one another's wisdom and insight as they develop the capacity to reflect and to install new forms of pedagogical action. The question is how action research can sustain focus on institutions and individuals, singly or in teams, as it seeks to match institutional structure to epistemology. Sanger (1989) sums up one aspect of the situation clearly: "Action research tends to empower individuals in their battles to improve their articulation and implementation of educational understanding with regard to professional practice. But dealing with institutionalized politics may be another thing" (p. 6).

Hollingsworth (1990) distinguishes from her work with teacher researchers four major obstacles to teachers' emancipation or freedom to write:

1. There is a lack of opportunity to engage in conversation about personal views of teaching before writing

2. Projects are too big to tackle while doing full-time teaching
3. The method of analysis does not fit the problem
4. There is a lack of sufficient guidance, support and expectations.

How can teachers actually get time to do action research if it is not regarded as central to their work? How can teachers be trained for it? Can they treat some of the tricky institutional problems as research problems, pregnant as they are with the possibilities of interpersonal friction? Much depends on what we think comprises teaching and therefore what counts as the framework for professional development within a career. If teacher-research is just an optional extra for a few dedicated souls within the conception of a career, rather than a primary avenue for professional development and teacher emancipation, time will obviously not be made available. This present situation is a reflection of the epistemological power of educational research as usually understood and the massive federal, state, and university bureaucracies that supports it. The development of a single professional community, through professional development opportunities and in other ways, has to be seen as the creation of opportunities for individuals, freed from the bulk of petty restrictions and constraints, to contribute to the aspiration of a profession. With that the emergence of a single professional community would be facilitated.

My claim in Chapters 2 and 3 is that we should work toward a single professional community of teachers. I have taken professional development as the common theme, since forms of collaboration and partnership are necessary therein. I have indicated what a framework for a career in teaching looks like and suggested principles for the education of novices and for the construction of master's-degree programs in education. This change in the academic–practitioner relationship must presume a major change in graduate education in which the focus turns away from theory to understanding and changing the practice and intellectual focus of individuals in their complex roles and workplaces. I have stressed the significance of the academic as coach in teaching and as partner in collaborative research. I have taken the argument into action research (of which teacher-research is an example), suggesting that we have been moving toward a single community through beginning the development of a common culture. Although both institutional and individual development are important in this process, it is individual emancipation, not empowerment, that is a primary theme in the development of the individual's career and of the professional community. That applies, I believe, to all teachers, whether they be professors, classroom teachers, or district superintendents.

CHAPTER 4

Professional Expertise as Virtue

We turn now from considering the professional community to professional expertise, a topic that is at the heart of professionalism. How are we to describe the professional expertise claimed by members of the teaching profession, most of which we would call professional knowledge? The longstanding adherence to positivist epistemology in the theory and practice of education is now discredited. Addressing the problem of professional expertise, therefore, demands an attempt to construct an alternative. Here and in chapter 5 I sketch one possible approach.

In this chapter, I start from the moral character of teacher professionalism and try to illustrate how five major virtues are central to an understanding of the practice of teaching: honesty (S. Bok, 1978), courage (D. N. Walton, 1982), care (Noddings, 1984), fairness (Rawls, 1972), and practical wisdom (Shulman, 1987, 1988, 1989). Following illustration and discussion of each of the five virtues, I will attempt in Chapter 5 to suggest how we might begin to construct an epistemology of practice for teaching from this virtues base. In writing of a specific human quality as a virtue, I mean a sustainable moral quality of individual human character that is learned. Virtues carry standards immanent in them. By *professional* virtues, I mean the collection of these acquired moral qualities that are embedded in the social practice of teaching and that are necessary to the particular professional task.

These five virtues are at the core of professional expertise in teaching and seem to me to be constitutive of teaching. Teaching necessarily demands these virtues—although many other virtues may be contingently significant. First, since teachers deal in knowledge and trade in truth, questions of *honesty* and deceit are part of the logic of their situation. Second, both learning and teaching involve facing difficulty and taking intellectual and psychological risks; that demands *courage*. Third, teachers are responsible for the development of persons, a process demanding infinite *care* for the individual. Fourth, *fairness* is necessary to the operation of rules in democratic institutions or, indeed, in one-to-one relationships. Finally, *practical wisdom* is essential to the complex process teaching is and, of course, may well demand the exercise of those other virtues (such as patience) that are contingent to the teaching situation. At first examination, these seem to be virtues of intellect and emotion in a way that, say, modesty is not. However, my primary concern is whether we can develop an epistemology of practice through a perspective on virtue. I need to begin that task by showing what knowledge is revealed when we use a vocabulary of virtue to illuminate teaching. (The tone of this chapter is not intended to be a moralizing one. I certainly do not hold myself up as an exemplar of virtue, nor am I setting forth from some kind of superior moral position what others ought to do.) I begin with honesty and its companion, deceit.

HONESTY AND DECEIT

Few would dispute the need for honesty in social life generally. It seems difficult to imagine how a society could cohere if, as a general rule, people did not tell the truth. Without it, when Elizabeth asks the way to her new school, she might be directed to the gas station. She would have to regard road signs as works of art rather than sources of information. When Mrs. Simpson picks a can labeled "beans" off the supermarket shelf, she might be getting asparagus. Our use of language as a tool for social living simply breaks down without the assumption that, in general, people convey the truth—whatever complicated explanations are given for this fact—for our social life is built on the assumption of truth, not the other way round. We cannot imagine a coherent social life if we could not proceed with our day-to-day lives knowing that, by and large, other people are proceeding on the basis that they, like we, will tell the truth.

Assumptions apart, this is not to be naive about the actual extent of people's deceptions or their most frequent causes—namely, that people do not care for themselves or others, that they cannot trust others, or that they are congenital liars. None of that negates the significance of honesty. The towering work in this fundamental area of human life is Sisella Bok's (1978) *Lying: Moral Choice in Public and Private Life*. Its authority derives from the way in which practical judgments for action are derived from both concrete situations and rigorous philosophical reasoning. What Bok produces is not simply a set of sensible nostrums, but grounded prescriptions for action. She begins with an important distinction about truth and truthfulness:

> In all such speculation, there is a great risk of a conceptual muddle, of not seeing the crucial differences between two domains: the *moral* domain of intended truthfulness and deception, and the much vaster domain of truth and falsity in general. The *moral* question of whether

you are lying or not is not *settled* by establishing the truth or falsity of what you say. In order to settle this question, we must know whether you *intend your statement to mislead*. (p. 6)

In teaching, however, deceit can arise through neglect as much as from direct intention to mislead, and it is on deceit that we must focus. Its ramifications are seen in such issues as censorship, the withholding of relevant information, the hiding behind institutional power, unexamined bias, and, perhaps most important of all, the neglect or lack of concern for what is true. In teaching it is as much a matter of neglect as of direct intention to mislead that underpins cases of deceit, for so much hangs on the teacher's attitude to the truth. This is a part of a teacher's character and professional integrity (see Chapter 7), as well as being both methodologically and substantively important in his or her expertise. Puzzling over problems, living with ambiguities, being prepared to countenance alternative positions is both a way of teaching children (a means) and what they are being taught (an end). Bok (1978) shows implicitly how there can be no harsh separation between content and method, enabling us to ask what the techniques are for becoming honest. Yet eschewing neglect and intention to mislead demands authenticity and integrity in the teacher as a person, as a citizen, and as a teacher, and maybe as a parent too. But that authenticity has to be hammered out in the classroom anvil as case after case after case forces moral decisions on the teacher.

Five different aspects of honesty/deceit are central to a teacher's professional expertise: an understanding of fact and fiction, a concern for the search for truth, an ethic of belief, creation of trust, and a passion for truth. Each are different, though the terminology seems similar.

Fact and Fiction

First, teachers must themselves understand the distinction between fact and fiction and teach it to children. This is not simple. The imaginative portrait Tom painted for the children was understood *as fiction* by the children, but the fiction in that case was still set, like a good historical novel, within a firm framework of accuracy about the actual events. Indeed, Tom demanded accuracy in the work the children did on their own galleons. He was not the sort of teacher who thought that provided the children were drawing soldiers, it did not much matter whether they wore caps, fezzes, helmets, bandannas, or busbies. If they were sixteenth-century Spaniards and were officers, they wore this type of helmet, not that. He would have been complaisant in deceiving his class if he did not bother to get them to get such evidence right.

There is well-known developmental evidence about children's cognitive growth in distinguishing the imaginary from the real, a capability central to human life (Piaget, 1968). Egan's (1986) valuable and perceptive comments on the use of story in teaching, particularly to young children, indicate how important the development of the imagination is as a balance against what is real. He also makes us aware of how fiction can be a vehicle for us to understand the world and the truth about it: Witness the relevance of fairy tales to the emergence of a child's understanding of good and evil (Bettelheim, 1977). Mrs. Simpson and Gabrielle Johnson, for example, are teaching children at precisely the age at which this is most important.

Take some examples of teacher deceit that involve neglect of facts, bias, or misrepresentation. A student is grossly misled if, in a senior literature class, the Freudian view of *Hamlet* is neglected or, equally, taught as the only interpretation. In science, the teaching of nuclear physics without attention to its environmental and political effects is, I would argue, deceitful. In kindergarten, stories that children enjoy but that carry an implicit bias are deceitful, as are many sexist or racist practices. In history, anything that makes a student think that "this is the case"—when it is disputable—is a case of deceit. Teachers may feel they need to go with the flow of jingoism and patriotism, but what is the truth about this campaign, that invasion, this massacre? Honesty and deceit are right in the guts of teaching. Virtually everything a teacher says or does could be measured in terms of its relation to the truth. Avoiding deceit is a pervasive teaching skill. This is morally important because deceit, as Bok argues, puts a person arbitrarily in the power of another.

Questions and the Concern for the Truth

The professional teacher displays a concern for the truth and how it is to be sought after. What does that mean? Tom's virtuous expertise in part lay in his moral skill of opening up questions for children, enabling them to search for the truth. Questioning, from this perspective, is not simply a set of techniques appropriate to analysis, recall, and so forth; it is a matter of *which* questions (in line with content) open up a search for truth. Recall the somewhat tendentious scene at the beginning of *Dead Poets Society*, a movie which portrays the rigidity of the traditional codes, mores, and expectations of an established prep school where individual and peer-group challenges to the boys' intellects and loyalties are developed by John Keating, a newly appointed maverick-nonconformist alumnus teacher. Keating is drawing out a philosophy of *carpe diem* (seize the moment!) with his class while he and they look at heroic alumni photographs. He leaves the philosophy itself unexamined, and we have to ask whether his questions show he is interested in examining the truth, or whether this is a manipulation, a form of indoctrination, a deceit with its immorality lying in the arbitrary power that it gives the deceiver.

Another example: What place do questions in multiple-choice tests (which invite guessing because they contain no penalties for incorrect guessing) have in a moral pedagogy of substance? Are we misleading children when we know their answers are guesses at what they think we want (as opposed to what the evidence suggests)? Another example: Are the questions a teacher raises when taking the position of devil's advocate in discussion just a technique? When is it appropriate—and at what age of learner? Under what circumstances is the technique justified when it *depends* on insincerity?

Does having children guess answers convey an attitude to the truth? An anecdote: As a student teacher, I was supervised in a London grammar school by a well-known historian of education, A. C. F. (Rudolph) Beales. He was an excellent teacher of novices with a superb feel for classrooms. Beales once saw me invite a student in a class I was teaching to guess the date of a battle. He was furious with me. In our consultation afterwards, he dressed me down for betraying history and historians, for displaying a lack of concern at how to get at evidence. Historians *never* guess, he said, we have to work with what there is.

One huge trap for a teacher is to confuse a search for truth with promiscuous open-mindedness, visible in sham questioning. "What do you all think of Custer?" says the novice student teacher and gets every answer under the sun. And there it rests. The novice fails to help the students move to a thought-out position *backed by evidence*, but resorts to the banal "everybody's entitled to their opinion," the detritus of values-clarification (Sockett, 1992). For an open-minded teacher, this form of intellectual liberalism can easily become a way of backing away from rigorous examination of conflicting positions. It can become a way of shuffling off the responsibility for facing hard choices and decisions about what is true. Censorship of textbooks sometimes prevents teachers from doing this, but it may not be as powerful as the self-censorship that often masquerades as open-mindedness. Without an enriched view of honesty as a professional virtue, and a sophisticated understanding of the many ways in which deceit can undermine the educational enterprise, a teacher cannot address these issues of developing ways of seeking for the truth.

An Ethic of Belief

Children have to be taught an ethic of belief because they are not born with one, that is, they need to learn that it is morally wrong to believe things for which there is no evidence (Quinton, 1987). That sounds terribly dogmatic, but an extreme case illustrates the point. What exactly is so pernicious about Nazi textbooks saying that Jews are subhuman monsters manipulating the world's finances? Two things. First, they teach children beliefs that are totally immoral and factually incorrect. Second, they undermine the fragile capacity in each child for getting one's beliefs in line with what is true. They sever the connection each child needs to understand, namely, that between belief *and* truth. Believing what is true—or what there is good evidence for—is itself of moral importance (see Chapter 5).

Positively, this requires that children have to be shown how to search for truth and also, whatever their personal predilections, to form beliefs on the basis of the best evidence. This is a formal statement of a principle that has many substantive complexities. Yet teachers have to demonstrate by instruction and by example, as well as by support, the real-life moral complexity of facing up to the facts and the courage (see below) that implies. If students do not face the facts, difficult though that may be, they cannot become citizens in a complex democratic society that is riddled with hard choices demanding attention to evidence. In some societies (e.g., Northern Ireland) people have been raised within a context of myths so powerful that a balanced view of what is true is virtually unobtainable. If we are to confront our prejudices, racist and sexist, we have to be aware of the moral importance of believing only what is true, difficult though it may be to establish what is, in any given case, true.

Indeed, that can be very hard for any teacher, at any level. In the context of a troubled civil society like Northern Ireland, I encountered many graphic examples of teachers who were totally nonplussed by some children's answers. For example, a teacher I know correctly told a class in a school in a Protestant area that the pope had struck a medal for King William III (the Protestant hero) after the Battle of the Boyne, a truth that runs counter to the myth-ridden conflicts of Northern Ireland. One child not only said he did not believe it, but told the teacher that if he did not retract the statement, his family would come to the school to beat him up. Bravely, the teacher persisted—and was indeed threatened in the community. One of the many problems in this story is that the child is refusing to confront the evidence and explain it. Trying to teach him an ethic of belief was of primary importance.

Trust in Classrooms

The professional teacher constructs a classroom complex in which trust, among other things, is paramount. The classroom situation can invite children to trust a teacher not because of his or her hectorings about honesty, but because the children know they will not be deceived, cheated, or in other ways ripped off (Nias, 1975). One major obstacle to such a climate of classroom trust is the prevalence of the paternalistic lie, whereby we deliberately do not state the truth (and thereby deceive someone) because we (as paternalists) judge them to be unfit to know it—because they are not old enough, or mature enough, or whatever. We prevaricate, or we are simply blind in other ways. Maggie, a young student teacher in a high school, assigned her junior class a research project on Prohibition. She was trusted enough to receive as one project a video-taped discussion by three of the class, drinking beer in a family room/wet-bar, of whether Prohibition would be possible these days. In the classroom, she wisely interrupted the video when it became clear what was going on. It would have been easy for her to have put over a maternalistic message about alcohol. She sensibly chose to engage them in debate on the topic as the important issue, and gave them a grade of 75 for their bad judgment in producing this as their research project. In so doing, she treated them seriously as young adults—which of course was why they felt able to invite her into their life and their conversation. At no stage was there any dissembling, deceit, or maternalism in her actions.

Sisella Bok (1978) argues that there are no good grounds for lying to children in general, that is, because they are children. Although paternalistic lies may be sometimes easy to understand and sympathize with, they carry very special risks. First, they can lead to having to lie more to keep up the pretense. Second, if and when they are discovered, the paternalist's credibility is seriously threatened. Third, a paternalistic lie is a huge threat to the relationship within which the deception takes place, for deceit undermines the quality of any relationship. Finally, there are risks of exploitation of every kind for those who are being deceived.

The implications for a teacher are very serious. If we (paternalistically) lie, we are likely to have to lie more. If we are discovered, our students may no longer believe anything we say. If that happens, the professional relationship with the children is drastically undermined. Then children may not care about the truth, simply about what to do to please the teacher and get the grade or pass the test. (For an account of the development of trusting relationships within institutions, see Chapter 6.)

A different form of (paternalistic) deceit is the misuse of authority. Another anecdote: I was privileged as a student teacher to have dinner with Beales and one of his friends, a well-known Piaget scholar, Edwin Peel. Peel was telling us how he had been examining a student teacher of science that day. She conducted an experiment in front of the class in which she told them that the litmus paper would turn blue to show that the solution was alkaline. The litmus paper did not change color. In Peel's account, the young woman turned to the class and said, "Well, it should have turned blue."

She conducted the rest of the lesson and had the class describe the experiment as if the paper had turned blue. So, Peel immediately gave her a failing grade. A person who has not understood the fundamental principles of science and who is *prepared to use his or her authority to deceive the children*, he said, cannot and should not teach.

Caring About the Truth

Finally, teachers must care about the truth. Brandon (1987) argues that they do not. For little of what goes on in schools, he argues, has anything to do with passing on the truth. Teachers very often misrepresent the status of knowledge. In making it accessible, they are falsifying it. We teach children "facts," he argues, whose status is very uncertain; we do not indicate the different ways in which such facts may be viewed. We fail to transmit a defensible view of the world or of our cognitive dealings within it. Far too often, value is taught as fact: The "desirable masquerades as the inevitable" (p. 77). We sometimes allow our unexamined biases free rein. Too often, we accept censorship that distorts the real world. We can even become expert at withholding information, thereby deliberately deceiving children. In each of these cases, what we do and what we say as teachers is a central piece in the quality of our practice. Yet it is rarely featured in research studies of teaching.

Professional expertise, then, is partly manifest in teachers' dogged pursuit of the truth because it matters and because telling the truth has become a moral disposition (Williams, 1987). These five areas of teaching are related to the virtue of honesty and the avoidance of deceit: teaching the difference between fact and fiction, displaying a concern for the search for truth, teaching an ethic of belief, creating trusting relationships with children, and displaying a deep-seated personal commitment to truth.

This account of the ways in which issues of honesty and deceit enter into professional expertise needs much greater descriptive enrichment. It needs intensive "reflexive ethnography" to inform and develop our moral understanding of teaching. It indicates enough content for the analysis and evaluation of pedagogy seen within the professional virtue of honesty. As we look at classrooms, reflectively as professionals or as evaluators, we could begin our evaluations through the lens of honesty along these five dimensions. Some teachers might be "technically" competent; but if they do not care about the truth, in Brandon's phrase, they would be incompetent.

Perhaps Brandon is right. The issue of deceit, in all its forms, has ceased to be part of the vernacular of the staff room. Perhaps it has been crushed by a we-them perception of the situation engendered by mass schooling.

Perhaps it has become part of the equipment needed to survive in schools in an industrialized system. Perhaps bureaucracies have created such complex, rule-governed systems that school life has become unworkable without deceit. Perhaps we cannot face up to honesty as the virtue of the professional expert because our institutions, our universities and schools, are corroded with deceit. What seems incontrovertible is that honesty and deceit are central to teaching, but right now no one seems to be paying them any particular attention.

COURAGE

Robert Graves (1966) records the bravery of Captain A. L. Simpson, who fell mortally wounded 20 yards out from the front line on the German front in World War I. He was so much respected that three men were killed and four wounded in the attempt to recover him. His orderly eventually reached him, but Simpson sent him back, apologizing for making so much noise. When Graves found him that night, he was dead, with his knuckles crammed into his mouth so that he could stop himself from attracting attention by making more noise. He was wounded in seventeen places. Another example: D. N. Walton (1982) tells a World War II Dutch story of how a German soldier on firing squad duty refused to obey an order to shoot innocent hostages. He was promptly court-martialed and shot along with the hostages, an unusual example of exceptional moral and physical courage. That men and women confront horrendous physical dangers and difficulties with little thought for themselves is a human treasure. It formed the basis for Plato's account of courage in *The Laches* and for Aristotle's elaborations in the third book of the *Nichomachean Ethics*.

There are good moral actions, and there are superb moral actions. However, not all courage is physical, nor is it to be defined as a response to physical or mental fear, nor is it restricted to men. The heroine of France in 1990 was Florence Arthaud, who enthralled the world of sailing by winning the solo transatlantic Route du Rhum race from St. Malo to Guadeloupe, one of the most difficult boat races in the world. She broke the record for the crossing in 9 days, 21 hours, and 42 minutes, bleeding from cervical problems, according to newspaper reports, for more than two days. A more challenging example of bravery in 1990 was Anna Rosmus, portrayed in the German movie *The Nasty Girl*, who was subjected to various kinds of personal attacks and threats because of her attempts to make her home town of Passau, Bavaria, face up to its Nazi past.

Kennedy (1956) tells the complex story of Senator Edmund Ross whose bravery was political rather than physical. After the Civil War, Andrew

Johnson as Lincoln's vice-President succeeded the assassinated leader. As President, Johnson sought to continue the policy of reconstruction and reconciliation with the South in the face of "radical" Republicans in his own party who wanted harsher treatment and continued military occupation, and passed several bills Johnson vetoed as unconstitutional. The radicals managed, for the first time in history, to pass some legislation over the Presidential veto. The struggle intensified between the two branches of government, with vociferous and unrestrained argument. The conflict on policy became so fierce that the "radicals" began the process of impeaching Johnson, even though they were formally members of his own party. Counting the votes, the radicals could be sure of success if they could get the two-thirds majority and here they looked to a young Kansas senator, Edmund Ross. Ross was virulently against Johnson's policies—indeed he had been elected on a "radical" platform. But the essence of the issue of Johnson's impeachment was political, a titanic struggle between the legislative and executive branches of government. In publicly casting his "not guilty" vote in an atmosphere of great hostility and intense political drama, Ross said he looked down into his open grave. He became a political outcast in his own party and thus sacrificed his career. His reason was that the office of President would be degraded if a President was forced out of office upon insufficient proof and partisan considerations. Thirty years later, the press who had vilified him saw that his vote had saved the country from a strain that could have wrecked its form of government. Courage is shown by Ross as a determination to stick to one's principles and one's judgements in the face of overwhelming odds.

Defining Courage

D. N. Walton (1982) points out the features of Ross's case that make his behavior an act of courage where no physical danger was involved. First, he did his duty (i.e., examined the evidence) under extraordinary countervailing pressure. Second, he displayed quite remarkable ability for practical reasoning. (He was also proved historically to be "right"—had he been wrong, in Walton's view, he would not have been courageous, merely misguided.) Walton argues that when we judge someone to be brave, we make at least two judgments. We judge an action first on its merits (whether it is worth doing) and second on how the action was carried out (the practical reasoning behind the action and the context in which it is placed). Courage as a moral quality can therefore best be defined as deliberate practical reasoning in circumstances of difficulty, turbulence, or trouble. In some such circumstances, Walton stresses, to be courageous means to be calm in the eye of the storm.

So the courageous person makes a judgment in troubled circumstances. That judgment is a judgment in practical ethics, that is, about the worth of what is to be done and careful practical reflection on how to accomplish it. Moreover, that practical judgment has to be measured to the task and its demands. But there is a difference between an immediate response to danger, wherein a person acts courageously, and a long-term commitment to ideals that are pursued through difficult circumstances. Captain Graves is an example of the former. Jessica Seigel, the teacher portrayed by Samuel Freedman (1990), is an example of the latter. Courageous may describe the ways a person acts. Where long-term commitments of an ethical character are involved, the pursuit of them encourages us to talk of courageous persons.

Philip Jackson's Foreword to Vivian Paley's book is instructive:

> The fundamental requirement is courage. Vivian Paley is courageous. She excels in the capacity to look at herself as a teacher in an unflinching way. . . . Reading of her occasional blunders as a teacher and of her efforts to correct them, all fully admitted and wholesomely confronted, we are encouraged to face up to weaknesses of our own and thereby to begin the often painful business of doing something about them. (Paley, 1984, p. iii)

Neither Jessica nor Vivian can set out every morning to "do something brave today," as if they were going shopping. Nor can they be brave in quite the way in which they have opportunities to be honest most of the time. Courage and honesty seem to be moral *dispositions*, each with a different context of possibility, although being honest can demand being brave. We display courage, hopefully, *on the occasions when it is required.* A continuing determination to stick to one's principles in the face of all kinds of adversity is not formally different from Vivian Paley's gutsy self-examination of her own teaching or the courage Jessica Seigel shows in facing the daunting tasks of the teacher on New York's Lower East Side. For Jessica, "there is a double requirement of courage in caring: I must have the courage to accept that which I have a hand in, and I must have the courage to go on caring" (Noddings, 1984, p. 9). Courage in teaching might be manifest in a single instance. More often it will be long-term, like Vivian's and Jessica's.

In every kind of worthwhile human activity, therefore, courage can find a place. But what counts as courage is dependent, in part, on context in which it is played out. Courage can also have such other virtues as determination, self-confidence, and other virtues of will embedded in it (Sockett, 1988). From this brief discussion of courage so far, three of its features are germane to my purposes in this book:

1. Courage is not related solely to fear or to physical action.
2. Courage demands the use of practical reason and judgment, *either* in a situation of immediate danger *or* in pursuit of long-term commitments that are morally desirable.
3. Courage, as excellence, will be found in different sorts of social and institutional practices.

Teaching is a social and institutional practice; teaching acts demand practical reasoning and judgment in pursuit of long-term commitments. These three characteristics are found in teaching, specifically in the common pedagogical terms of encouraging and discouraging, central in all teachers' relationships with their students.

Encouraging and Discouraging

What teachers do to support children in contexts of difficulty, personal or academic, is central to the task of teaching. The virtue finds its way into the classroom context through the terms *encouragement* and *discouragement*. Presumably encouraging means putting courage into people, while discouraging conveys something connected to sapping their will.

We can seek to encourage our pupils in all kinds of ways, for example, by praising their work, and they can be discouraged when they are blamed. Consider how subtle that task is, as opposed to the soft soap of self-esteem. Encouragement must be distinguished from praise and from reward, and discouragement from blame and from punishment. *Learning* presents people with difficulty often accompanied by fear, as many people grappling with statistics will testify. Children learning are constantly in situations of difficulty, struggling to master what they do not already know. All learners have to face difficulty. A painless pedagogy of the kind advocated by B. S. Bloom (1971) is a charade. Things worth doing do not drop into our laps. Children, like adults, get *frightened* by the difficulty and the consequences of what they perceive as their inadequacy. They are terrified by failure, or they become so identified with it that they will not risk struggling with the difficult.

The situation, therefore, is not simply that children are trying to learn things they do not understand. The learning situation is frequently invested with fear, and we need only recall our own experience as child learners to remember its power. To encourage a child is to give the child particular kinds of support in these contexts of difficulty. It is not, per se, to convey propositional knowledge. Moreover, as we consider the classroom, it is manifest that the ways in which teachers do this is crucial to pupils' learning, connected to questions of moral character (such as making an effort, being conscientious and careful, and learning to concentrate) that children deploy as they face the variety of learning tasks the teacher presents. Encouragement and discouragement (as opposed to praising and blaming, rewarding and punishing) are highly sophisticated moral acts, the purpose of which is both to get the children to learn whatever is to be learned and also to summon up their will in these situations of difficulty and fear. They require extraordinary professional expertise.

Courage in Teaching: Two Cases

We need to remind ourselves again of what courage is. It is a virtue that describes how a person, often selflessly, behaves in difficult and adverse circumstances that demand the use of practical reason and judgment in pursuit of long-term commitments that are morally desirable. It is not an exclusive property of those under physical threat. Does this mean teachers themselves have to display courage in order to encourage? Probably not—but they must be highly sensitive, preferably through reflection on experience, to the demands on a child's will that learning makes. Two excellent educational examples were available to the movie-goer in 1988 and 1989: *Stand and Deliver* (the factional portrayal of Jaime Escalante an outstanding mathematics teacher in a Los Angeles High School) and *Dead Poets Society* (the fictional story of John Keating, teacher of literature in a very traditional prep school). These examples illustrate the significance of courage across the range of teaching as a social practice. They also show that the major way in which courage can be demanded in teaching is when a teacher's educational beliefs are put to the test, often in the development of school policies.

Escalante is a model of courage, struggling with extraordinarily rugged determination against all comers—the department chair, the kids, the school, the parents, and finally the testing service—at the cost of his own health. As portrayed, we have to describe his work in its initial phase as courageous. It meets the criteria for courage—displaying practical reasoning in situations of great difficulty for purposes of great value. Of professional significance too is that, being a courageous man, he seeks to *encourage* his pupils. Escalante chooses different tactics to encourage different kids. Sometimes he seems to be discouraging one or two pupils as he pursues the ultimately more important goal. In being discouraging, he is not being immoral; rather he is testing the real resolve of his pupils, finding out the limits of their courage. Thus they learn to be courageous, to attack and defeat the establishment of testing rather than emulate the boorish hostility of some of their fellows. They also learn calculus—and calculus results matter. But consider the man's moral example for his students!

John Keating, the teacher in the *Dead Poets Society*, is more complex. Do we view him as a sad eccentric, simply creating a stir and losing his job through incompetence, or *is* there something much more profound at stake? He is portrayed as working with students to challenge the educational establishment and to make the "dead" literature they are taught come "alive." (It requires some daring, I would say, to encourage a class to tear up the basic textbook.) Recall the moral skills Keating displays in the classroom (but are they wise?) to put *courage* into the reluctant but bedazzled students. Notice the connections among life inside the classroom, on the playing field, and in the school assembly, as well as the interconnectedness of the teacher–pupil relationships, relationships hard to replicate in public education.

Why does Keating do it? He is not simply an iconoclast. He does it because of his passionate commitments to literature, to its purpose and place in human life, and to education as the vehicle in which these passions can be handed through the generations, a commitment matched by Escalante's devotion to mathematics. His demonstrable courage encourages or emboldens his pupils. They break rules, smashing all manner of conventions, upsetting rotten-apple carts of desiccated teaching and learning. They challenge the mores, root and branch. They threaten good order and discipline in doing so. With Keating and Escalante, it is how they *are* that matters. It is the moral cast of the men that so offends the hierarchies and their conventional colleagues, and attracts the students.

If we do not support the direction Keating is following, then we will see his behavior as eccentric, even crazy and irresponsible. His substantive values are in question. Assuming we think he is right, we admire his courage. Why? Because of our sense that the passions of the intellect get crushed by educational institutions. The weight of social control seems inexorably opposed to the variations of the human spirit. The courageous teacher, in this sense, evokes our special regard because of the attack on an institutional framework that stultifies, oppresses, and in the end *misleads*. That kind of courage is controversial and special in this case, as with others, because it dares to treat young men (or women) as adults, to help them experience life, and with it to accept that they may go off the rails and—in the case of one student—commit suicide. After that tragedy, when other students are asked to show their courage against their parents or the principal, none can do it. The example of courage has not been followed. Maybe courage needs more practice.

These kinds of courage are not as rare as we might think. They are central to the moral practice of teaching and what teachers know and do not know. Freedman (1990) simply picked out Jessica Seigel, a teacher in a New York school, and wrote about the courage (and other virtues) that he found. Courage itself is discouraged in teaching. Keating is fired, not treasured, for his courage; nor is he helped when tragedy strikes. Escalante gets recognition only for the pupil results, not for his courage. Faculty colleagues pity him, as they do Jessica, for the doggedness of their respective commitments. We may ignore "courage" as a concept through which to see and understand classrooms, and institutions may dislike it because it is so frequently used against them. It is difficult to be courageous in times of accountability, performance evaluation, management by objectives, outcome-based learning, and all the other bric-a-brac of the kind of institutionalized system we have developed, let alone its politics. But we should remember that a teacher is not the only example of courage children may encounter. They may often find it in their own homes and circumstances and in the lives of those around them whom they emulate. The teacher's particular concern is with intellectual courage.

None of this discussion will make any sense to a teacher without passions for subjects or for children, or who believes that education is a matter of facts to be stored, skills to be acquired, interpretations to be memorized, tests to be taken, and human values to be ignored. Passion in teaching and the courage to pursue it do not spring full blown from the heads of student teachers. It has to be fostered and nurtured in teacher education, and in the colleges and universities where they confront their teaching subject and through which they first meet with children who are learning.

Courage in Teaching: Professional Expertise

Where, then, is professional expertise visible through a concept of courage? It appears in the classroom as teachers help students learn through the encouragement and discouragement they give. The promotion of educational principle we witnessed in the cases of Vivian, Jessica, Jaime, and John indicate that it is an occupation fraught with demands on our courage, inside and outside the classroom.

Teachers can take great risks and be courageous with content and method. Content disciplines and subjects are traditions. They are not artificial "bodies" of knowledge, but complex living sets of ideas sustained by individuals and groups and powerfully influential in human life (see Chapter 5). They are great human achievements into which even the critical theorist has to be inducted. They can be approached with timidity, obeisance, or daring. They can be challenged. In matters of method, there is the set of risks that Elizabeth set herself to confront as a student: persisting in the creation of the most desired classroom climate, never giving up in the battles for individuals, assuming one's own power and ability to affect and change, never hiding behind an institutional structure, and so forth.

Courage is a necessary virtue in teaching. The connection between courage and encouraging/discouraging, the fact that learning is difficult, and the continuing opportunities for bravery in dealing with content or struggling with method give it a central place. To seek to make life and learning easy is, I think, simply to ignore the actual human condition and the fact that when things become easy people search for something more difficult. The teacher who cannot provide examples of courage, however mild they may look to the professional soldier, cannot exemplify the one virtue that is critical in the life of the intellect and the condition of learning. But courage, like honesty, is only one piece of professional expertise as virtue. Care is another.

CARE

I am regarding *care* as a virtue. This is not a familiar word in the pantheon of virtues. *Carefulness* is the nearest traditional usage, but that is more concerned with objects than people. The grounds for my stipulation are the implications for morality that spring from the view of the moral life that, for Noddings, Gilligan, and other writers, is distinctively feminine. A "caring person" has this specific, sustainable moral quality related to carefulness (Sockett, 1988) and, like most other virtues, it is affectively grounded (Peters, 1979b). The educational situation does not seem to be predominantly one where care predominates.

Care and Custody

In the middle of a bright schoolday morning in the spring of 1990, a student at a Virginia high school left a message under his helmet and killed himself by driving his motorcycle at 80 miles an hour into the wall of the boys' locker room. The reports from his stricken friends were, roughly, that school was the only place where he had friends. Remembering Durkheim's work on *Suicide* (Durkheim, 1951), I find myself haunted by this dreadful tragedy and its symbolic character. It ought to keep me awake more than it does because, unlike the suicide of the student in *Dead Poets Society*, it is so perplexing, even inexplicable. Children and the individual people who teach them develop all kinds of signals that, to the witness, are signs of trust. That relationship is morally more valuable, Noddings argues, than any content that might be taught, for the child is infinitely more important than the subject. But that, as she later insists, does not mean that schools should ignore the training of the intellect. A strong intellectual purpose in a school is not incompatible with its being a caring community.

For the Virginia student, it seems the school was not sufficiently caring to have taken note of his troubled life. On the other hand, school seemed to have been an oasis for him, particularly through his friends. The complexities of this death oblige us to think about the dimensions of our custodial institutions as we seek to make them caring institutions. Can a person's trust in an institution simply break down? Maybe our caring in schools becomes too routinized, too official (see the counselor!), and too detached from the problem of being a person, as opposed to having a problem to solve. Perhaps bureaucratic care—sophisticated custody—has come to define the limits of teacher perceptions. Perhaps in some of our schools there are no signals of trust of any greater intimacy than that between players and a referee.

Perhaps many schools, especially high schools, are too male? That the dominant approach to professional expertise and knowledge is in a cul-de-sac is becoming clearer to us because of the influence of femininist approaches to education. The "different voice" and the "voice of the mother" are transformative and powerful in the way we conceive our professional art. Indeed the concept of in loco parentis is critical to a sense of caring for children, but vox parentis must include both father and mother—their special difference of tone and pitch; the need is for harmony, not unison.

The problems are very striking:

1. Care rather than custody defines an educational situation. Custody, for the most part, defines contemporary schooling.
2. Care for each individual pupil defines education. Competition and depersonalized bureaucracies define much contemporary schooling.
3. Educational caring involves affection, regard, and feeling. Deep personal relationships can be both inhibited and destroyed, especially in the contemporary secondary school.
4. Care in education demands in loco parentis; it has been driven out by due process.

Dialogue between students and teachers seems inhibited by the pressure of test-driven curricula, and opportunities for caring cooperation can scarcely be achieved in competitive frameworks. High school climates then become antithetical to caring, for student motives are routinely suspect. However, professional expertise in the role of the caring teacher can be viewed through two main perspectives: the extent and limits of care, and care in the social climate of schools.

Extent and Limits of Care

Professional teachers can develop an understanding of the extent and limits of individual caring, specifically in teacher education (Arnstine, 1990).

They come to know when caring shades into overprotectiveness, when caring becomes corrupted into sentiment, when caring is sham because it fails to be tough, especially since the ethos of schools, particularly high schools, no longer seems really to foster the robust caring relationships important for excellence in teaching (Elkind, 1984). They get to stretch the capacities and responsibilities of their role, understanding that it has to be a professionally personalized role. They are not afraid of showing that they care, nor are they ashamed of wanting students to appreciate them, to like them, to reciprocate care. They may also need to neglect in order to care.

In his paper on "Skillful *Neglect*" (emphasis added), Labbett (1989) looks specifically at a curriculum problem: He is searching for instructional strategies to ensure that children in a world of information technology understand it as a world of purposes. (Now there are some moral issues!) He argues that teachers have to care enough about children's introduction to that world to neglect (skillfully) those children's expectations or, more properly for a world of intentions, to neglect to fulfill their own pedagogical routines.

Neglect as used by Labbett is hyperbolic. Yet it is not a technical term. It draws attention to the complex world of conflicting and differing purposes in classrooms—not between a recalcitrant child and a put-upon teacher, but between a curriculum world of ideas and directions (as yet new to education) in which there are no received dogmas, no social priorities, just an unexplored landscape, a wild frontier of learning. What Labbett seems to me to be doing is drawing morally sophisticated distinctions of teacher actions that simultaneously describe the pedagogical acts a teacher should follow.

Labbett has come up with what can only be described as a *moral* hypothesis for action. It is open to testing, but only in part empirically, because the evaluation would have to be primarily moral, just as any assessment of a person's courage demands moral appraisal and an appraisal of "what the facts were." It is also one in which the limits have been closely defined. Yet Labbett's hypothesis is not restricted to personal care; he conveys that what the teacher has to put before children is always conditional, specifically in respect to truth, even though that does not imply a relativist account of truth. Labbett provides an example of a teacher who cares for his or her subject and for children. What the teacher cares for is embodied in his or her practice. Teachers must want children to care for what they learn and for each other with what Bailey (1984) calls "affective conscientiousness." Bailey extends the notion of caring into a commitment to traditions and disciplines that have to be loved and protected, in Holmes's (1988) view, if they are not to be trampled upon by the barbarians at the gates.

Care and the Climate of Schools

Teachers require the space to critique the climate of the schools and institutions in which they work, particularly in relation to the social backgrounds of pupils they work with and especially in terms of the gender character of the institution. This is not simply a matter of becoming autonomous as a critic. It means showing a concern and care for the frameworks within which children have to grow up, to accept responsibility for them, and to seek to match institutional experience with domestic upbringing and relationships.

Care and dialogue.   Noddings (1988) has argued for the development of the moral skills of dialogue, so often present in the talented kindergarten or first-grade teacher but so often resisted in many high schools. She simultaneously describes and prescribes for classroom actions, not merely educational ends, using the ethic of caring to examine the relationship between researcher and subject in teaching (Rogers & Webb, 1991). So, if we witness a lesson, we need to be able to identify the moral sophistication of the questions the teacher asks and the quality of the conversation, given the individual pupil, as the teacher works one-on-one. I was only able to record Mrs. Simpson's dialogue—but recall how her response showed she "cared for" Wayne, the one who said, "The painter's clothes get very mucky." His remark was a challenge (the painter's clothes get very mucky, so [implicitly] what's wrong if ours do too?). She did not ignore it, tell him to stop being silly; rather she *cared* for him by taking what he said seriously and presenting him with a good reason for making the distinction between his clothes and the painter's. Sometimes teachers talk of individual children and their problems as somehow subservient to the artificial "needs of the class," as if the class somehow was *educationally* more important than the individuals the class contained. Mrs. Simpson displayed care. The topic may not have been of huge moral significance, but her focus on the individual pervaded even such an apparently insubstantial occasion.

Individual and group needs for care.   The carefulness in handling pupils and classes, balancing individual against group concerns, goes beyond the problems of dialogue with individuals. Nor does carefulness here imply "being too careful," placing restrictions on actions "just in case." It is how the teacher establishes the sets of interindividual relationships within a class. For example, the composition of groups in cooperative learning is of critical importance, with balances to be struck between personalities, leadership, gender, and learning needs in terms of team work as well as academic context. The teacher is establishing moral learning groups and determining moral and pedagogical issues.

Modeling care.   Teachers can model care, and then teach children to care and to be careful. Indeed, they can model and teach a broad set of virtues of will, such as concentration, patience, and determination (Sockett, 1988). This balance of modeling virtue and teaching it goes right through the school context. Institutions can also set morally caring sights for children. For example, some schools find no difficulty in raising immense amounts of money for known individuals in distress (e.g., a local child needing a bone marrow transplant) or for their own clubs. But their horizons may not extend beyond the parochial (e.g., to the refugee, the famine-struck family, or the international organization). Teaching people to care and to be full of care demands asking whether and in what ways the subject is worth caring for. These are moral issues once more.

FAIRNESS

"Being first virtues of human activities, truth and justice are uncompromising"; John Rawls's comment at the outset of his *A Theory of Justice* (1972, p. 4) is as important for teaching, perhaps more so, as for other areas of human life. In one of his early papers, Rawls (1963) suggested that no child could grow up with a sense of justice without having had parental love within a framework of rules. Indeed, it remains a commonplace for teachers of young children that the issue of what is fair arouses the most profound passion in their students.

However, the problems of justice are philosophically complex. Briefly there are two types: distributive justice (where the problem is to allocate benefits) and retributive justice (where the problem is to right a wrong or sanction a lawbreaker). Both are important at every level of teaching, although school systems do not have full-blooded codes of retributive justice built into them. Aristotle's famous remark provides a key to the meaning of justice at the level of particular decisions or acts. Justice, he wrote, consists in treating equals equally and unequals unequally—but in proportion to their relevant differences. (For example, where the horses are all three-year-olds, no handicap is needed—equals are treated equally. But where they are of varying ages and have won more or fewer races, then weight handicaps are sensible—unequals are treated unequally to make the race "just.") Applied to horses or to people, this implies the principles of both impartiality and equality. Just what forms of handicap or different treatment are relevant has to be decided on the basis of merit, need, and desert.

Lawrence Kohlberg (1981, 1984) built a scheme of moral development around the concept of justice. The influence of notions of development of justice clearly influenced Rawls, whose work grew from a view of justice as something of a natural law (Barry, 1973) to claiming that the desire to act justly is somehow a central aspect of human development. The human desire to be just and to cooperate in the maintenance of a just society is something humans have to do or they will be somehow morally stunted. Kohlberg's stages are constructed on this basis too, as a path to full altruistic justice-as-fairness, an argument Carol Gilligan and others have criticized as being gender-determined (Gilligan, 1979, 1982; Gilligan & Attanucci, 1988; Gilligan, Lyons, & Hammer, 1990).

Fairness is not the central moral principle or virtue in teaching, but it is one of them. As with the other virtues outlined, its ramifications reach deep into pedagogy. Fairness also reaches into educational provision in general, for instance, into questions of equity, where the distribution of benefits have to be weighed against merit, need, and desert. Yet fairness is central to teaching in one particular respect. Teachers are the first adults most children meet who are in positions of authority but are unrelated to their personal family lives. Teachers represent adult life. Their determination to instill a sense of justice alongside a sense of caring is an initial model of the outside world.

However, the argument is often made that since life in the outside world is nasty and brutish, unfair or even rough treatment in school will not do children any harm. But if children never receive fair treatment at school, they are not likely to expect it outside, and they will certainly not work to support it in social institutions. Educational programs of all kinds should aspire to contribute to human betterment without being outrageously unrealistic and with the knowledge that a school is not a replica of society. A moral ethos in the school, its character as a just and fair institution, is essential for children's social, civic, and moral growth. In practice, teachers assume at least three roles that involve questions of fairness: distributing time and attention, imposing discipline and sanctions, and monitoring fairness as a member of the school faculty.

Fairness and the Distribution of Time

Mrs. Simpson exemplifies the proper way for a teacher to distribute his or her time and attention to individuals. She distributes attention through directing questions. These questions are not aimed at the child with the "right answer," nor are they used as tools of discipline. She weaves the questions, *fairly*, across individuals. A researcher or another teacher could view her question distribution simply as technique. But it must also be seen as a professional practice in which the effort to focus on as many different children as possible reflects a respect for the children as individuals by giving each *a fair share of the teacher's attention*.

This problem is writ large for classroom teachers. How do we resolve the clamor for help from both ends of the ability range with the needs of

the "average" child? Teachers search for techniques to deal with this problem, often resisting such innovations as mainstreaming because they feel
inadequate to meet the demands of being fair. Too frequently the naive
assumption is made that the ideal of fairness is "equal time"—but remember Aristotle and the horses: Equals equally, unequals unequally. There is
a technical question: "How can I marshal techniques (e.g., in cooperative
learning groups, use of teacher aides) to reduce the clamor, and with it the
problems of overconcentration on one group?" But the more important
question governing issues of technique is: "What is *fair* in such situations?"
The two questions must constantly interact in the teacher's reflective practice. The empirical possibilities inform the moral problem (see Chapter 5).

Aristotle's construction of justice is highly instructive for teachers and
for the consideration of fairness. It recognizes differential weight for different parties, but it demands that assessment of empirical issues (e.g., the
practical reason we discussed earlier as necessary in courage) inform the
moral decision regarding "relevance," "equality or inequality," and "merit,
need, and desert." Issues of the distribution of time and attention do not
stop at the classroom door. They spill over into issues of time and attention in respect to the teacher's *own* time: first, in respect of the teacher's
duty to him- or herself. Jessica Seigel works fifteen hours a day in teaching,
grading, preparing and assisting children out of school. That is not morally reasonable as a *general* expectation for teachers. Second, in respect of a
teacher's family: many issues are raised in the Escalante family by Jamie's
apparently unencumbered open commitment to teaching adults as well as
children. With whom should he spend his time? Third, bureaucracies and
their occupants are also frequently oblivious to the trivial demands they
make on professionals' time, too often making paper mountains out of
organizational molehills. In this sense they constrain the teacher's opportunity to distribute time and attention fairly.

Fairness in Discipline and Sanctions

These matters primarily fall upon the institution and its authorities.
Yet fairness, as a moral issue, is found in strange places. It is most marked
in the constancy with which—throughout the history of schooling, I suspect—recidivism (offenders repeating offenses after having been punished)
occurs in schools. That must raise questions, which may be simply answered
in a particular context, about the fairness of the *system*, particularly when
the punished group is usually made up predominantly of black males.

Two issues stand out for the classroom teacher: (1) the frequency with
which any individual deserves discipline and sanctions and (2) the application of the system of rules. The obligation to be fair is clear to most teachers, and with it the obligation to try to make the institution a "just com-

munity." Most classrooms have sets of rules and sets of expectations for social or individual behavior, whether these are formalized in a statement or are simply norms understood by the students. Teachers need to be morally alert to the opportunities for unfairness that come in the application of both rules and norms to individual children, especially with those whose behavior creates in teachers expectations of further unruliness. The recidivist in school as in society at large, attracts deep suspicion and is sometimes treated unfairly for that reason.

Recidivism is not by itself an indication of unfairness in a context of the social rules of a school, but it is an indication that, for whatever reason, the school and its teachers are somehow failing with the recidivist student. The problems of fairness are especially acute in a school, since children are forced to attend; thus the obligation to make the experience valuable is greater than it is, for example, in the army. The principles of social control in the classroom and the sanctions or rewards that are meted out are constant factors in professional expertise.

Fairness and the School

A teacher is a member of a faculty. A school staffed by professionals is one that is influenced by the concerns and commitments of its staff. In some schools, teacher isolation has prevented the emergence of morally powerful school communities, but this may also be due to poor leadership and oppressive bureaucracy (Hill et al., 1989). But a teacher's schoolwide role and the classroom role do not simply interact. For the students to experience a coherent moral community, an moral ethos of fairness must pervade classrooms and the wider school. However, if there is no common policy of, say, discipline and sanctions, or if there is no common attitude within classes about the importance of any virtue, but particularly fairness, then that is itself unfair. Students working with conscientious teachers are receiving educational benefits denied to others. Or, to put the matter differently, teachers need to ensure that the school's ethos of fairness pervades their classrooms, not simply because it is a good thing, but to give children fair and equitable opportunity and experience.

The most important feature of distributive justice in terms of schooling is the access children have to the "best" teachers. Parents often try to bring pressure to get their children out of one teacher's class and into another's. The distribution of educational benefit is perhaps unavoidably uneven, since the quality of schools varies (Good & Brophy, 1986; Kozol, 1991). That is sometimes a matter within the classroom teacher's grasp to correct. But distribution need not be uneven in one respect—in the determination with which teachers seek to be good practitioners. Inefficiency or incompetence in teaching is not just unfortunate. It is unfair to children. Positively and negatively, the primary way in which teachers, in their professional roles as members of a faculty, can create an equitable system is by working to the highest standards of which they are capable. This is not to say that teachers can be the same, or that some teachers will not be better or worse than others. But it makes efficiency, and the commitment to self-improvement, a moral matter internally connected to what is fair.

PRACTICAL WISDOM

Finally, teachers should have practical wisdom, which requires qualities of reflectiveness and judgment interwoven with the four other virtues of professional expertise that I have stressed. Practical judgment in a classroom accrues from reflective experience, enabling the professional to know what to do when and why. Within this fifth virtue constituting professional expertise in teaching, I would place all those aspects of what is usually thought of as pedagogical skill (method) and the subject knowledge (content of what is being taught). Our familiarity as teachers with this part of our expertise makes it unnecessary for me to belabor its importance.

Wisdom in Courteous Translation

The most important component in practical wisdom is, to use Bruner's (1974) phrase once again, a matter of courteous translation—introducing children to material they may conceive of as difficult. How? In Mrs. Simpson's case, the objective is clear—to get the children to understand that the reasons they must take care with the painter's work *are* the interests of the other parties. The wisdom she displays is manifest in the techniques she uses (e.g., questioning), which are based on moral criteria. Tom is a quite different case of professional wisdom-in-practice and professional virtue. We could look at him only through the concept of practical wisdom, and notice the kinds of interpretative understanding, expository skills, and so forth that mark off part, but not all, of his distinctive expertise. With Tom, we miss what distinguishes his teaching if we only look at him through practical wisdom, critical though that wisdom is. We need a broader context of virtue to describe his teaching. His enthusiasm for his subject is *authentic*; it is not a show put on to "bring about children's learning." That authenticity is part of his integrity as a person, part of his moral integrity, part of what makes his role as a teacher congruent with his personal values. His risk in telling the story like *that* is an instance of the practical moral reasoning that is an element in courage. But he is also a pedagogue of substance (Shulman, 1990). Elizabeth's determination to reduce noise, however, has a different moral purpose—the creation of a learning community. The "means" each of these teachers uses, the "techniques" or the "strategies" they employ, are not simply *efficient*; they are selected and developed with moral and technical criteria. They exemplify practical wisdom as one component of moral knowing-in-action that is only fully constituted when all five virtues are present.

Wisdom and Practical Skills

What characterizes practical wisdom is, I think, different in kind from the four other virtues. First, practical wisdom, while itself a virtue, brings into focus the epistemological and technical aspects,—that is, matters of content and method—that are not *specifically* the domain of any one virtue or virtues. Second, what is practically wise depends on characteristics of the subjects or disciplines themselves (whatever the grade or college level at which they are being taught). For example, teaching science is going to require skill and judgment in running laboratories (or simulated laboratories for younger children), a feature of science not needed in history, where the discipline requires other kinds of techniques and skills for teaching. Forensic skill by a teacher is important in the humanities, but not so relevant in mathematics. So while the methods or techniques may ultimately be moral, they are derived from the nature of disciplines that are not intrinsically moral or nonmoral.

Hence Shulman (1987) has suggested that teachers' competence is domain-specific. His work on wisdom-in-practice has great power, and the supporting case studies by his co-workers are critically important material for our understanding of teacher expertise. I think Shulman would say of Tom that, as a teacher of history, he is able to transform his knowledge of content into a pedagogy which makes that knowledge accessible to students. The ability to do that, he would argue, is a specific ability distinct from any content knowledge Tom might have. The key word here for the purpose of the practice of teaching is the word *accessible*. The depth of insight into a subject is a perception of it as learnable, which is also an insight into aspects of its teachability, in Shulman's account. That is only possible, I think, if the teacher self-consciously views him- or herself as a learner of that content, such that the account of teaching may be in fact an account of one's own learning viewed from the standpoint of teaching.

For any teacher to obtain practical wisdom, it is a *sine qua non* to be educated in one or more of the great human traditions—art, literature, science, mathematics, history, music, philosophy. Teachers must know their material if students are to become liberally educated persons with some kind of grip on the ways of thought that have been hammered out across the centuries and that are found in all cultures, albeit in different manifestations. Just as we may have lost some of our moral sensibilities because we have stopped using a moral vocabulary, so we will lose much more if we ignore our world-culture—its history, artifacts, conventions, and styles—and settle for some empty hybrid like critical thinking. A teacher cannot understand many practical issues within teaching without being learned.

THE INTEGRATED VIRTUES?

I have argued that we can understand professional expertise as constituted by five virtues—honesty, courage, care, fairness, and practical wisdom. It may be argued that where the action is, where the teacher "acts" in the classroom, what is displayed is practical wisdom, into which the four other virtues are assimilated. Practical wisdom would then be the virtue within which others were integrated. Perhaps.

One difficulty for me with this kind of assertion is that it seems a relic of the way of thought that I have been at pains to dispense with, one that looks only the primacy of the observable behavior of practice. As a teacher myself, my sense is that while I am teaching I am involved in practical actions. I am accountable for outcomes, and, with a professional commitment to continuous improvement, I am constantly changing my processes. The trouble with this is that, while I am teaching, my mind is full of questions about whether what I said just then was accurate, about whether I can take this kind of risk, about whether I am being unfair to this student, and so forth. I am not just a bundle of actions, but a bundle of thoughts and actions as I teach. That seems to me the illuminating character of Schön's (1983) notion of knowing-in-action. I may be "technically less proficient" than a teacher without such thoughts, but is it too arrogant to say that I am a better teacher for the moral perplexity I so often find when I am teaching (Lyons, 1990)?

Another difficulty is that the notion of practical wisdom slips away too easily from practical virtue. What is wise is the result of judgment, but those judgments are themselves always to be assessed from the perspective of the other virtues of significance. Hard choices frequently have to be made, as illustrated in the phrase "the best [wisest] is the enemy of the good [the right thing to do]." The constant need to balance the wise with the good may be lost if we elide professional virtues into one single virtue—practical wisdom. So I strongly resist the notion of some kind of integrative account under the single virtue of practical wisdom. I find perplexing the urgent need to categorize, to find some "solution" or "explanation" that will simplify the teaching endeavor. Once we understand teaching as moral above all else, we can live with the ambiguity, the difficulty, and the uncertainty that understanding brings. If we continue to believe in teaching as something reducible to laws and generalizations, then we will have a highly etiolated conception of teaching and only the illusion of certainty.

CHAPTER 5

Professional Expertise and an Epistemology of Practice

In the conventional view professional teachers, like men and women in other professions, are experts because they have a special body of knowledge that they draw from in practice. Yet precisely what it is that Mrs. Simpson, Tom, and Elizabeth *know*, either as individual teachers or as exemplars of teaching excellence, remains uncertain. In recent years the inadequacy of teacher education and the insistence on finding appropriate means of assessing teachers, either at entry or as part of performance evaluation, has led researchers to believe that capturing that knowledge is just around the corner (Reynolds, 1989). These optimistic claims made for the delineation of the knowledge base of teaching have partly been a result of the conviction that scientific knowledge of all aspects of teaching is growing. If my characterization of the moral complexities of teaching so far is correct, then such searches for a knowledge base are premature, if not mistaken. I will show that the methodologies and assumptions being used in this quest are limited, if not discredited. To conduct a search for a knowledge base assumes an epistemology that is clear and defined; that does not seem to me to be the case in the study of education, any more than it is in the field of morality.

I have shown in Chapter 4 how profoundly our understandings of teaching are influenced by moral concepts of virtue and how all techniques (of the kind that might turn up in the knowledge base) are determined by their moral acceptability as much as by their efficiency. I have done this by using moral terms to describe major aspects of the teaching task. In the first section of this chapter, I explain why I am teaching professional expertise as a matter of professional virtue. In the second section, I begin the defense of these claims by outlining four views of the theory–practice relationship in the study of education, and in the third section I point out three apparently insuperable difficulties for the applied-science view of educational theory into which accounts of the knowledge base of teaching are presently intended to fit. In the fourth section, I define a criteria for a (moral) epistemology of practice. Finally, I examine knowledge *and* knowing-in-action in a moral framework as the potential basis of an epistemology of practice applied to teaching. This chapter will thus conclude this provisional and sketchy account of the second dimension of teacher professionalism, namely that of professional expertise.

THE SKELETON OF THE ARGUMENT

If we begin to use a language of virtue, what range of understanding of professional expertise opens up? What will that yield, especially as we have also begun to take seriously the voice of the teacher—and the voice of the woman and the mother in addition to the father (Sadker, Sadker, & Klein, 1991)?

Professional teachers are experts because of their professional virtue. By virtue, to repeat, I mean a sustainable moral quality of individual human character that is learned. By professional virtue I mean the collection of those qualities embedded in the social practice of teaching that are necessary to the particular professional task and that, as such, form the core of expertise needed. How teachers come to have those virtues is a matter of their autobiography (Harre, 1983). That they must come to understand these qualities and their far-flung influence on teaching is of paramount importance. Building on the account of virtues I have given, the skeleton of the argument for an alternative epistemology runs as follows:

1. Education/teaching is directly concerned with human betterment. It is thereby a moral business. There will always be argument about what constitutes that betterment, but every teaching act both presupposes and is invested with moral considerations of both ends *and* means. This applies at the general level (what should the curriculum be?) and at the individual level (how shall we help young Johnny?) (Buchmann, 1990; Sockett, 1989a).

2. Human betterment through education demands at least the development of and the capacity for choice and for care. These can only be learned in a context where both are possible, which implies that the learning students do must be volitional (Peters, 1966) and relational (Noddings, 1984). An educational context therefore has to be a partnership between teacher and learner, one in which learners can also be teachers and teachers, learners. We need to work to these premises wherever and whomever we teach.

3. The moral complexity of teaching, however, cannot be captured if it is wrenched from its context. Teaching is not an act or activity but is primarily a role created by individual men and women teachers, by traditions,

by moral and other theories, by particular school cultures, by parents, children, politicians, and so forth. The teacher can never simply "teach" (in the sense that a knitter knits). For limited purposes, of course, teaching may be viewed partially as a sequence of acts or a performance (see, for example, Rosenshine, 1971).

4. The role is constantly being redefined. It is also filled by both men and women, and gender differences bring different qualities and perspectives to the definition of the role and to what counts as professional expertise. Embedded in such differences are morally complementary ways of viewing the world (Belenky, Clinchy, Goldberger, & Tarule, 1986).

5. A comprehensive account of professional expertise, therefore, must be moral and multidimensional. Thinking, reflecting, or theorizing about—or by—these experts must also squarely reflect that moral complexity, including the fact that the expert professional teacher must have varieties of knowledge of the empirical world and of what is to be taught, all of which are part of the value-laden exercise of the professional role. The knowledge a teacher has could not be just a matter of an internalized "knowing-what-to-do-when" technique, for only technique influenced, comprehended, and individually expressed within a moral framework provides a basis for describing the role.

6. Professional expertise has to be captured in a moral language of personal attribution, that is, professional virtue. These human qualities (virtues such as fairness, honesty, courage, care, and practical wisdom) are integral to the individual attributes, competencies, and capabilities the teacher (in his or her role) possesses, because we can understand ourselves in our roles through these concepts of virtue. These virtues are necessary qualities in teaching for the effective exercise of the role. They are also the content of teaching and have to be learned or acquired by students.

7. The teacher, as a professional man or woman expert, can have a profound moral knowledge within a range of virtues. These virtues are not a kind of optional framework; they reach deep into the substance of the social practice of teaching such that teaching, as a practice, can be described in terms of them. Primarily such language allows us to achieve a balance between the voice of the father and the voice of the mother as we work back to a renewed conception of the role as *in loco parentis*.

8. An epistemology appropriate to teaching is rooted in such a social practice, but it requires agreement on central moral purposes (and thereby on some moral truths). It will be highly sensitive to the moral claims of individual learners and can be characterized as "knowing-in-action" reflecting the context-bound, fast-changing fluidity of what professionals do day-by-day. It is also a jargon-free, nontechnical, but highly sophisti-

cated language providing a common framework for personal and professional life.

9. The characterization of professionalism built on this virtue-centered view of professional expertise is radically different from one which places a view of technical knowledge at the center. It influences how we judge ourselves as teachers, how we invite novices to see their own career development, and how opportunities are created for practitioners. It asks us to question the virtues in ourselves and the virtues in our own work.

This sketch provides a way to link the role, the men and women who occupy it, the moral demands it makes on us, and the practical arts of teaching to the institution of education. Distinctively different valuative approaches to education will still exist, forcing the debate on educational ends and means and the complexity of their interrelations, up into the culture of the profession. A profession can have unity of purpose with distinctiveness of perspective.

CONCEPTIONS OF EDUCATIONAL THEORY
AND THE RELATION TO PRACTICE

However, we presently have no common epistemology on which professional expertise and knowledge can be based. There is a noticeable gap between teaching knowledge and educational theory in the language used to describe, explain, and justify phenomena of schooling. Sometimes practitioners use theory-laden language in slogan form; they talk about "developmental stages" or "reinforcement" as if these were facts of nature. Sometimes academics remain locked in intellectual positions that have been discredited. Sometimes practitioners, particularly those in the social sciences, describe classrooms with "natural" languages drawn from their major disciplines. Sometimes there are subtle languages within teaching (as Elizabeth Beck showed me) that are rich in explanatory content but that academics, withdrawn from practice, do not recognize. Frequently the practitioner dismisses the academic's languages as jargons that simply do not fit the practitioner's frame of understanding, thus undermining any potential these languages might have for forwarding understanding of classrooms or schools in general.

Without a shared epistemology, how are we to understand what is the formal (rather than the substantive) relationship between theory and practice? What different views are there of the relationship between the knowledge (some of which at least must be theoretical) and the action (what a teacher does)? It is a reflection of the queasy state of education as an academic study that these questions are much disputed. At least four different accounts of the theory–practice relationship have adherents in the professional community. These are a commonsense view of the relationship, a philosophical view, an applied-science view, and a practical view (Carr, 1986).

First, there is a "commonsense" view, in which practice simply means acting and thinking in conformity with a tradition and the place of theory is to encourage the use of an existing and developing stock of skills (P. W. Jackson, 1986). Many teachers as well as those teacher-educators whose primary allegiance is to a discipline they teach would adhere to this conception—as would, of course, laypersons as the proprietors of common sense. Second, there is a "philosophical" view of the relationship between theory and practice in which practice is indeed tradition, but this view is based on ideals and principles that need to be articulated and justified in theory as a way of reflecting on and transforming practice (Hirst, 1972). Many liberal educators, egalitarians, philosophers of education, and all manner of ideologues who put their faith in the transformative power of well-articulated ideals would be allied to this view.

Third, and dominant in houses of educational theory, is the "applied-science" view. Here practice is seen as a collection of technical skills, while theory provides the scientific knowledge in terms of which the efficiency of these skills can be determined. Positivists of all descriptions, notably behavioral psychologists and curriculum designers, many educational bureaucrats, and "official" education itself cling to this view. These people see no difficulty in separating means from ends in education; in their work they are mesmerized by the model of instrumental rationality that is incapable of application in their lives (Oakeshott, 1967; Peters, 1979a).

Fourth, there is a "practical" view of the theory–practice relationship in which practice is seen as a moral activity requiring judgment, wisdom, and prudence in complex, changing situations; here the task of the theorist is to make morally defensible decisions by developing the art of practical deliberation among practitioners in order to facilitate the improvement of practice. Curriculum researchers focusing on action, naturalistic evaluators, and the educational followers of John Dewey and Joseph Schwab are attracted to this view (Walker, 1990).

Three points deserve notice: (1) In describing these different views I have related the beliefs to the believers, the knowing(s) of the knowers— albeit in caricature; (2) each view contains an implicit ideal of pedagogy and with that, an ideology of educational process; and (3) these different approaches mirror ongoing debates in the social sciences. So what are we to make of them?

There is probably no commonsense view per se. Rather there are commonsense views of each of the other views—for example, "if only we

could get the ideals, aims, and goals of education sorted out, then education would improve" (the philosophical view); "if only we really applied what
research tells us, then education would improve" (the applied-science view);
"if only we thought out properly the context and the complexities of what
teachers do, empowering teachers as we did so, education would improve"
(the practical view). But the practitioner is happily eclectic, willing to draw
on ideas and conclusions from each or all of them. If it works, it is useful;
forget the theory. For the academic, this is not just a theoretical game of "choose
an educational theory." Indeed there is a hot-blooded controversy among
the academic partners in the professional community, who are engaged in
a major and deep-rooted conflict of epistemology. That war is fought in the
columns of journals, around the board tables of foundations, in promotion and tenure committees, and within the fabric of many educational
institutions. At stake is intellectual status (and coherent theory–practice
relationships). Clearly the absence of a technical subculture is not, as some
claim, the practitioner's responsibility, but a result of the confusion in the
educational epistemology that is properly the academic's responsibility.

However, each of the alternative rival views discussed implies a particular kind of academic–practitioner relationship. The applied-science and
philosophical views elevate the academic, while the commonsense view denies
the need for the academic; only the practical view demands close, mutual
understanding between academic and practitioner. My ideas in Chapters 2
and 3 about the development of the single professional community will
thus be differently perceived within one or the other of these four epistemological positions. The dominant power of the four is, of course, the
applied-science view of the theory-practice relationship, and it is important
to see now how my earlier remarks on its inadequacy can be justified.

THREE DIFFICULTIES FOR THE APPLIED SCIENCE ACCOUNT OF KNOWLEDGE AND PRACTICE

The present dominating power is sometimes referred to as educational
empiricism or, more popularly, positivism. Like an aging feudal empire, or
a fundamentalist church, it clings to life and power even though the intellectual world outside has long since passed it by. We seem unable to get
away from its power, for it seems to control our institutions as well as the
way we think. I have pointed out that its main contemporary manifestation in thinking about teaching is the belief that all we have to do is to
"capture the knowledge base," and I have indicated the political and hierarchical relationship that follows. Once the knowledge base is fixed, then
academics teach it to teachers, and they in turn will go out into classrooms
and apply it.

There are three major difficulties for this view of theory–practice and the consequent attempts to construct an account of knowledge in teaching. First, theorists interested in the knowledge base rarely have an adequate epistemology of value, or of the fact–value distinction, thereby allowing their knowledge construction to pose as value-free when it is value-laden. Second, those who attempt to describe the knowledge base usually ignore the severe problems they encounter through being wedded to a simple view of action, wherein a harsh distinction is made between means and ends. This view of theory–practice thus has an inadequate view of practice because it has an inadequate view of action. Finally, it is procedurally and epistemologically difficult to separate the teacher-as-person from the knowledge being used.

The Values Difficulty

What we decide will count as education (and thus open to educational theory) presupposes a decision of value. I discussed this problem in Chapter 1 from a different angle, namely, how moral discourse is central to education. One does not see experiments in universities on whether children learn math better through being hit with a stick 3 or 20 times an hour. Why not? Because moral considerations have already entered in. We have already ruled out some ways of learning as noneducational. Our techniques are themselves rooted in values and moral selections. The upshot is that if one advances a claim to (educational) knowledge, it has to be hedged about with value conditions, rarely made explicit. Indeed, what we are prepared to count as education—the vast range of social and other constraints that are placed on what teachers do—*ipso facto* constrains the scope of "educational theory" and riddles it with "values." We therefore have the values difficulty, the problem of acquiring educational knowledge (on a scientific model) untainted by those worrisome values or attempting to divide fact from value in some simple-minded way (Schrag, 1989). The applied-science view of educational theory aspires to an unattainable norm, namely, that values can be separated from facts. Dependence on the so-called empirical thereby becomes unintelligible as an epistemology for a practice like teaching. It faces only minor difficulties in this regard in theory development in, say, natural science.

The Means–Ends Difficulty

John Stuart Mill (1843/1950) articulated a significant distinction for rational action that has dominated the logic of sciences ever since. This is the distinction between the ends (which we value and decide on in advance of acting) and the means (the techniques that have been tested as the scientific best to attain our ends). Ends and means are separately describable, in Mill's view, and connected only contingently. That seems fine when we are building a brick wall. Dewey claimed that in any form of human action ends and means are constantly interacting (Eames, 1970). Oakeshott (1967) goes further by claiming that we cannot do justice to practical contexts and describe means and ends separately. In any case, he claims, this prescription for rational action is untenable because no one could actually conduct themselves according to its prescriptions. It is not a cogent account of action. So, when we try to imagine what the practice looks like, we are given an implausible picture: that of a teacher taking action by summoning up knowledge and applying it, always selecting ends before means.

It is facile to use Mill's distinction within the social complexity of education, for which it was not intended. Consider Elizabeth: The politeness and consideration she shows her children is not just a means to an end. She is also trying to teach them to be polite and considerate (as an end) by being polite and considerate (as a means). She has multiple teaching "ends" and "means" simultaneously. Consider Tom: It would be misleading to describe his enthusiasm as technique, a mere strategy he uses. (It would also be insulting, because it would indicate that it was not quite authentic.) Consider Mrs. Simpson: How can we unravel the ends and means in her teaching of moral standards? More particularly, why should we be saddled with a dogma that insists that our failure to do so is some kind of intellectual heresy? If we also try to take examples from these three teachers and teach novices from their work, are we bound to package this knowledge in some kind of empirical formula for application? I call this problem the means–ends difficulty. What Mill's followers in educational theory try to do for the purposes of analysis often distorts the practice rather than keeping faith with it.

One characteristic manifestation of this difficulty is the extent to which we believe that proven strategies can be implemented anywhere, based on a development with an experimental group. Theory puts pressure on context. To be coherent, context must pressure our theorizing so that it becomes aligned with the actions of the practitioners and their situational complexity. That implies a far more sophisticated conception of what rational action is in teaching (Bennett, 1964), even if we recognize its historically and philosophically distinctive roots (MacIntyre, 1988).

The Knowledge-and-Persons Difficulty

This is also true for the third problem, the knowledge-and-persons difficulty. Take Mrs. Simpson, Tom, and Elizabeth again. If my account of their good teaching is compelling, how do we ascertain exactly what it is that they know that is somehow independent of them as persons (Downie, Telfer, & Loudfoot, 1974). There is a continuing procedural difficulty about capturing the knowledge base of teaching. We still seem to be left (even when we think we have isolated the "knowledge") with some kind of reference to Mrs. Simpson as a person and as a knower—to what she thinks, to what she values, to how she decides and judges, and to how that interaction of personality, held values, and knowledge occurs in the activity of teaching. Perhaps we need to talk about her understandings, tacit and subtle as they may or may not be, if we are to be accurate about her professionalism. Better still, maybe we could find some way to let her speak for herself.

Scholars, when faced with this third difficulty, have tended to give it a label—"tacit knowing" or "judgment"—and to regard it as a puzzle that does not upset the basically empiricist account of teaching they offer (Shulman, 1987, 1989). That seems quite wrong and leads, in conceptions far less sophisticated than Shulman's, to the creation of a picture of her as a teacher that does not accurately reflect her. We persist in that error, usually for the convenience of a theory. Teachers are portrayed as individuals who "use" a knowledge base in much the same way they use a knife and fork—much like other people, but with occasional idiosyncracy. We fail to connect the knowledge base (or the conception of knowledge) to the agent as knower.

These three problems seem insuperable in trying to establish the basis of teaching knowledge in an applied-science model. It cannot be value-free. If that is right, then we need to look to an epistemology that admits of value statements. If its view of action (particularly classroom action) is too narrow, then we should develop an epistemology that reflects that complexity. If it fails to connect knowledge to the person-teacher, then we need a far more sensitive account of understanding what teachers do in the roles and with the individual personalities that they have.

However, pointing out these major weaknesses in the dominant house of educational theory is not done for the purpose of supporting a "know-nothing" movement or claiming that therefore we are ignorant, that there are no empirical facts in education, and that no headway has been made in educational research. Far from it. Empirical methodologies and skills are useful, for example, in evaluating the practice of teaching. Conclusions and methodologies are important. They are simply inadequate for the whole enterprise of an epistemology of practice. For, within this tradition, what has been and is being described as knowledge is not set within the occupational framework of teaching, that is, persons in roles pursuing moral purposes. Present attempts to describe technical teaching knowledge based on the applied-science view seem to fall into the traps laid in each of these issues, and we have not been able to overcome them satisfactorily. Philip Jackson's (1987) uncertainty about progress made on the knowledge base in the last ten years is therefore well founded. Educational theory has been in a long, confused nightmare in which we have regarded education within the domain of science.

The nightmare may have persisted because of the social and political battles for supremacy that take place in houses of educational theory rather than because of any serious attention to the nature of the theories themselves, a point reiterated volubly by critical theorists. It is important to see that each of the four accounts of theory I have discussed could, in principle, form a useful (if incomplete) framework for understanding educational phenomena. Yet we lack a unifying overview. As in England's (1986) view of social work, education could be seen as a legitimate part of the humanities rather than a social science, and within that framework its status as a moral endeavor could easily be understood.

THE CONDITIONS FOR AN EPISTEMOLOGY OF PRACTICE

If these criticisms of the applied-science model are correct, then we first need to establish criteria for an alternative epistemology that takes moral practice in teaching seriously. Without criteria, we cannot determine whether an alternative is arbitrary. Thus the following six criteria for an epistemology of practice are offered.

First, an epistemology (of practice) is a theory of knowledge (of practice). Knowledge, whatever its social determinants, must contain a view of meaning and truth (Hamlyn, 1970; Taylor, 1970).

Second, it has to search for a common language of description, explanation, and justification, which will not be exclusively a moral language (Hirst, 1972). Like history, it will include the use of concepts, laws, generalizations, and so forth from other disciplines (Dray, 1964).

Third, it needs an account of objectivity that is not determined by empirical observation but rather allows intersubjectivity as an appropriate way to make judgments about human actions. Intersubjectivity is well understood in history, where grounded judgments, using moral character concepts, are crucial to the explanation of human behavior. To say that Senator Ross (see Chapter 4) was courageous is a judgment based on evidence, not simply a round of moral applause. We may also be able to work with such notions as subjective generalizability (Hollingsworth, 1992), and, as I suggest in Chapter 7, we can reexamine the relationship between the universal and the particular from idealist metaphysics.

Fourth, the focus of educational and teaching inquiry is practical, not theoretical. Thus any epistemology must be comprehensive in scope. It must provide for description and explanation of teaching technique and of human behavior and action, of the work of institutions, of the range of ideological standpoints that inform educational activity, and so forth. It must find its primary point of reference in action not just in interactions or results.

Fifth, it must have a view of rational action that matches human conduct. The kind of instrumental account given by Mill is adequate for controlled experiments but is inadequate for the vagaries of human life outside a laboratory. Two things follow. An epistemology must develop a sophisticated view of reason-in-action by plotting and understanding the way human beings act reflectively (i.e., using their reason) as they teach in the context in which they are placed. It must also seek to understand such phenomena as the tacit in teaching as an adjunct or a part of that reason-in-action.

Finally, as the central theme in this book reveals, an epistemology must stand up to the question of its relationship to the moral, a task neither Shulman nor Schön attempt. We have seen that the practice of teaching is the heart of the matter. It is necessarily interpersonal, and it must thus be governed in all its aspects by moral criteria. Precisely because teaching is interpersonal, we need the richness of the moral vocabulary to describe and explain it. But as with moral understanding, a moral epistemology of practice as such can only be developed on the basis of grounded empirical observations about human or institutional behavior.

In sum, an epistemology of practice must contain:

1. A view of meaning and truth
2. A common language of description and explanation used by practitioners and theorists
3. A view of objectivity
4. A comprehensive reference to practice and to human action
5. A view of rationality in action
6. A view of its relationship to the moral

AN EPISTEMOLOGY OF PROFESSIONAL PRACTICE

Unsurprisingly, the above specifications fall into three categories: knowledge (meaning, truth, concepts, and criteria of objectivity), action (rationality and individual and social practice) and their interrelations, and the moral (worth, purpose, quality of actions, attitudes, and beliefs).

I have so far dealt with the moral in this book in the following way. In Chapter 1, I set out an argument for seeing how we understand teaching in primarily moral terms and from that argued that professionalism should have a moral core. In my preliminary discussions of Mrs. Simpson, Tom, and Elizabeth, I claimed that professional knowledge and understanding must include not simply subject and pedagogical knowledge, but also something that we might call character and commitment. In Chapter 2 I discussed these four elements as embodied in different elements of career progression. In Chapter 3, I stressed the significance of teachers as moral individuals in institutional roles and in the professional community. In Chapter 4 I developed an outline of the argument for the centrality of the moral through delineating five central virtues and showing how each has a major place in our understanding of the moral enterprise of teaching. Following this line of argument, an epistemology of practice will be a moral epistemology, but the viability of that argument will depend on (1) a coherent account of knowledge, and moral knowledge in particular, and (2) how knowledge and action relate to each other in the social practice of teaching, as well as how we understand both.

Knowledge and Its Components

A conventional philosophical view of knowledge is as follows: What a person knows can logically be divided into three groups—knowledge of propositions, knowledge displayed in skills, and knowledge of persons. I will concentrate here on knowledge of propositions only. Propositional knowledge can be understood as justified true belief (Brandon, 1987; Hamlyn, 1970); when a person (A) claims he knows that p (where p stands for a proposition, such as Berlin is the capital of Germany), three conditions must logically apply for that person accurately to be said to know p, or to make that claim himself. These conditions are (1) A believes that p; (2) p is true; and (3) A has good evidence for p. So if A says, "I know your last car was a Volvo," A must believe that my last car was a Volvo; my last car must in fact have been a Volvo; and A must have good evidence for his claim, viz., that I drove him to work daily in my Volvo, that he saw my registration documents, that he borrowed my Volvo to go to New York, and so on. There are three conditions for knowledge on this account—belief, truth, and evidence.

Belief is not often disputed, for there is a sense in which—ethical issues apart—people can believe anything they please. Characteristically people find the truth condition difficult because they want some overarching view of Truth (with a capital T), something that is "absolutely" true. The alternative to truth being always absolute, it is thought, is that truth is always relative, with people saying such things as, "well, that's just your view of truth." Part of the problem with the many variations of the dispute about whether knowledge exists, whether it is relative or subjective, whether its rooted in ideology, or whatever is that examples such as "God is love" or "Capitalism works" are cited as the standard cases, rather than mundane, everyday things such as what make of car I possess and whether A knows that for a fact. The central issue, in my view, is *not* just how belief and truth are connected, but how truth and evidence are connected—for we find out the truth by looking at the evidence.

The type of evidence you want depends on the type of statement you are making in your knowledge claim. For example, it does no good for A to claim that he knows I have a Volvo by saying that Volvos are made in Europe. The evidence A is then citing does not apply to the nature of his claim. Similarly, you do not have to go searching in a laboratory for the "evidence" that $2 + 2 = 4$, since that is analytically true, or true by definition. Again, it makes no sense for me to go hunting through a biography of Newton to find the right evidence for the law of gravity. What is stated by the law of gravity is true irrespective of Isaac Newton; indeed it was true—obviously— before Newton formulated it. Of course, types of evidence do not neatly separate into analytic and empirical categories. For example, I know (have a justified, true belief) that the Japanese attacked the American base at Pearl Harbor in 1942. That historical truth depends on reports and records, gravestones, and, right now, human memory. It does not depend on observation or replication, the acid tests of the empirical. Evidence for the truth of any statement depends on the kind of claim being made. Many scholars (Eisner, 1985; Hirst, 1972; Phenix, 1964) have argued that these differences of evidence are captured in different traditions where central distinctions exist that we must all learn if we are to understand the differentiated nature of our world. Incidentally, that leaves open the matter of how we teach them.

Toward Moral Knowledge

These are extremely important matters when we look at education. For we seem to have been trapped by positivism into the dogma that only empirical knowledge is knowledge. Moral knowledge has been thought unattainable because it does not conform to scientific norms. If you could have moral knowledge, then you could have moral knowledge in teaching.

This is an exceedingly complex and well-worn philosophical problem, and I will not do justice to it here. Is it possible? First, recall the case D. N. Walton (1982) makes for courage, namely that we can and do make judgments about incidents on the basis of the facts, on the worth of the person's ideals and their practical reasoning in carrying them out. We can with perfect propriety say that we "know that Senator Ross was a courageous man." Our use of "know" there is not tendentious. On the contrary, it is a justified true belief that meets the criterion of being a true statement and therefore a proper claim to knowledge. But, although it contains empirical facts, it is a claim to moral knowledge. If it is correct to call our claim about Ross a statement of moral fact, then in principle we can do the same for statements about teachers and any of the other virtues they possess and display. We can have justified true beliefs (i.e., knowledge) about a person's moral behavior (and that can apply to the living as well as to the dead). For example, I have described Mrs. Simpson, Tom, and Elizabeth by using evaluative words to describe their work and their character. I believe that I can justify my claims—by providing you with evidence that I know that Mrs. Simpson was morally highly sensitive, that Tom was brave, and that Elizabeth showed determination. My further claim is that these qualities are important professional qualities in teaching.

As we observe people and observe ourselves and our contexts in moral terms, we are engaging in what Stout (1988) calls *reflexive ethnography*. He uses the term briefly, but it is highly suggestive, in that we can study situations, as it were, ethnographically, but with a system of moral concepts. That is, we can study our own contemporary (and historical) social life in teaching as we work at moral issues, and from such a base we can build from and back into general moral truths about teaching. Indeed, from such a base, he argues, it is possible to develop a continuum from those values that may be judged to be less well founded (i.e., more subjective) to those that have come to have the status of truths (i.e., more objective). According to Stout, moral claims and propositions fall along "a spectrum of relativity." This spectrum enables us to say, at one end, that "slavery is wrong" is a true moral statement—indeed, a fact. At the other end of the spectrum, heaping moral blame on individuals who practiced it 150 years ago is much less open to epistemic justification. Stout writes (1988):

> I propose a metaphor. Propositions imputing moral blame and propositions describing people, practices, or institutions as evil (*or good*) fall at opposite ends of a spectrum of relativity. The truth value of the former, like the truth value of propositions about epistemic justification, is relative to certain features of the circumstances of the people referred to. The truth value of the latter is not similarly relative (p. 87; emphasis added).

We can thus develop propositions about the evil or goodness, vice or virtue of people, practices, and institutions that "seem no more problematic, on reflection, than other relational, context-dependent, or context-sensitive propositions, including propositions about epistemic justification and explanatory success in science" (Stout, 1988, p. 90). We can, in other words, properly talk of moral knowledge.

What might this imply? I have attempted throughout the previous chapters to follow Stout's metaphor of moral philosophy as reflexive ethnography by describing factual, fictional, and hypothetical cases in the social practice of teaching. I rehearsed at the beginning of this chapter the kinds of perspective-taking that teaching as a moral affair raises. Each of my diagnoses of virtue can be set out as claims to knowledge necessary in the professional practice of teaching, for example, that avoiding deceit implies doing this or that. We could expect, as we undertake our reflexive ethnography, to develop a corpus of knowledge about, say, honesty in teaching and to be able to share that understanding with novices in the profession. (I would guess we already do). We could use that knowledge for self-evaluation. The claims I made in discussing each of these virtues—honesty, courage, fairness, care, and practical wisdom—indicate that statements can be made using these terms that can then become candidates for moral truth and for moral knowledge. Within the social practice of teaching, we can expect to develop a central continuum of moral knowledge out of our understanding, insight, and intuition. In some cases, I suspect that claims to truth and knowledge will be palpable. Other claims, on careful examination, may turn out not to have the strength we might expect. Each would need mixed empirical and evaluative inquiry, as in the examples of courage.

Other important features of the criteria I have suggested for an epistemology of practice are implicit. If we are to make shared statements about what we know, then we also have to share the language, its concepts and modalities; we have to share a sense of meaning (necessary to sharing truth). Moreover, Wittgenstein (1963) suggests that "if language is to be a means of communication there must be agreement not only in definitions but also, (queer as this may sound) in judgments" (p. 88e). Where these things are shared we can then, in principle, get objectivity—or at least intersubjective statements about individuals and institutions. Objectivity may become intersubjective judgment. The language of description will be an increasingly sophisticated moral language. It will be more comprehensive as it centers on practice, and its view of meaning and truth can still strive for the objective without trying to survive in a relativist quagmire.

That may be acceptable for the purposes of describing a general view of professional expertise and knowledge. But would not our discussion of individuals be always relative, like the "propositions apportioning blame" of Stout's examples? Sometimes—but certainly not in principle. Take Mrs. Simpson once again. We may be happy to admit (1) that she had moral knowledge that she was imparting to the children (i.e., about respect for others) and (2) that her professional practice celebrated that. But how do we judge *her*, as Senator Ross was judged, and expect to come up with true statements about *her*, especially if we are completing her performance evaluation form? The judgments will be moral judgments, but would they have a claim to objectivity?

The Senator Ross model of making judgments on individuals is significant for us. For Walton (1982), judgments about incidents of courage are made (1) on the basis of the facts, (2) on the worth of the person's ideals, and (3) on the practical reasoning in carrying them out. Following this model into the social practice of teaching, there will similarly be

1. Many empirical, local, and contextual factors, as perceived by observers and participants
2. The established generalizable claims to knowledge of professional virtue and expertise in teaching
3. The individual's use of "practical reasoning in carrying them out" (i.e., Schön's knowing-in-action)

Within the framework of knowledge and expertise are all kinds of know-how in teaching—skills, strategies, and tactics—that have been sifted through the net of moral appraisal and are idiosyncratically deployed by individuals. Generalizations from such disciplines as psychology based on a scientific model of objectivity can be incorporated, as they have to be in history. We therefore create common understandings of best practice and in their light judge individuals like Mrs. Simpson, just as we do in every other walk of life. That may be the impartial best, epistemologically speaking, we can do. But that *will* be the best we can do—as we fit understanding to practice and abandon the attempt to drive practice from a limited basis of theory.

Practices, Persons, and Actions

We can now start talking (hesitantly) of moral facts, truths, and knowledge about education and subject technical knowledge to moral criteria. As we look at the best actions, as we look at a practitioner's first-rate professionalism, it is not mere knowledge (of facts or of skills) that can be evaluated as excellence in teaching. As with Mrs. Simpson, Tom Stevenson, and Elizabeth Beck, there is something much more complex involving who they are and what they do with what they know. We cannot just apply evaluation criteria. Perhaps, indeed, professional quality rests in the moral cast of different individuals below the performances and speech-acts. What we can begin to see is that truly professional acts are a complex of many virtues, including practical wisdom, related to contexts and situations through the individuality of the professional.

For the purposes of analysis I separated knowledge, action, and the moral as necessary criteria for an epistemology of practice. But, as I have complained about the applied-science model, distinguishing these for the purposes of analysis does not mean that they can be separated when human beings are actually doing things. Schön (1983) reminds us of Ryle's (1963) remark "when I do something intelligently . . . I am doing one thing and not two. My performance has a special procedure or manner, not special antecedents" (p. 32). So, of knowing-in-action, Schön (1983) writes that it refers to "the sorts of know-how we reveal in our intelligent action—publicly observable, physical performances like riding a bicycle and private operations like instant analysis of a balance sheet. In both cases, the knowing is *in* the action. We reveal it by our spontaneous, skillful execution of the performance; and we are characteristically unable to make it verbally explicit" (p. 25).

The critical knowledge instantiated in the *individual* professional's actions is an understanding of the five central virtues of teaching. Recall my account of Mrs. Simpson once again. She revealed her understanding of the importance of teaching the children respect for others, but she also embodied that respect in her own dealings with the children and how she described the feelings of others, for example, the principal, Mum, the painter, and so forth. She revealed her knowledge by her spontaneous, skillful execution of the performance. While individual teachers may become virtuous in these respects for all kinds of different reasons, it is of paramount importance that they understand their significance and focus on them as bases for reflection in and after action. The knowing (of these virtues) is then rooted in the (professional's) action.

But Mrs. Simpson, like all teachers, is an heir to teaching as a social practice and to the roles as described in particular *institutions* (see Chapter 3). We need not, as Stout argues, accept MacIntyre's (1984) particular historical arguments to see the force of the philosophical account given of virtues as constitutive of social practices (like medicine) and of institutions. MacIntyre's analysis of institutions is inescapably moral, and we understand institutional social practices through constitutive virtues that are the internal goods of such institutions. Institutional roles carry implicit definitions of rights and duties conceived in moral terms. The constituent virtues of teaching—honesty, courage, care, fairness, and practical wisdom—will also be the primary elements in such role definition. The commitment to improvement of practice has also to be construed in terms of virtues. Olson (1991) writes:

> It takes certain virtues in order to learn from experience how to be a
> better practitioner. As MacIntyre points out, a practice gets better be-
> cause people are willing to take criticism (= being honest) from those
> whom they recognize as fit to give it (= being fair), and are willing to
> act on that criticism (= being courageous). . . . Because of such vir-
> tues it becomes possible to learn from experience as well. (p. 23)

These virtues are not just descriptive of individual persons. They are
embedded in the character of institutions through the roles exercised therein.

Teaching as a social practice is thus constituted by virtues. They
appear in the rights and duties of specific roles. To attribute virtue to a
person in a role we need a mix of the moral and the empirical as a basis
for claiming knowledge and evidentially justifiable beliefs about professional
knowledge in action. Expertise and excellence are here defined. While
individuals themselves may not be able to give accounts of "why they do
what they do when," substantial accounts can be given of the basis of knowledge, moral and empirical, in terms of which they act as professionals.

I have now set out, in a rudimentary form, a rough-hewn line of argument for an epistemology of practice that is moral. I have expanded it
beyond Schön's architecture example to the social practice of teaching set
in a moral frame. It is an epistemology (the knowledge) of practice (the social
practice of teaching) as it is apparent in professional expertise. Theory and
practice, in this account, are not separable because we both act as teachers
and observe ourselves and others within a framework of knowledge and
action differently understood.

Obviously, like any other account of an epistemology, my argument has
a persuasive function. It is distinctive as an alternative to the traditional
account in the following main ways:

1. It respects the complex mixture of value and fact rather than try-
    ing to separate them for theoretical purposes.
2. It seeks to build knowledge from practice and the phenomenology
    of practice only.
3. It searches for a common moral language through which techniques
    and technical concepts can be framed in such a way as to incor-
    porate science and narrative.
4. It denies a separation between epistemological issues distinct from
    ethical issues in teaching, and it promotes the notion of epistemic
    justification in ethics.

The argument of this chapter remains at this stage a skeleton requiring developed argument and detailed studies and self-studies of teaching.

The philosophical directions have been portrayed as yellow brick roads rather than the mind fields they in fact are. However, if the argument is on the right track, we can reconstruct the ways in which professionals conceive what they do. For example, the central issues—"What did we achieve? What were the results? What was the learning product?"—would remain important, but each would have to be viewed in terms of such questions as "Did we do our best? Was that fair and honest? Was that result worth achieving?" Outcomes noted thus appear in a different frame. That would be a radical alternative, a way out of the cul-de-sac in the development of how we understand teaching and how, as teachers, we understand ourselves. So our professional lives would shift their focus. Another example will be discussed in Chapter 6, namely, how we explain the complexity of what we do to our constituents by reconstructing our perception of our accountability.

Such a brief account of underlying approaches to this complex topic is inadequate in several respects, particularly in that it does not attempt to deal with the weight of countervailing literature on any of these matters and does not contend with critical theory. Its brevity also does not do justice to the complexity of the different positions I have cited. My justification, to repeat, is that I am trying to set out a broad picture of teacher professionalism and to open it up for critique.

CHAPTER 6

A Professional Code of Practice

Moral agency is nothing very fancy—simply, that a person considers the interests of others, does not make discriminations on irrelevant grounds, and has a clear set of principles or virtues in which he or she believes and on which he or she acts. Taking the teacher as a moral agent and taking education seriously as a moral business now has to be applied to the accountability dimension of professionalism. In this light, a system of teacher accountability must be compatible with three things: (1) the existing best standards of practice, (2) professional teachers' search for improved quality in their practice, and (3) ethical standards across the roles of teaching. The focus of that accountability can include not merely classroom conduct, but also every aspect of the role, for example, relations with colleagues, parents, and the community. Not only the teacher but also the school as an institution can be seen as accountable. For both individual and institution, the task of education is a contribution both to the individual and the public welfare.

The moral obligation on teachers for accountability is therefore palpable. A professional teacher, seen in a moral role, is under a moral obligation to provide to the public in general, to parents and other constituents, as well as to his or her employers and supervisors, an account of his or her endeavors and outcomes. To improve educational relationships, especially with the immediate constituencies of parents and students, a professional teacher will also want to find ways of acquainting the public with educational actions and explaining achievements and failings in recognition of the critical need to build trust in the practices used and the judgments made (Sockett, 1990).

Unfortunately, our conceptions of accountability are not couched as arguments about the ethical or moral character of the teacher's responsibility to the constituencies he or she serves, but as items in a bureaucratic audit (Darling-Hammond, 1990; Kirst, 1991; Kogan, 1986, 1990). Accountability has come to be seen as a panacea for the improvement of education, and the experience of its practice so far is as an expensive bureaucratic nuisance. Teaching and other professions have been reined in by legislation sometimes because they have neglected accountability to their clients, but often for other, political reasons. Our present systems of accountability have been developed because the public began to distrust teachers and *in loco parentis* gave way to *due process*. The social and historical origins of these changes are complex (Bell, 1973). Governmental bureaucracies at many levels in the industrialized world faced an economic crisis in the early 1970s and needed to cap public expenditures (Macdonald, 1977). Political attacks on professional incompetence among teachers provided a convenient rationale for imposing tighter control of personnel and finance (Derber, 1982; Ehrenreich & Ehrenreich, 1979). Although some recent deregulation of teachers has engendered some legislative enthusiasm, and although there is contemporary talk of teacher autonomy and creativity in *America 2000* (U.S. Department of Education, 1991), that enthusiasm could be short-lived without a strong political will, particularly in the context of a continuing recession and declining state budgets.

If a quest for *professional* accountability with its moral core is to be sustained, it will be up to the profession to lead the drive to resolve the tension between public and professional control by promoting forms of accountability that are publicly acceptable. Otherwise an increasingly bureaucratic system will continue to grow.

In this chapter, I attempt to articulate a new approach to the question of professional accountability that is consonant with teaching as a moral endeavor. This proposal relaxes the administrative demands on teachers but heightens their moral obligations. To achieve this end I will argue for four main positions:

1. Accountability may sensibly mean something akin to moral obligation.
2. *Trust* is a primary condition for the development of professional accountability.
3. A professional code of practical guidance provides a potential vehicle for accountability that can be congruent with the public's claims.
4. A moral stance toward professional accountability is central in professional development at all levels.

TWO VERSIONS OF ACCOUNTABILITY

Can accountability mean something akin to obligation in a moral dimension? There is an apparent incompatibility between the notion of accountability and autonomous moral agency. A man selling goods in a convenience store is, in terms of role, doing what he is told. He is just the *agent* for the owner, standing in the owner's stead. He can be defined as a person who acts within prespecified limits and directions and who does what he is told by others. On the other hand, where a person is a fully fledged moral person, he or she acts autonomously, making decisions about principles as well as immediate events. This person is not someone else's agent, but is a *principal* (in the legal sense—with the right to make decisions). In terms of his or her role, compared to the salesman, a doctor has this kind of autonomy. The doctor is more like the independent professional familiar in law, medicine, universities, and elsewhere (Carr-Saunders & Wilson, 1964; J. A. Jackson, 1970), whereas the salesman is more like millions of others in the typical hierarchy of accountability familiar to manufacture or commerce (Langford, 1978).

But accountability is not merely a matter of whether a person acts independently or acts under orders; it also defines the character of the relationship between the parties involved. Look at the salesman as a model. He is responsible to the owner; the owner also benefits from his work to the extent of the man's skills in selling goods. More formally, accountability, in this view, refers *to an agent's responsibility to a provider, the provider being the beneficiary as measured by the results produced through the agent's skill in handling resources.* While the salesman has customers or clients, and the owner may make the salesman's skills available to other customers, the salesman is accountable to none but the owner. Moreover, the benefits the owner wants are very limited—cash in the till. (In principle, both agent and provider here could be a group of people or an institution.) This "salesman" model of accountability was put in place in state systems in American education during the 1970s. The teaching account was delivered to a single provider, the local educational management representing the public, rather than to individual citizens with differing wants and expectations, such as parents, churches, employers, and unions. The measure of accountability, like the store owner's money in the till, was restricted to measured student learning outcomes.

The salesman model in fact has very limited applicability. The heterogeneity and complexity of knowledge-driven industrial, entrepreneurial, and professional activities could not be conducted if there were not immense freedoms for individuals to make decisions and to act as they think professionally appropriate. Employers and employed alike know that that kind of independence is crucial to success. But teaching (like any occupation) *could* be forced to fit this salesman model through unremitting legislation limiting teachers' freedoms and the accompanying overwhelming bureaucracy. This may well have been the purpose with teachers in the 1970s. Conceived as a role with complex *educational* ends, teaching cannot coherently accommodate the salesman model or the definition of accountability that goes with it.

In the alternative model, the doctor is not using her skills to benefit the people who own the hospital she works in, as if the hospital was like the store owner. The doctor is accountable to her patients as clients, to the families of the patients, certainly to her fellow professionals for maintaining its reputation, to the hospital and others. The accountability of the agent, in this version, is not to the provider as beneficiary, but to providers, client beneficiaries, and professional peers for results achieved and for the quality of standards maintained through occupational practice. The doctor has to look at results and at standards of practice as well as at the variety of constituents to whom she is accountable.

Teaching as a profession seems to require some kind of developed sense of accountability of the second kind, but a satisfactory format has yet to be developed. If the teacher is not to be limited to trivial ends in the classroom, the exercise of teaching will demand much greater autonomy than the salesman model would allow, while also demanding an appropriate formulation of achievement in terms of student outcomes. The teacher is frequently going to have to act as "principal" (legal sense, again) not just as someone else's agent. The teacher must also not be limited to an accountability relationship with, say, the school board seen formally as "the provider." For there are many different constituencies of accountability for the teacher—parents, colleagues, and students among them. Finally, many valued educational objectives cannot be captured for measurement within the simplistic views of performance-contracting and so forth that found favor in the 1970s.

The implications of this more developed conception of accountability are profound. First, the teacher has multiple constituencies to whom an account is due. The context implies differences of demand and the public interest is not necessarily reflected in private wants, nor is it just an aggregation of those wants. Second, attention is devoted to professional standards of practice. Provision must be made for standards to be maintained and promoted and the conditions of competence set out that enable a practitioner to meet them. Third, the teacher is responsible not only for maintaining the occupation's standards of practice but also for *showing* that this is being done (Lessinger & Tyler, 1971).

This conception of accountability speaks more directly to the educational context and to the tensions created by the individual rights of teacher, parent, and the public interest. It accepts the rights of individuals—as parents, or as children, or as colleagues—but does not posit unanimity. It addresses the complexity of teaching as an art by implying constantly changing standards. Some researchers have used different terms to highlight the significance of different constituencies by distinguishing answerability to one's clients (moral accountability), responsibility to oneself and one's colleagues (professional accountability), and accountability per se to employers or political masters (contractual accountability) (Becher, Eraut, & Knight, 1979). Professional accountability will cover each and all of these, so there is no need to regard professional *accountability* as a contradiction in terms. This conception of accountability therefore fits the profession of teaching with the underpinning conception of moral agency. It also has the teeth to bring about improvement and to prove to the public and to individuals that improvement is being accomplished.

ACCOUNTABILITY AND MORAL ACCOUNTABILITY

Two problems arise in this view of accountability-as-obligation for professionals in teaching: (1) the pluralism of moral ends and (2) the conflict between private wants and the public interest.

Pluralism of Moral Ends

The problem of pluralism of moral ends and moral agency is reflected directly in the two interpretations of accountability. There is a major distinction in ethics that is reflected in debates on accountability and in the two differing versions offered of it. This is the difference between a teleological and a deontological ethic (Frankena, 1963; see also Chapter 7). Briefly, the former is interested in consequences, or ends; the latter in principles. The former is interested in results, the latter in standards. Honesty is valued in the former insofar as it brings about desirable results; in the latter because it is valuable in itself. "Act always so that what you do brings about the greatest happiness of the greatest number" is rather different from "do as you would be done by." Very different practical policies would result from these imperatives. The emphasis on *standards* of practice, as opposed to achievements deriving from competence, provides a different moral basis for development of the second version of accountability. Yet the demand for *results* seems still the very stuff of teacher accountability as practiced across the nation.

Private Wants and the Public Interest

In any democratic policy there is conflict between private wants and public interest (Barry, 1965). In the United States, the complexity of that conflict is very great indeed. It is present in debates on virtually all legislation, but it is in the workaday circumstances of social life that the persistent power of the conflict is revealed. The typical parent of a schoolchild wants public education both as a matter of the public interest, no doubt, but also because education gives that child positional goods—a maximized position for economic superiority (Hirsch, 1977; Hollis, 1982). The steps that the parent takes to achieve private wants, particularly in a community of aggressive self-aggrandizement, may not match the public interest. Private pressure groups make efforts to turn particular sets of private wants into "the public interest," for example, in terms of family-life curricula. In their working lives, teachers face the sirens of private wants and the public interest. From students and parents, the cry is for "better grades"; from crisis-happy government, the demand is that schools deal with the problems of the day (drugs, AIDS, teenage alcoholism), inviting the wrath of socio-political groups of different kinds. The drip of mandates has become a flood from state legislatures. In that conflict of private and public interest, the development of teachers as professional practitioners is no easy task (see Chapter 7).

Of greatest concern, however, is the apparent difficulty of even bringing moral considerations proper into public life and debate about teaching, whether we are talking about accountability or anything else, because of uncertainties about the present practices in our political life (Dunn, 1980). If we are seriously seeking to construct a view of accountability that is congruent with the moral agency of the teacher, we are putting moral issues firmly where they belong—in the public forum. Yet some religious groups feel bound not to observe the principles of tolerance and personal conscience familiar in the secularized Protestant constitution. Most difficult of all, Bellah and colleagues (1985) conclude that Americans have lost the vocabulary for ethical debate. Allan Bloom (1987) paints a picture of a young intellectual cohort of undergraduates enmeshed in an individualist materialism in which there exists only a vestige of understanding of moral agency. Teachers are not somehow above and different from these social manifestations.

With different individual perceptions of morality, with the deep-rooted conflict between results and standards as the core of judgment, with a pluralist society that may be losing its moral vocabulary, the task nonetheless remains the promotion of a comprehensive vision of the profession of teaching, where the individual professional teacher is a reflective moral agent. The tension is clear: An acceptable form of professional accountability consonant with public rights needs to be forged. That development is utterly dependent on one particular condition among many, namely trust. If trust were to be properly established, a practical proposal for local codes of practical guidance, out of which a more powerful professional code of ethics might be constructed, would be viable. What such codes could do is connect both standards and results to the variety of constituents to whom the teacher is accountable in a professionally appropriate way.

This seems the only cogent framework for accountability if education is the enterprise, because of its diversity and the need for autonomous teachers. The professional's accountability extends not to a single provider, like a school board, but to a multitude of diverse constituencies. The professional builds trust through accountability. He or she is more like the doctor with broad responsibilities for results and for standards than like the store salesman who is accountable only to the owner. Nevertheless public moral debate is not sophisticated, and practical proposals for a professional version of accountability are needed. Maybe the deliberations of the National Board for Professional Teaching Standards (1989) will foster a cogent view of professional accountability. Any practical proposal, however, is dependent entirely on recognizing the significance of trust.

THE SIGNIFICANCE OF TRUST

The change from in loco parentis to due process was an indicator of the collapse of mutual trust between parents and teachers. If it is true that the level of trust in the school-based professional is low, then professional teachers have to accept that part of the social reality and seek to win it back. Many of us who have been or are parents of children in schools, as well as being teachers, can easily understand exactly why some teachers are not much trusted by parents. What is the significance of trust as a condition of the development of professional accountability?

Trust is a relational condition between individuals. It has an outside, where formal systems and client individuals are linked through effective role holders, and an inside, where professional relationships become personalized. (Outside—the Principal of Highway School, Dr. Clarence Jones, may be trusted by parent Mrs. Cynthia Lee and the chairman of the school board, Dr. Maria Rodriguez. Inside—Clarence may be trusted by Cynthia and Maria). Trust is established through stability and reliability of conduct according to particular virtues but is totally dependent on the absence of deceit if it is to be authentic.

For the outside relational condition, Nias (1975) has argued that trust demands two things. First, it implies being able to make accurate predictions about such things as individual attitudes, reactions, and technical competence and consistency in role behavior and in organizational procedures. However, people and routines become predictable only as one gains knowledge of them. Second, perceived agreement over ends is also necessary. Where there is disagreement about ends, there will be greater need for formal procedures. These conditions are the basis of our sense that we trust the system. A common phenomenon of Gallup polls is that people think the schools their children attend, or the teachers they know, are just fine. That seems to indicate a strong degree of trust. On the other hand, they will say that education, as a system, is in a mess, indicating a level of low confidence and lack of trust at an outside level. Trust may be excellent inside, but not outside, a fact that applies to both institutions and systems.

The significance of trust in this outside sense is that it provides the opportunity for clients to trust a system, but it does not guarantee it. Teachers may not trust the school district but have solid trusting relations with individuals in it. Where trust exists, individuals have confidence both in the system and in the people operating it. Trust is created on the outside because the procedures are clear, public, and understood and because the officeholders want to promote their effective use in order to benefit participants. That outside is what is seen by the public at large as well as the participants. Public satisfaction is not, however, the sum of private perspectives, nor do the judgments of realtors and politicians necessarily reflect the educational value of a particular school or the levels of trust enjoyed on the inside.

The establishment of trust thus demands a meaningful interplay of persons and their roles. Schools, like other institutions, cannot establish trust if they are impersonal. A high school senior of my acquaintance liked and trusted her classroom teachers, but whenever she had to deal with the assistant principal her confidence in the school was grossly undermined because he was cynical, rude, and demeaning about faculty and students. Tellers at a bank may be extremely friendly and helpful, but the computer appears consistently hostile. The family atmosphere of the small school, where the nervous parent feels at home, contrasts with the bureaucratic halls of the huge urban high school, where that parent might fear to tread.

For the parent as much as for the teacher, establishing trusting relationships is a matter of personal knowledge and to some degree dependent on an individual's idiosyncratic capacity for knowing more or fewer people. This is where the outside and the inside sense of trust meet, and, for the teacher, it is a major part of his or her moral agency. He or she must contribute to creating trust in the system through working at trust inside the institution. For trust is not simply the *outside* relational condition of persons and systems, mediated by role holders. It is a relational condition of the *inside* life of a school, between individual teachers and children, between colleagues, between principal and staff, and so forth.

Yet how can this condition be described? Only in terms, I think, of the virtues that constitute trust—namely, fidelity, veracity (honesty and an absence of deception), friendliness, and care. It is not enough for a trusting relationship with a school and its teachers for the system to be understood as "pro-kids" in a parade of sentimentality. Mrs. Simpson, the teacher, has to be known by Ms. Calvoressi, the parent, as someone she and her son Romeo can trust. One administrator in Jaime Escalante's school, as portrayed in *Stand and Deliver*, finds Jamie's altruism and beliefs different to stomach and does not trust him for that reason. The trusting relationship so desperately needed is very difficult to build, and it is rarely if ever achieved by transactional leaders (Goodlad, 1990), who, as powerbrokers, rarely command the full confidence of anyone.

Trust is equally important with children, and we have seen some examples of that in Chapter 4. The need to shield young children from danger, to encourage them, and to protect them from greedy or ambitious parents, the idiocy of some bureaucratic rules; the problems of being precise and accurate with information; and the general difficulties of that exquisite task which defines teaching, that is, conveying understanding to someone who does not understand—all create opportunities for deception, for lying to children. The effects of deceit are visible in its impact on the deceived. To be deceived is, as we have seen, to be in the power of another person to which no one wittingly surrenders and which must be anathema to the educational enterprise. The principle is veracity. "Trust in some degree of veracity," writes Sisella Bok (1978), "functions as a foundation of relations among human beings: when this trust shatters or wears away, institutions collapse" (p. 33). Veracity is also the crucial underpinning for other central virtues of education, such as treating people fairly, looking after their interests, and not harming them. If a person's word cannot be trusted, why should anyone think that he or she would be fair, concerned, and incapable of injuring? Why, in other words, should that person be trusted?

As with veracity, so with caring. Noddings's (1988) virtues of dialogue, responsiveness, and response, also noted in Chapter 4, are part of this framework of trust. More complex in trusting interpersonal relationships in an education context is the problem of friendship. To create and develop the inside sense of trust, people and children have to come into the kinds of close relations that mediate between them and the system. The closer the relationship, the greater the opportunity for it to turn into a friendship, as opposed to friendly relationships (see Chapter 7). But friendship creates obligations that go beyond the rights and obligations of a role relationship, for friends have privileged access to each other. The development of friendships between teachers and students (as opposed to friendly relations) as well as between teachers and parents, is complicated by the need to sustain a professional accountability relationship. Friendships have a measure of exclusivity about them and those outside the friendship relation (e.g., other students or parents) may see it as a threat to the ordinary role relation they have.

For an institution, fidelity is perhaps as important to trust as veracity. For the child or the parent their "faith" in the system or the individual teacher or principal can easily be undermined. So a teacher who sexually molests a student, or the teacher who is attacked in a school because the institution is out of control, or the counselor who talks at a dinner party about a student's private life, or a principal whose special confidence is betrayed by a board member, or a superintendent who ignores incompetence in a teacher who is a friend—each of these breaks faith or is a victim of such a breach.

Fidelity is thus the virtue of which trust is the condition. A person may keep faith but not be trusted, for trust is a mutual condition of a relationship. Each participant to the educational enterprise—child, parent, teacher, and principal—is entitled to fidelity. Together with veracity, care, and a sense of friendliness, rather than friendship, it forms the core of the trust that is critical to establishing professional accountability. Trust is fragile, not easily built up, and has to be earned. On the basis of trust, partnership is possible. Trust provides the basis on which an accountability system, while recognizing human weakness, can presume professional integrity. Or perhaps the other way round. It is only on the assumption of professional integrity that a system of professional accountability can be built (Goldman, 1980). That integrity can still countenance complex moral compromises, situations where there is no obvious "best" way forward.

The task for developed professional accountability is therefore twofold: (1) how to create trust within the profession and in its dealings with the wide range of constituents it has, and (2) how to convince a skeptical public that, in matters of peer-group judgment and much else, teachers can be trusted. Right now, in my experience, many parents want the privileges of *in loco parentis* with the rights of due process. They seem prepared to trust the teacher, but are not yet convinced. These parents are usually of the vociferous middle class. That need not be the norm. A committed teacher can pick up a strong *in loco parentis* role and have her work valued and applauded by pupils and parents (Freedman, 1990). Maybe the profession's retreat from the *in loco parentis* role (albeit under pressure) has, like much else, satisfied the middle class but penalized the poor, whose children no longer garner its benefits except from those teachers who respond to human need as they see it. The significance of trust is therefore paramount in professional accountability relationships with clients, especially in teaching.

THE BASIS FOR PROFESSIONAL ACCOUNTABILITY

A system of professional accountability incorporating trust will need to be developed that has a moral basis, allows for multifaceted judgment, is locally accessible, and is adequately maintained by teachers. It also needs to be cognizant of codes of ethics as models from other professions.

Criteria for Professional Accountability

First, such a system must be built on a common moral basis. Accepting that there will be some valid moral differences between professionals and their constituents, it must embody a basis of agreed-upon principles. Usually great stress is laid on the diversity of moral opinions among people. Yet just to have children in a school implies some measure of agreement, and ways have to be found to extend the scope of common understanding. Teachers, in the generic sense, need to work with a clear and common notion of what trust actually amounts to in school X or college Y.

Second, multifaceted judgment will be involved. If the accountability is to be sufficiently comprehensive and wide-ranging, it is myopic to rely on students' test scores as the only measure. The accountability system must contain the potential for agents, professional peers, and constituents to have a rich account, so that they can make judgments on the basis of standards *and* results, for example, to the broad professional expertise of the teacher and the social character of the school, in addition to various measurements.

Third, a system of accountability has to be locally accessible. It must have primarily a local focus, answering to students, colleagues, and parents—the private persons within the community—and only secondarily to the public at large, or even the school board. It also has to offer a framework for the redress of grievances, not because all teachers are devils, but because they are not all angels. Without that local focus, constituents lose interest and the school cannot negotiate and create the appropriate levels of trust. If they complain and nothing happens, their trust in the institution is weakened.

Fourth, teachers must see that the system is maintained. It must be constructed in such a way that professional teachers have a stake in maintaining its integrity and the public trust it develops. As with so many things, people have to have a sense of ownership if they are to feel that what is to be done matters. So teachers need to feel that the issue of accountability is important and that they have this stake in public trust.

Codes of Ethics as a Source for Professional Accountability

What examples might be borrowed to develop a system on these criteria? The history of professions in respect of self-government is mixed, usually involving legal status of some kind proposed by the particular profession. This is necessary for civil protection against professional misconduct. Some rhetorical aspirations for accountability are to be found in professional codes of ethics, but they have a purpose well expressed by Price

(1922): "A code of ethics becomes necessary not only to assist the mechanical engineer in his conduct, but to acquaint the world with what it may expect from a professional man" (p. 73).

Codes of ethics have become a familiar part of the rhetoric of professional self-government and professional control. From the Hippocratic oath to the code of ethics of the National Automobile Dealers Associations, a declaration of commitment to ideal behavior has provided a source of unity for members of an occupation. Yet the status and influence of codes of ethics are uncertain. There is usually some ambiguity of purpose. Sanctions, other than the legal, have to be used to stiffen the ethical resolve. Codes require policing. Moreover, they cannot solve major ethical dilemmas—for example, the Hippocratic oath can be used either way in the abortion debate. Generality of expression also contributes to their rhetorical character, although the automobile dealers' code runs from a general commitment to the "highest ethical standards" in the first of its ten clauses to the rather specific "never alter the odometer readings of any motor vehicle" in the ninth.

The American Sociological Association (1984) has a detailed code of ethics that is meant to "sensitize all sociologists to the ethical issues that may arise in their work, to encourage [them] to educate themselves and their colleagues." It is also seen as an "attempt to meet the expressed needs of sociologists who have asked for guidance" (p. 3). It also provides the association with a Committee on Professional Ethics, which both reviews the content of the code and is responsible for the investigation of complaints under it. The more specific ethical guidelines for high school psychology teachers issued by the American Psychological Association (1983) is an equally precise code of practice for teachers. Codes of ethics in teaching have been produced by teacher unions too, but it remains unclear how they relate to practice in a non-self-governing occupation or how unions see the resolution of the public–professional tension.

Could a code of some kind be the vehicle to meet the criteria for a system of professional accountability? The task, it should be recalled, is to find some way, consonant with the moral and professional autonomy of the teacher, in which the tensions of public control and professional control may be resolved.

A PROFESSIONAL CODE OF PRACTICAL GUIDANCE

One possible way to resolve the problem of professional accountability would be through a reinterpretation of the notion of a code of practical guidance. However, the word code carries with it some negative baggage. It implies strictness, lack of flexibility, and detail, as in a code for driving on

the highway. Even honor codes (which clearly contain injunctions to virtuous conduct) carry a connotation of rigidity.

Notwithstanding that, suppose that the word *code* is softened by talk
of a code of practical guidance, more like a *creed*, perhaps, for which one
stands accountable. A discussion of a code of practical guidance within and
outside a school may open up and sustain a dialogue for the reestablish-
ment of trust where that is necessary. Each school has its particular milieu
and its modus operandi. Each school may know or may need to find out
just how far trust is present, and whether it needs to work out such a code
of practical guidance to get its accountability relationship right. Although
there are these variable patterns and differing contexts, discussion of a code
may serve as a process of parental or community socialization into discussion of the school's purposes and its practices. Clearly the quality of the
discussion is going to be crucial, but only local community and parental
contributions can facilitate appropriate professional accountability, as rigorous school-based management developments indicate (Hill & Bonan,
1991). The school becomes the locus of accountability if the criteria I have
described above are met, and if trust, in particular, is to be established.
Such a code of practical guidance must emerge from the habits and reflections of teachers if it is to be owned by them as professionals.

What might this program for professional accountability look like? To
fill out this practical proposal for professional accountability, and simultaneously to examine some of its strengths and weaknesses, we need to look
at the three items that any putative code of practical guidance must cover—
form, content and status. Form describes the shape a code of practice in
teaching might take. Content describes the substantive areas of the code.
Status describes how a code might be implemented in practice.

Form

The characteristic form of such a code of practial guidance might be
as follows:

1. It provides guidelines, not prohibitions, which set standards or norms
   in matters of individual or institutional conduct to be followed by a
   teacher as a moral agent, in the same way that he or she follows moral
   guidelines or principles.
2. Guidance refers to all, but is used particularly by the novice, the per-
   plexed, or the wayward teacher.
3. A wide variety of sources (empirical observations, law, and convention)
   contribute to the content, but its force is moral when it describes interpersonal relations.

4. Interpretation will often be needed, for new situations will demand new interpretations of what the guidelines mean for that situation.
5. The code needs a responsible body or authority to administer and look after it, for example, keeping it up to date and taking responsibility for the processing of grievances.
6. Public accessibility must be provided to the guidelines, with comments, suggestions and contributions to the code in the course of its construction.

These formal characteristics require substantive dressing. Suppose Principal Smith's school, in discussion with parents, determines it will become a "caring community," a general principle all teachers will seek to follow. It will apply to everything they do, for example, what behavior they choose to discipline or not to discipline in the classroom. Weak and incompetent teachers will find the practical guidance that emerges helpful, as will the new teachers who have to find out how to behave in school X. A process of self-monitoring, or mentoring, or teacher-research, or external inquiry, together with reflective discussion among teachers about what they do and why, will all serve to develop the guidelines within the school. Here it will not be enough to concentrate on organizational health; one must seek to characterize the moral significance of the school's ethos (Cusick, 1983; Cusick & Wheeler 1988; Grant, 1988; Lightfoot 1983). Moreover, no guideline can be totally unambiguous. Discussion and controversy is inevitable.

Clearly this code of practical guidance has a particular kind of status for children. Because it contains values about appropriate interpersonal behavior, it contains content that should be taught to children. Because children need to learn how to work with authority, it deserves to be a framework for children to use as a resource not just for learning, but also for redress. Manifestly, there are dangers in such arrangements, but the "school within a school" that has grown out of Kohlberg's notion of the just community at Brookline High School achieves a quite distinct relationship with teachers within which individual professionals are accountable (Power, Higgins, & Kohlberg, 1989). However, the context for this discussion, we must recall, is the tension of public and professional control. To construct such codes of practical guidance only within the workplace misses that point. The public are, rightly, concerned with two issues—accessibility and sanctions.

The traditional professional codes of ethics or of practice are publicized but rarely displayed. One finds diplomas across the walls of a doctor's office, but never the medical code of ethics, though one *can* find a code of ethics posted in some automobile dealerships. How could a professional code of practical guidance in teaching, established at the local level, promote public access to it?

First, the composition of the code demands parental and public input. This is not a matter of public relations but of common experience (and common sense), since the process of education looks different to the parent of the child than it does to the teacher. It behooves the profession to attend to the perspectives of its clients if the school is to provide a fundamental life-enhancing experience for every student. Teachers can be blinded by their role as easily as other professionals. The process of code composition, when the rules are being written, should not be judged by the professional in terms of the question "is this within my present competence?" but "would this satisfy me as a code for the teacher of my own children?" This "what-if-it-were-my-kid" test is not a trivial sentiment. It is an expression of one of the deepest moral principles, namely moral equity, which obliges the teacher to take a detached point of view.

Second, the code of practical guidance has to be made publicly accessible for consultation and use, and detail will have to be balanced against accessibility. Many schools already publish brochures, plans, documents of all kinds for parents and the public. There is no reason why such a code should not be part of the publicity, for it implicitly states what the institution expects of its professionals and what they expect of one another. But mere publication is not enough. The code of practical guidance has to be used. It may need to be referred to at parent–teacher conferences, in PTA meetings, and in public discussions to ensure that it becomes a living thing in the minds of the public to whom it is *owed*. The form of its presentation is important too, since it should become a *document for consultation and guidance*, not like an insurance policy or a set of rules and regulations. The connection between sanctions and public accessibility is now clear. It must be possible for a constituent client (e.g., a parent or a child) to hold a teacher or a school to account in terms of the public commitments made in the code. Cynthia Lee must be able to have redress if her youngster is not cared for within the new caring community—the inside and the outside must meet.

I recently observed a discussion in which parents were talking with a principal and wanting information about discoveries of drugs in a middle school. Were there any, and if so, of what kind and what was done? The principal treated the parents as if it was not their business except in terms of what the school board might publish in statistical terms. Apparently they could go no further. They had no redress. Yet accountability without sanctions is empty. If professional teachers want a system of accountability that will work, then a code of practical guidance must contain the opportunity for sanctions, but more particularly for redress. It must be possible for a parent who so wished to seek redress and to use the code of practical guidance as a way of getting it, rather than using the hierarchical management systems of the local bureaucracy, which, no doubt, had instructed the principal not to give out information about drug abuse in the school.

It may be argued that in a community like a school, where collegiality is critical, the very presence of a code of practical guidance that contains possible sanctions will harm rather than promote professionalism. The problem is *not* just that there are lazy, shirking, incompetent, or downright unprofessional people in teaching as there are in every occupation and profession. "Sanctions," writes Hart (1961) of legal systems in general, "are required not as the normal motive for obedience, but as a *guarantee* that those who would voluntarily obey shall not be sacrificed to those who would not . . ." What reason demands is voluntary cooperation within a *coercive* system (p. 193; emphasis added). Sanctions thus provide a safeguard for those who suffer under the pressure of the informal system: They protect the weak. The willingness to put oneself under a sanctions system is, in part, to offer trust. We may wish we did not need the coercive framework to ensure our voluntary cooperation, but building a system of professional integrity does not mean ignoring the need to take account of human weakness. To a person concerned about accountability, it looks empty without sanctions. To an autonomous professional, accountability with sanctions can seem inappropriate. That gulf has to be bridged by finding a modus operandi for professional accountability.

At present, there are many areas of professional life that are left to convention, for example, in matters of relationships between colleagues. These are usually completely outside formal sanction. Sets of group habits have grown up within the profession—consider the habits of the "jocks" in the high school faculty lounge. Good habits can develop, as in the early days of the wearing of seatbelts, without legal pressure, but for the majority of us the presence of the legal rule ensures that our habits change. We do not subsequently come to wear a seatbelt because it is law, but because we see the point of it. Similarly, the construction of a code, with sanctions, would not mean consistent litigation. Its effect should be to turn *desirable* professional habits into *regularly observed* habits. Ultimately a code with sanctions provides the professional with two things: (1) pressure to adhere to the code as a guide to follow, not as a set of regulations to obey, and (2) confidence that competence, standards, and results can be measured within the opportunity for the public to seek redress.

The form of a code of practice, developed from many sources, is a set of rules and guidelines. It will require constant reinterpretation and maintenance under an authority that will also ensure an effective system of sanctions and public accessibility, particularly while under construction. This is its *form*. For the purposes of this chapter, it is necessary only to refer briefly to matters of content.

Content

A code of practical guidance is intended to govern action, not belief. Practice is the target. The content will thus describe what practitioners should do in their work:

1. In formal instructional settings and informal contexts with students
2. In collegial relationships within schools
3. In formal and informal relations with parents and other appropriate clients
4. In management relations
5. With the discipline to which they have an allegiance, a discipline which is itself a living community of scholars with its own traditions

The sources for the content are numerous and could be derived, for example, from the effective-schools literature and its critics (Feiman-Nemser & Floden, 1986). But its primary use will be in controversial areas where the issues are difficult. It is important that the code of practical guidance be prepared to address some of the stickier problems teachers face, and perhaps do not know how to face up to. It is the inclusion of these problematic areas that will ensure that it is a living document. Here are some examples:

1. Under what sorts of circumstances should a teacher *not* inform a parent of facts about a student? For example, should a teacher tell a fundamentalist parent if a youngster spoke of his loss of faith (see Chapter 7)?
2. In general, what are the ways in which a teacher should protect a student's right to privacy against his or her parents?
3. How can the rights of the child of parents who are conscientious objectors be protected in classroom discussions of war? Or vegetarians in discussions of farming? (And, isn't the "right to withdraw the child" the most banal of managerial and professional responses to this type of situation?)
4. Should teachers respect without question the "right" of colleagues to be, or to behave, as they wish in classrooms? What is the line between collegiality and toleration of inefficiency or immorality?
5. Are there general "discipline-based" rules that teachers ought to observe in instruction, derived from the character of that discipline? Does it

matter if children "guess" in history or science, "get the right answer" by accident in math, or learn things that are false, even though they are commonly accepted as true? (See Chapter 4.)

6. What ought management to do to respect the rights of teachers as citizens within schools? To what extent is management undermining a teacher's citizenship by restricting political discussion in classrooms?

In differing ways, each of these questions points up areas that will have much greater significance if greater teacher autonomy and professional responsibility exist. But the alternative to professionals taking the initiative in working out codes of practical guidance that have been negotiated with relevant publics is a situation in which a school board determines, inevitably on the basis of least difficulty and the advice of a bureaucrat, the actions that a teacher is to take and the limits of his or her freedom. On that basis the teacher is neither autonomous nor a moral agent, but rather a purveyor of someone else's views.

Status

The goal of a system of professional accountability is to resolve that tension of public versus professional control. On the one hand, there must necessarily be some form of public control of standards and accountability, if not of management. Professional aspiration implies a measure of autonomy, and thereby some professional control. Could a code of practical guidance satisfy both justifiable claims? Only, I think, through a partnership of the public and the professional.

School-based professional codes of practical guidance could be adopted as part of the system of public control alongside more traditional forms of accountability. They can be incorporated into new systems of school-based management. They can be built by schools in discussion with their constituencies. They can be viewed as a recognizable, justifiable, and necessary element within teacher and school accountability. They offer, for many large school districts, a way of optimizing relations with parents and the community. They will have a moral basis, refer to multifaceted judgments, be locally accessible in the full sense, and be maintained by teachers. That is not, I believe, either a radical or a revolutionary suggestion, and the proposal would fit with some contemporary developments in the United States—whatever their substantive merits. Such developments include:

1. The use of a model of instruction across a school system
2. The development of annual or biennial plans based on individual schools/communities

3. The spread of a movement toward collaborative decision making in schools
4. The development of the use of mentor teachers and teachers as evaluators of colleagues
5. The movement toward school-based management, with much greater local responsibility within schools

The use of one instructional model serves to focus on elements of classroom instructional behavior that act as a "code of instructional practice" for teachers to follow, although I have strong reservations about this practice for other reasons. The development of annual or biennial plans provides the occasion for public declaration of "results to be achieved." Such an occasion could also provide an admirable opportunity for a statement of "standards of practice to be maintained and developed." School-based decision making exemplifies the reliance of the institution on a teacher's professional judgment outside the mere acts of instruction. The use of mentor teachers or teacher evaluators is crucial in developing standards of practical professionalism, for here is peer-group judgment at the cutting edge, that is, focused on instructional practices. The true professional does not simply put up with peer evaluation. He or she must *want* it in order to improve his or her standards of practice.

The most significant of these different movements is the hesitant shift to school-based management (Hill & Bonan 1991). School-based management takes extensive responsibility from school boards and administrations and delegates it to the building level—within the proper confines of local and state standards. It recognizes professional responsibility, thereby illustrating perfectly what the local implications of the second wave of reform (Darling-Hammond & Berry, 1988) are and what they imply for the professional teacher. Central administration becomes not an extensive bureaucratic control mechanism responsive to the political will, but a responsive support mechanism for the school in its social responsibilities. This developing practice still contains the unresolved tension of control. There will be no professional accountability proper until the pattern of accountability is much more localized and professionals can put the standards to which they are committed on display; until professionals, aware of their own problems but thoroughly confident of their own competence, can invite individuals and the public to judge and call a teacher to account in terms of those standards; *and* until there is a developed partnership between public and professional control.

It is necessary to broaden the scope of public accountability systems and persuade those who control the systems on the public's behalf to realize the significance of developing local trust by promoting the notion of a code of practical guidance that the profession, in partnership with its publics, administers. The public and individual citizens and parents need to see these and other developments as a move toward professionalism for teachers. They need to see the comprehensive unity it implies, and they need to be drawn into the discussions of institutional means that will resolve that tension of public control and professional autonomy. Although it may remain true that professional status is most effectively guaranteed when professional codes are safeguarded by law but enforced by their own members (Corwin, 1965), the intimacy of the relationship between the professional and the parent in bringing up children is not something served by increased opportunities for due process.

Of course, such a code of practical guidance may be unworkable for all kinds of local and political reasons. The notion itself is not, I think, totally incompatible with my stress on virtues in professional practice, provided we do not have in mind a rigid notion of a code. While it could provide a basis for discussion, the balance between trying to produce a document that is specific without being litigious is a challenge! Locally, it will depend very much on teacher leadership within a community and a degree of openness for which teachers everywhere are not renowned. Politically, it runs into all kinds of issues, from performance evaluation upward. The problem of how the teacher as a professional moral agent makes him- or herself accountable will remain. To the extent that other suggestions take the responsibility out of the hands of the teacher, the aspiration of a profession is defeated. If the outline proposal I have made in this chapter is unacceptable, the task of resolving the professional–public tension remains to be addressed in a more creative way. That may mean formulating the problem quite differently.

CHAPTER 7

Professional Ideals
and the Professional's Role

Jessica Seigel's biographer, Samuel Freedman (1990), leads us through the working days of this young woman teacher who is deeply committed to the welfare of children. He records the patterns of self-aggrandizment, petty bureaucracy, and status problems that she faces, all of which serve, in different ways, to humiliate her. She suffers. She makes sacrifices. She endures. She gets trapped in the plots and the greed of others. Yet she sustains passions and beliefs. She works herself to a standstill for what she believes in. Richard Rorty (1989) could have had her in mind when he wrote: "The best way to cause people long-lasting pain is to humiliate them by making the things that seemed most important to them look futile, obsolete and powerless" (p. 89). We can imagine, and some of us may even remember, just how painful the progressive annihilation of one's ideals is. We often cannot articulate the passion we feel for social ideals (Zeichner, 1991) whose countenance we cannot even describe.

Jessica gets caught in a bonfire of vain ideals. She is committed, and commits herself, to the flames. In that morally repugnant phrase, she gets "burned out." Valves in engines, electrical condensers, and cathode-ray tubes burn out. Buildings, barns, and factories get burned out. Human beings do not, morally speaking, have anything in common with buildings or with worn-out machinery. When we use such phrases as "burn-out," there is a pervasive danger of taking seriously the analogy of a person as a machine, and thereby dehumanizing ourselves and others. Loss of moral vocabulary leads to loss of moral indignation. We need to work with an anthropomorphic, not a mechanistic, model of persons (Harre & Secord, 1972). To do that, as is the prevailing theme in this book, we have to get back to using a moral language.

An *ideal of service* is the fourth and final dimension of teacher professionalism. Even against the preferred background of the professional community with its professional code of practical guidance and an epistemology of practice rooted in professional virtues, the phraseology of ideals carries us further into the realm of moral language. All major professions have a commitment to human betterment in a fundamental sense, for example; health, justice, or education (Goldman, 1980). What counts as an ideal provides a basis for thought and conversation about guiding fundamental purposes, a topic that must be at the heart of a professional community's view of itself and shaped by its history (Cremin, 1989; Holmes, 1988). But the ideal is not unitary. It can be a cluster of ideals, for example, about the nature of the role, about ideal curriculum as appropriate to a conception of service, about the ethos of institutions, and so on, all of which bear on the core ideal. To seek to state professional ideals is not, I think, to be blindly utopian but rather to bring out into the open fundamental issues about the nature of teacher professionalism that are locked up. In the first half of the chapter, I will outline certain fundamentals in the character of ideals. Teaching as an ideal of service to developing persons, I will argue, demands constant change and improvement if that service is to be properly pursued. An ideal, however, is an unrealizable picture of a desirable good that can function both as a guide and as sustenance. Our understandings of what ideals might be are enriched by different definitions of them. Importantly for teaching, we can learn specific ideals as we learn different roles, and those ideals can be construed as the internal goods of social practices that are constantly being extended.

In the second half of the chapter I will examine three very different problems as material for the development of an argument that the ideal role of the teacher should be *in loco parentis*. The argument is not intended to be complete, but is intended to illustrate the relevance of different issues when we discuss ideals—in this case, a more precise ideal characterization of the teacher's role. The problems described are (1) a dilemma of trust in an individual teacher-student relationship, (2) parental choice of school, and (3) how we characterize integrity in teaching. Many ideals in teaching, other than the ideal role, need to be articulated and argued for, especially those connected to the nature of democracy (Dunn, 1980; Guttmann, 1987), but I focus on only one here, beginning with a general description of ideals and their place in moral conversations.

AN IDEAL OF SERVICE AND THE INDIVIDUAL TEACHER

How do ideals fit in the moral firmament of our personhood, and how does that personhood fit with the role of the teacher? Materialism can blind us to people who do things for their own sake or for the good of others as opposed to personal gain, and psychoanalysts are apt to tell us that all that we do is "really" for our own pleasure. So the idea that teachers or doctors or other professionals could try to live up to a proper professional standard for its own sake will seem incomprehensible to the materialist, who will ask—What's in it for me? It is therefore impossible for a professional educator to be a serious materialist, since his or her life is bound up with service (of some kind) to others for their (not his or her) benefit.

Teaching as a role implies the provision of a service that enables others to learn. Any ideal of teaching must therefore contain a notion of some ideal of service. That service extends to a responsibility for a person's *developing* to full human moral agency, during a period of learning and growth that makes special moral demands on the teacher's nurture and care. The struggle for the teacher moved by an ideal of service is how that ideal can be extended to all children, whatever their handicaps, natural or material wealth, backgrounds and conditions.

Such an ideal is not defeated by the profound difficulties of its realization. The fact that we have not yet learned how best to enable the world's children to benefit from education, or even how to handle our own classrooms, does not mean that we should abandon the ideal. Nor is the ideal defeated by such striking examples of corruption as the drug-pushing ex-principal, or by the more common failures of competence that Mrs. Old manifests. Nor is it defeated by inequity between the natural endowments and privileges of status that children have, nor by the fact that educational goods are, in Hirsch's terms (1977), *positional* goods that give children opportunities to achieve different social status.

An ideal, in other words, is not defeated by the actual conditions of life. Those conditions simply provide the challenge and the test for both quality and commitment. The value of an ideal of service lies not in attainments but in its worth as a moral guide. This contrasts with individualist and materialist societies that place high value on achievement, the acquisition of positional goods. Schools are apt to follow society and prize the elite pupil. Yet this creates for teachers two problems: (1) how to balance accomplishments against other personal qualities of an individual pupil, and (2) how to recognize the value of all pupils as persons whatever their actual achievements. Such problems only occur where the moral value of persons *matters*. Tom Stevenson clearly expends great energy and considerable thought on the teaching of that group of disaffected 14-year-old students. He recognizes them as having value *as persons*, although their achievements as students amount to very little. Many of them will have qualities of character—personal qualities of loyalty, determination, and hard work (if not in school)—that schools do not measure but that teachers recognize.

This commitment to serving every child can provide the justification for stalling the claims of ambitious parents, of greedy pupils, or of elitist pressures. Without such an ideal of service and a moral conception of the role, it is difficult to see why teachers should have *any* rights in the upbringing of children, except the minimum technical discretion afforded them in contracts. However, as Lortie's (1975) teachers indicate, some awareness of the overarching goals of the enterprise are perceived and valued by many teachers independently of whether they feel themselves especially suited, for example, by vocation, to fulfill them, just as Goodlad (1990) notices a commitment to the improvement of schools among teacher educators.

Ideals in a Moral Life

When we use ideals in our moral discourse, we need not reject the use of reason. Ideals and reason need not be mutually exclusive, as they appear to be in theories of ethics that distinguish *ought* (the notion of obligation) from *good* (the notion of what is best—for myself or others). For Kant and his followers, *ought*—duty or obligation—is primary (Frankena, 1963; Peters, 1966). For the variety of idealists since Plato, however, the notion of the *good* is, in Iris Murdoch's (1970) phrase, sovereign. An ideal is a picture, a vision, a perspective on what is the good for a person or for humankind. So we can distinguish a person who lives on the basis of ideals *from* one who only works out on the basis of reason what he or she ought to do and is thereby committed to fundamental moral principles like the Golden Rule. Murdoch describes an idealist as a person who works out a moral life by having a model or a picture in his or her mind that he or she seeks to realize in life. An example of this would be a follower of a highly esteemed religious or political figure, such as Christ or Gandhi.

One problem about this distinction between *ought* and *good* is as follows. The Kantian is said (roughly) to operate solely on the basis of his or her principles. But this is surely also an implausible view of human life, for in which direction is the Kantian headed? What sorts of moral ends seem worth pursuing—for example, a life of contemplation or a life of action? While reason may assist in making such a choice, is it conceivable that what a person does be based solely on reason as opposed to either a nonrational preference (as created by, e.g., by upbringing) or a belief in, or a commitment to, an ideal of some kind? Human beings can choose a great deal—their jobs or careers, what kind of family they wish to create, and what political or social aspirations to embrace. Between these kinds of choices, reason and moral principles are often pragmatically, if not in logical principle, neutral. A person's political views, for example, are not just a conception of what ought to be done in the here and now but are governed by some ideal picture, however hazy, of the way society should be. Philosophy, as Winch (1968) puts it, can no more show a man what he should attach importance to than geometry can show a man where he should stand. Interestingly, very many of those who profess a moral form of Kantianism are political liberals, liberalism being a cluster of democratic principles and unrealizable ideals such as equality of opportunity (Barrow, 1982). So the Kantian, faced with (moral) choices that influence what is to be done, cannot rely solely on obligations derived from *reason* but must have *preferences* (at the very least) about which reason has something, but not everything, to say.

On the other hand, a thoroughgoing idealist cannot simply snatch out of the air a set of insights, say, into what following Gandhi or Christ is—or what education or teaching is—and expect that to be enough for his or her moral life. It is not enough to say I must love my neighbor, for, as countless prelates have urged sleepy congregations, reasoning must determine who is one's neighbor. A person must work out in the here and now, on the basis of reason, what would be the Christ-like thing to do. Similarly in political ideals; it is not always clear what is the Gandhi-like thing to do when it comes to passive resistance and civil disobedience. The path ahead demands constant retreading, getting the signs right, working out the ways to go, through reason and with intuition or insight into an ideal. Both ought (and reason) and good (and insight) seem integral to the moral life.

Some mix of reason and ideals thus seems central to the way a person conceives him- or herself as committed to the service of others. But what does an ideal of service imply? It must, of course, relate to the real context of children, especially in terms of the fact of children's changefulness. Indeed, if a teacher asks why he or she should be constantly improving practice, the answer has a naturalistic flavor. The service is to persons, and the persons are constantly changing. Teaching often becomes routinized. We arm ourselves with a set of categories within which the situation and the children may be classified. We define the context as a repeat performance of previous encounters. That may be necessary for personal survival in some classrooms, and, indeed, children may manifest stereotypical behavior. That should not disguise the *fact* of their uniqueness as persons.

Fact? Advisedly so, in that children actually do have sets of individual experiences in their lives and they are more or less well endowed with talents of differing kinds. Where teachers ignore that uniqueness, by stereotyping children, they are ignoring the claims that the individual person is making upon them as teachers. The subjects in front of the teacher are constantly changing individuals. For the teacher to provide any effective education there must be constant shift, change, adaptation, and adjustment to established routines of practice. This is the human condition. That condition makes severe demands on the professional's expertise, and it is why those who "teach as they were taught" cannot respond to children with proper professionalism. They will fail in part because they assume that people are static, and they fail to see the need to see the students' goals as their own. Elizabeth Beck could have shouted her way through the experience and blamed her failure to master it on Mrs. Old. This commitment to a process of change and adaptation equips a teacher with new strategies and new repertoires.

The ideal of service is to persons who are themselves developing and changing (especially if they are children). The ideal must therefore in part be constituted by some notion of what a child as a person is to become. Recall the ways in which Mrs. Simpson is not content with simply telling children to keep off the paint. She sees the development of reason and autonomy within a framework of consideration for other people (the principal, the painter, Mum) as essential for even the very young if they are to emerge as moral persons. She has a implicit or explicit ideal for these youngsters and a conception of her place in their development. Teachers like Mrs. Simpson make both formal and informal contributions to the task of the human and moral development of children.

Mrs. Simpson's students, as beneficiaries of education, will achieve rational autonomy and become free human persons where "person" is both a conception of an *achievement* and a *moral status*. For personhood, unlike physical strength and puberty, does not emerge from within. Nor does it emerge simply from the basic categories of human understanding (cause-and-effect relations, conceptions of time and space, and self-awareness). To be a person issues from a development of mere self-awareness at birth into that of an individual with moral identity through childhood and adulthood. We understand that development in terms of a complex spectrum, that is, the cognitive, conceptual, moral, affective, and social and other pieces of what it means to be a moral human being. Such a concept of a person underpins any ideal of service. The problems of its realization do not need to be belabored—what improvement of practice amounts to, how it can be institutionally effectively conceived, how the constraints of classrooms and schools affect it, are further questions. But to the ideal of service and the improvement of practice, a single professional community and its members are necessarily committed.

This is all very well as far as it goes—and it is not here argued in enough depth. It is very formal and insufficiently sensitive to the issues of *gender* for morality. Feminism, in its various forms, seems to be arguing for what looks like a naturalistic morality. Women have different priorities. Great importance is placed on caring or connectedness in ways that seem foreign to men (Belenky et al., 1986; Gilligan, 1979). Women do this, certainly, but they regard these characteristics of morality, as they perceive them, as ideals to follow. It is with that good in mind that they nurture their children as they do (bearing in mind Hare's [1962] comment that the dark places of ethics are enlightened by considering how we bring up our children). We must also be careful not to surrender to a gender determinism in ethics, for example, because I am a man, I must care about justice more than connectedness.

Caring is not therefore a simple replacement for a utilitarian teleology (the greatest happiness of the greatest number) or an alternative to reason or justice. Rather we are listening to the voice of the woman articulating a moral ideal, providing pictures of care that differ from such ideals as love (agape) or justice. Caring or connectedness are ideals constantly to be pursued and worked out. Indeed, caring is itself the activity of service to others. But just as one can only understand, say, what following Christ is by living like Him, so we can only fathom what the ideal of caring is by acting within its framework. Read this way, feminism is philosophically an idealist challenge to an objectivist morality. It is no accident that it should be a woman, Iris Murdoch, who is the major living exponent of idealism.

Three Characteristics of Ideals

If, therefore, we are to be moral agents, we must have some kinds of ideals in our lives, although we have to understand their function. Neither an idealist metaphysic nor a straightforward objectivist view of moral principles by itself provides an intelligible view of moral life. Following ideals as guides (however unformulated) is important for moral coherence in our lives if they are seen as definitions of some good state we pursue as individuals. But ideals also have three interesting characteristics: (1) They are subject to different definitions, (2) they are unattainable, and (3) they can guide and sustain us.

The pledge of allegiance speaks of "one nation, under God, indivisible, with liberty and justice for all," a fine statement of ideals, which is manifestly capable of many interpretations. One person's conception of liberty and justice may differ from another's. Human creativity, too, as an ideal to pursue in one's own life, can take many forms—in the plastic arts, in terms of the development of a scientific rationality, in literature and music, and so on. There can also be ideals that are evil, such as racial purity or white domination (Malan, 1990). So ideals are thus not ribbons to wear around our necks. The words in which we couch ideals are continuously contestable definitions of life's primary purposes, and they are thereby liable to different interpretations.

Moreover, we do not reach or realize the ideals in our lives, although they act as guiding endpoints to help us move in a certain direction. Self-realization may be coherent as a personal ideal, but there can be no obvious point at which I wake up one morning to say "today I will complete my self-realization." The goal is unreachable, and in that sense is an ideal rather than a goal. The "promised land" of equality is portrayed as a dream in the sermon delivered by Martin Luther King shortly before his assassination. We do not expect to see the day when each child has a perfect education, however much we work within the framework of that as an ideal.

Indeed, ideals sustain us. Take a conventional, if increasingly unfashionable, ideal—a monogamous marriage. I guess most people who marry in a Western Christian tradition regard the commitments they make to the other person as very important. They regard marriage as, in some way, an ideal state within which to live with another person, to raise children, and so on. The ideal of marriage is valued, as in *Who's Afraid of Virginia Woolf?* The failure of a specific relationship need not mean that an individual thereby looses his or her commitment to the ideal. Indeed it may be the commitment to the ideal, as much as the particular relationship, that sustains the individual(s) concerned. There are countless other circumstances in which an ideal can (rightly or wrongly) also sustain a person. The dead of the American Civil War, the First World War, and many other wars across the ages bear witness to the power of ideals in people's lives.

Roles, Ideals, and Vocation

We define a role, as opposed to a function, by characterizing it as a set of rights and duties, the normative expectations that a person in a role takes on (see Chapter 3). However, an interesting connection arises among role, ideal, and individual. It occurs, for example, with a man in a family being a brother (as a class of people), being John (Sam Doe's brother), and being a part of brotherhood (or fraternity). We acquire brothers naturally, and from this natural state we learn to play, more or less well, the role in our differing social environments—compare the brothers Walton of the long-running television series of the same name with the brothers Corleone of Mario Puzo's *The Godfather*. From these natural facts of our relationships with our brothers we grow to understand what the rights and duties of being a brother are, and thereby in some degree what brotherhood *means*, as an ideal state.

Important implications follow. While we learn how to play the role we can also add to it, develop it, expand it, and certainly give it our own individual interpretation. That way, we do not merely play it, but we expand the possibilities within the conceptions of the ideal. We learn how to be a brother, and what brotherhood means in our own distinctive way. Such natural roles no doubt influence our behavior in life. As a brother, Tom Stevenson used to read to his young sister, "as big brothers should." Many other intervening roles will have been influential in his becoming a teacher, but brotherhood will have helped shape either his or his sister's career choice. There is no logical or chronological priority between the notions of self and role, for our development to maturity as human persons consists in the development of our selves through working or playing a wide range of roles and, of course, being ourselves. From these varied experiences we can develop certain kinds of ideals. As we play roles, we frequently expand our own understanding of an ideal state.

It is from this interplay that the notion of a vocation arises. Individuals will develop differing perspectives on their work, bringing to the job of teacher their own commitments, enthusiasms, and passions. These will be shaped by their role. In Piagetian language, teachers "accommodate" themselves to their role and their own perceptions of it as a chosen profession, perhaps a vocation, or a community. Would-be candidates for the profession are generally asked why they want to teach, which is sometimes thought to be a question asking for vocational commitment. Vocation, in this sense, has a metaphysical flavor—that an individual is somehow "called" to a profession. The notion of a vocation is, I think, more simply understood as where there is a fit, a complementarity, between what the task demands and what the individual has to offer in terms of temperament, makeup and character, interests, abilities, and desires (Emmett, 1958). For example, if brother Tom Stevenson were very impatient and liable to fits of temper, he would obviously not have a temperament fitted for teaching. Vocations have to be discovered. A person has to find out whether his or her temperament and natural abilities match the demands of the job. Sometimes, of course, whatever the person thinks, he or she may be disastrous in the classroom. Individuals misjudge their fit, however motivated they may be; such people have to be counseled out of training or advised to work elsewhere. Vocations, in this sense, do not just appear, as one did to St. John Rivers in *Jane Eyre*.

Many of us come to teaching with social ideals, determined to try to contribute to society, or to right some social wrong, or because we felt an affinity with children of a certain age, enjoyed their company and their peculiarities, quirks, or style. Maybe we felt we could be people who, as Noddings (1984) puts it, were the sort who "could be crazy about that kid" (p. 61), yet equally valuable would be a commitment to what we could be objectively good at and knew we had the patience for, to ensure that the fit between the occupation and ourselves is the right one. The ideal clarifies and develops as we work.

Feminist theory teaches us to expect the sense of vocation to differ between men and women. That is, there will be differing interpretations of the ideal of service. Indeed, if we look on the word *vocation* metaphorically, it is the *different voice* that calls. Our problem is to listen to the voices of the father and the mother when *in loco parentis*. We should seek different attributes from men and from women, *but* we should seek to ensure a balance of their presence in the lives of children. That is why the gender balance in the profession accompanied by the male character of many schools as institutions poses such a challenge to professionals.

But differing perspectives on roles, ideals, and vocations come from many places, including upbringing, gender, and our learned understanding of what the practices involve. Indeed, our dispositions and predispositions are rooted in the traditions of the profession. It has a history as a practice that individuals have sought to extend and develop. Across the years individuals have sought to interpret and manifest the ideal of service to which the practice is committed. MacIntyre (1984) writes:

> What is distinctive in a practice is in part the way in which the conception of the relevant goods and ends which the technical skills serve—and every practice does require the exercise of technical skills—are transformed and enriched by these extensions of human powers and by that regard for its own internal goods which are partially definitive of each particular practice or type of practice. (p. 193)

These internal goods, as MacIntyre describes them, are the ideals rooted in human practices. We can therefore only make judgments about the intrinsic satisfactions different teachers reveal on the basis of the ideal understood as a tradition of virtuous practice that defines teaching. The social practice of teaching is defined by (1) an ideal of service describing goods internal to the ultimate directions of the practice and (2) those virtues (honesty, courage, care, fairness, and practical wisdom) that describe acts and actions within the practice. These are not different ways of describing the same thing: Ideals and virtues have quite different functions in moral language, and thereby, in our lives.

THE NEED FOR A PROFESSIONAL IDEAL

People work as professionals. To understand their profession is in part to understand their shared ideal. I have characterized the ideal in teaching as a commitment to serve developing persons, with the rider that since those persons are constantly changing, there must be a commitment to changing and improving practice. An ideal of service will have different components that form the bedrock of moral discussion about ultimate purposes in the profession and from which major conclusions follow.

First, we can learn professional ideals as we learn our role, and we can bring our individual perspectives to them. We need initiations for novices that consist of education into the ideals of the profession—where teachers can contribute their own voice, where we see that self-reflection is necessary to our effective discharge of duty, and where we understand the different contributions men and women bring to discourse on professional ideals. Right now, the profession of teaching does not induct or socialize its initiates into a set of ideals, not even an ideal of service, nor does it incorporate in its selection mechanisms anything that weeds out those who are uncommitted, nor does it present an ideal sense of the teacher's role.

Second, some dissonance is likely between personal and professional ideals, and ideals may not be reflected in the institutional arrangements teachers are obliged to follow. That dissonance may or may not be tolerable, either for the individual or for the profession. That a teacher hold professional ideals is not to say that these are the only ideals they can hold as persons. Individuals have many other ideals in their life beyond those to which they subscribe as professionals—family, politics, social life, and so forth. Sometimes such commitments to ideals, particularly in terms of the time spent pursuing them, will clash with those of teaching, and harsh choices will have to be made. The ideal of service in teaching does not supersede all other individual ideals. What an ideal of service demands is commitment to it. For it governs the conception and the execution of the enterprise. Some ideals (e.g., fascism) make it impossible for a teacher to hold the requisite professional ideals.

Third, any professional will undoubtedly find conflict between what he or she may be told to do and how he or she conceives professional ideals. For example, a state may mandate a curriculum that runs counter to the teacher's conceptions of what or how a child ought to be taught. Or a parent may demand that a child be treated in a way that, to the teacher, is manifestly unsuitable or even downright immoral. Or a department in a secondary school may have an attitude toward the teaching of, say, *Romeo and Juliet*, utterly in conflict with the perceptions of the neophyte teacher. For many teachers battered by bureaucracy, the response may well be to keep quiet because there's the paycheck at the end of the month.

But teachers will give different interpretations to ideals, as do individual scientists or artists driven by creativity. Ideals are not carved in stone. These differences will be influenced by a teacher's epistemological views (see Chapter 5). Holding ideals is not exhibiting warm and fuzzy feelings but needs to be valued as part of intensive educational debate about fundamental purposes that we conduct even as we argue on specific issues. Major disagreement over some ideals should not mask the areas of agreement across a professional community. Keeping a constant conversation going on the broad range of our professional ideals can include every aspect of our endeavor.

So teachers may have a broad governing ideal of service to persons learning, but the extent to which the ideal matters to them will vary in interpretation between individual teachers, and individuals may be more or less committed to it. At the one end are the saints and heroes like Jessica Seigel who struggle along in circumstances of considerable privation teaching children in hostile surroundings. For these people, personal individual welfare is relatively unimportant. They work, as we say, above and beyond the call of duty (Urmson, 1969), putting themselves beyond the point where we can say that they ought to do what they do. At the other end are teachers pandering, say, to the whims of rich parents, just doing what is required efficiently and adequately; their "ideal" is filtered through the lure of the lucrative contract. The function of an ideal is to bring those perspectives into a moral conversation about education, the absence of which undermines the heart of professionalism. The function of ideals in our profession is thus of fundamental importance, but, as the second main section of this chapter now illustrates, that can be a conversation with very wide parameters.

TOWARD *IN LOCO PARENTIS* AS AN IDEAL ROLE
FOR THE PROFESSIONAL TEACHER

What should the role of the teacher be—ideally? This is a moral question. If we were clear about it, it would dramatically influence everything we do, especially our conception of career development and how we compose our lives (see Chapter 2).

Due process, I have claimed, has obliterated the conception of the role of the teacher as being *in loco parentis*. This section reopens that debate but does so by coming at the problems from quite distinct directions, each of which is primarily moral in character—teacher–student relations, parental choice of school, and a teacher's integrity. I am seeking to describe an ideal role for the teacher that is moral, not bureaucratic or technical. Such an ideal will play a part in the profession's conversations that I have described. Whatever conception teachers have of their role, it must involve a perception of relation to students, to parents, and to themselves. Even if the specific arguments are rejected within each of these areas as supporting the ideal of an *in loco parentis* role, they serve to provide an example of how diverse issues relate to the articulation of a professional ideal. I begin with the teacher's relationship with students.

Teachers and Students in Personal Relationships

The individual personality and character of the teacher, we can repeat, is a significant factor in expert teaching, not least because children are obliged to come to school (Kleinig, 1981; Krimmermann, 1978) which of itself can prove an initial handicap for the relationship. Where professional expertise is construed in terms of virtues, the personality of the teacher becomes enmeshed in the exercise of every aspect of the role. Mrs. Simpson is not just a mix of knowledge and personality. She is what she is, teaching children to care (Kohn, 1991). A teacher's classroom personality may or may not be different from the private self. Tom, for instance, brings warmth, friendliness, and security within himself to his teaching. He has developed his teaching personality, much like an actor develops a style, except that the interpersonal relationships in the classroom are genuine, not pretend, and an actor can play totally different fictional people. Teacher personalities are in part shaped by the age of the children they teach. We can talk of a classroom personality as we can talk of a courtroom presence or a bedside manner, as a significant part of life in classrooms (P. W. Jackson, 1968). Through all this run the various threads of expertise we have discussed. Thus the individual person within the role of teacher is as important for us to understand as is the role itself.

What happens as the person of the teacher engages with the person of the student? At this interface, there are three interwoven issues for the professional teacher:

1. The integration of conscious and unconscious modeling of personal behavior
2. The extent to which a professional relationship can be personalized
3. The extent to which children as students get the opportunity to care for the relationship with their teacher and through that, how much a professional can learn from a child

Modeling and intention.   The teacher is an intentional agent within a role, running a classroom or an office, grading tests, helping children, and so forth. But whether the teacher likes the idea or not, he or she is also a model, which may be partly intended, but much of which is unintended. Mrs. Simpson can intentionally model good behavior, but she does much of it unintentionally, that is, she has formed habits of classroom behavior that are now integrated pieces of her classroom persona. What she models as good behavior she hopes the children will pick up from her without direct instruction (P. W. Jackson, 1968).

Where the teaching is direct and intentional, a teacher can readily find out its effects, not simply in terms of results, but in terms of the interaction of his or her personality with those of individual children. "I can't seem to get through to John" is more a matter of the interaction of personalities than of the method or content of the teaching. Paramount, in my view, is how the intentional and the unintentional are perceived by the individual children. Is the teacher just a teacher to John or Sally? Is he or she a confidante or a friend of some kind? Or is the teacher modeling impatience, poor control, lack of enthusiasm, inefficiency, meanness, and a host of personal mannerisms? What is it about some teacher–student relationships that make them such dramatic failures or so successful, indeed so powerfully influential? We need to realize the precious value in the unintentional effect of modeling, but that can only arise where the quality of intentional agency is good (Ryle, 1973).

Personalized relationships.   Children's perceptions of adults, it is said, will be measured by their understandings of the world in general. In this view, at an egocentric stage of moral development, children would see teachers as instrumental to their wants; at a realistic stage, teachers would be seen as rule followers; only at the stage of autonomy would they be seen as persons. Maybe, but this seems not the whole story. The love and care a five-year-old can show for a parent (or indeed for a teacher) is not rooted in instrumentalism. If the schooling situation is not one where love and care abound, then children will see teachers much as they see policemen, shopkeepers, or any other adults they come in contact with.

What sometimes seems to leave us quite baffled is exactly why the warm, tender, caring relationships within good elementary schools seem so utterly foreign to institutions of secondary education or universities. But why the bafflement? Part of the teacher's assigned role in the secondary school or the university is to issue grades, which determine life chances (C. M. Clark & Peterson, 1986). The teacher in this role is inevitably a threat, possibly an enemy, even to the successful student. However brilliant, however solicitous, however friendly a teacher is to a student, the immutability of this institutional fact remains to foul up the personal understandings and relationships of teachers and students. If we were really concerned to build strong, professionalized, interpersonal relationships with students in our classrooms or seminar rooms, what might we do?

We have to move away from rule-governed to care-governed visions of contexts where, of course, rules have their place. Through a child's work, a teacher should get to know how he or she appears to that child. Everything a child writes or submits is an implicit evaluation of a teacher's work. Moreover, every piece of work deserves care, attention (witness Jessica Seigel), and constructive and detailed evaluation, not critical assessment. Children can be encouraged to want to be learning resources for one another, as cooperators in learning and the enjoyment of learning. They can share common pursuits with love and enthusiasm in the company of their teachers.

Caring for teachers. The center of a valuable student–teacher relationship is partnership. Bateson (1989) makes the point that men look in their lives for symmetry of relationships rather than the asymmetrical. We assume that age hierarchies are right and justified. We fail to see children as teachers, not learners; we fail to ask ourselves what we can learn from them, not what can we teach them. "Children might be better off," she writes "if parents were more aware of themselves as learning from them, rejuvenated by them, and ultimately perhaps dependent on them" (p. 107). We need to build as strong a partnership with students as with their parents, perhaps stronger. Can we not find ways consistently to make students our evaluators, critiquing our teaching as we critique their learning, and learning from them? How can we get them to share our passions and enthusiasms? How can we do that if we lack professional expertise and moral maturity and confidence in ourselves as adults and as teachers?

Part of our problem is that students do not see teachers as they are. Principal Smith as a citizen has a right to advance social causes outside the school. She happens to be a feminist working for changes in power structures, of which children in her school are well aware, but high-profile involvement in almost any political issue may well be seen as inappropriate for a teacher, let alone a principal, particularly when that stance "affects" what is done in schools, for example, when the feminist principal starts to attract attention among the students because of these views. This could be viewed contractually. For example, to what extent is the system effectively impinging on her rights as a citizen? What are the limits of political activism for teachers? But it is also a major problem for teacher–student relationships. For what kind of example does her reluctance to engage students with such political problems set for children if they are to be involved in the political life of a democracy? How can proper partnerships be constructed if children cannot see the private person within the professional role?

This kind of selectivity about what one can and cannot share with children undermines the possibilities of strength in a partnership that could only be built on respect and on trust. If teachers cannot or dare not share in aspects of a student's private life, partnership will be very formalized and shallow. The same is true if a teacher like Mrs. Simpson or a principal like Smith cannot share personal interests that are of public importance. If a school curriculum is to challenge a child's developing perceptions of the world, it must result in a child's exploring ideas about that world (whatever curriculum or discipline framework that is couched in). If the teacher is to be authentic, it must come from the heart. For the mutual purposes of teaching and learning it becomes utterly arbitrary to cut off areas of discourse by external fiat, or to produce a sterilized curriculum through a hygienic textbook that obstructs the development of strong interaction among teacher, child, and subject in a caring context. We cannot teach children to care without caring for them and they for us. Right now, we have shut down that debate almost entirely with the litigiousness of due process.

A Dilemma in Parent–Teacher Child Relations: Mrs. Simpson and Louise

We can begin to explore issues within *in loco parentis* with a hypothetical example. Assume that Mrs. Simpson is a generally religious person, the sort who goes to church irregularly. Her slightly skeptical attitude toward religion is not related to the quality we have seen in her moral beliefs and her life as a moral educator. Louise used to be a student in her first-grade class, and is now in the sixth grade. She always liked Mrs. Simpson and pops into her classroom regularly for a chat. Louise's parents joined a fundamentalist church when she was 3. As she has progressed through the school, she has begun to talk to Mrs. Simpson a bit about "going to church." Mrs. Simpson tried to get her to avoid the topic without hurting the child, although she was concerned that Louise was clearly in distress. Louise has now confided in her that she is "all mixed up"–she does not believe any of that "stuff" her parents believe.

What can Mrs. Simpson do? Should she try to help Louise resolve her crisis of religious belief? Should she tell the child's parents their daughter is no longer a believer? To whom is the teacher morally responsible in a public institution? I suspect our present system would have a clear answer: Mrs. Simpson has no problem; what a child does or believes outside of school is none of the teacher's business. That is a political answer, not a professional moral solution.

This problem is at an extreme end of teacher–parent–child relations, but it is instructive to try to follow through. The outcome may be that professionally Mrs. Simpson can take no action. Yet if Louise's plight is to be regarded as none of Mrs. Simpson's business, are we then stipulating

that, in general, teachers must not allow themselves to come into relationships with pupils where the kinds of close confidences Louise offers her
former teacher come out? What does it do to Louise when Mrs. Simpson,
a significant adult in her life to whom she turns for care, support, and
intellectual advice, rebuffs her, saying, "We shouldn't be talking about this"?
The problem can be posed in a number of ways, each with a different
emphasis, each inviting a different answer:

1. Does Louise have a right, in a democratic society, to be helped to
   see alternatives so that she can decide what she wants to do? Or,
2. Can parents be permitted to deny children freedoms (like those
   protected by the First Amendment) that are the rights of other
   members of the society? Or,
3. By what right could a school, or its teachers, teach a child things
   contrary to the parent's beliefs?

Each way of putting the problem alters the kinds of answers we expect, and
in a democracy, all arguments are contestable, though not all are equally
valid. Without dealing with all of these issues, certain things seem basic
for a professional teacher of children.

First, the teacher's premier duty must be to the child, while at the same
time recognizing that the child is a member of a family. Children are growing up in a democracy. Public education in a democratic society must have
as its central purpose the development in people of the ability and the will
to choose (see Chapter 4). Whenever a teacher misses out on an opportunity to examine alternative beliefs or lifestyles with as much professional
expertise as can be mustered, the opportunity to develop fundamental
democratic principles, on which the future of a democracy depends, is not
being fulfilled. The threefold description of the issues at stake only makes
sense within a democratic framework. In general, therefore, Louise ought
to be helped by her teachers to see alternatives to the lifestyle, including
the religious beliefs, in which she is growing up.

Second, parents should not be allowed to deny basic constitutional
freedoms to a child, such as freedom of thought and expression. The rights
a society affords to parents over children are not total, any more than persons can do whatever they want with their land. Parental authority is by
no means invariably benign, as we learn from child abuse statistics and
autobiographies (Freeman, 1983). Supporting the institution of the family
does not mean acceding to the bizarre wants of every biologically connected
group of people with minors who happen to dwell in the same household.
Indeed, the ritual obeisance we give in educational discussions to the

notion of the "family" contrasts with the general social failure to implement measures that could properly support it.

Third, public (or indeed private) schools in a society already do teach children to believe things that parents do not believe. The children of a serial killer would still, we hope, be taught to respect other people and not hurt their schoolfriends. In the Ethos Partnership—a university-schools project we have developed—a parent attacked an elementary school principal on the grounds that his child was being taught the virtue of honesty outside a theistic framework, but the principal rightly did not concede that this was cause for reprimanding the teacher. There are the obvious sensational cases, such as the debates on creationism, in which parents may be in outright combat with the schools. A much larger and noncontroversial area is the fact that children acquire knowledge their parents do not have because the knowledge is in some sense "new" or because the parents' education was incomplete. Religious beliefs, however, are often bound up with views of the family itself, and it is in this controversial area that Mrs. Simpson's difficulties with Louise are located.

One answer to the dilemma could be to say that fundamentalists or other minorities should create their own schools. Louise's parents may well choose to send her to a private school of their choice, and that is their privilege. But choice does not mean getting exactly what one wants, for it usually implies a compromise. Social regulations have to be put on what kinds of schools are legitimate, what kinds of schools might be publicly funded, what kinds of schools are appropriate within that framework, and what kind of certification or licensing of teachers is desirable. Of course, children can be educated at home, yet even here, the state intervenes with tests for children being so educated. So a democratic society, however open, cannot tolerate a Charles Manson sect opening schools. The democratic society has to draw the lines around the rights of the parent or the family. Once it is seen that lines *have* to be drawn, the question is *where*.

In responding to Mrs. Simpson's problem so far, I am arguing that the professional's premier duty is to the child and that the parent should be prevented from invading a child's constitutional freedoms. But this way of responding to Mrs. Simpson's dilemma hardly looks like a recipe for establishing good parent-teacher relationships. Yet maybe it is. The profession has to declare itself, to be outspoken about the standards that it believes in and the educational framework within which it must be pursued. The development of intellectual freedom in order to enable Louise to exercise her own choice of religion is, for a professional teacher, nonnegotiable. Working in partnership with parents does not mean kowtowing to their whims, but rather having the confidence and the expertise to engage them in debate about the future of their children in all its aspects (Lightfoot, 1978). If any parent brings up a child badly, teachers should say so—just in case no one else does.

This dilemma is fortunately not the general case. The implications of the discussion are that individual teachers and schools should be prepared to state more forcibly where they stand, especially in matters of moral education and educating children in such basic social principles as honesty, respect for others, considering other people's interests, and being kind and compassionate. Mrs. Simpson should support Louise in her difficulties, using the best expertise she has. Of course, the populace may then say they do not want education in their schools, but something called "custodial schooling." If so, there is no place for a role called a professional teacher any more than there would be a place for a professional teacher in a university if the curriculum was mandated by the state.

What we may discuss in principle may not be the case in practice. I fear most of us would advise Mrs. Simpson to follow the political route—let dear little Louise chatter on and do nothing to support her nor anything to anger her parents. Politically that may be the sensible thing to do, the structures being what they are. No doubt with regret. Poor Louise! Is it too harsh to say that it is professional negligence for Mrs. Simpson to do nothing?

This case depends on matters of freedom, but it is also dependent on what we think the role of the teacher should ideally be. To visualize that ideal, these issues are highlighted in the Mrs. Simpson–Louise case. First, the child is central—sometimes and often disputably above the rights of the parent. Second, that does not mean taking a permissive stance toward children and their wants. Third, it does not demand that a teacher behave like the actual parent, but rather within a framework of parent-like attitudes of an ideal kind, for in loco parentis does not mean taking the actual place of the real parent, but taking the role of an ideal parent. While these matters may be highly controversial, we cannot simply stand on one side shaking our heads at the controversy if we are to grapple with an ideal role for the teacher. Due process seems to have ruled such problems out of our conversations.

Parents, Teachers, and Schools

But what is a parent these days (Boyer, 1991; Clark, 1983; National Commission on Children, 1991)? The past hundred years have witnessed the continuing loss of power and the authority of parents and families over children (Coleman & Husen, 1985). The visual media are important reflections of social culture (Kubey & Csikszentimihalyi, 1990). They also education because both have a low status. Teachers expect support for what they are doing, irrespective of a child's behavior, successes, or failures, but they frequently meet parents only when problems arise. Parents in parent-teacher associations are organized into a group with which the school can communicate. Unfortunately, too often such organizations are not interpersonal but bureaucratized, which may make it difficult for many parents to participate, although such organizations are ones that are familiar to most middle-class parents.

There are a plethora of proposals that indicate how these relationships can be improved at state, regional, local, and school levels, involving everything from parent empowerment programs to home visits, adult education, and classroom volunteers. Most authorities recommend a negotiated and understood partnership between parent and teacher as professionally necessary, provided that we do not undermine parental responsibility still further (e.g., by taking at-risk children away from their parents). Yet if the notion of a partnership is to be authentic, notwithstanding the richness of the activities of contemporary practitioners, there must also be professional partnership specifically because a child going from kindergarten through twelfth grade changes schools. Institutional connections must be sustained across a pyramid of schools so that the relations established at elementary level do not collapse at intermediate and again at secondary level. That implies intimate working relationships between schools and between professionals across a pyramid, not a simple transfer of files. The child's move to a more senior school is as traumatic for the parent as for the student. Such practical initiatives have to be constructed at local levels.

Consider this example: We have been working with seven schools for the past 16 months, building the Ethos Partnership (Wilavsky, 1992) referred to above. Hoping to defuse the issues that words like *moral* raise in the public forum, we are a group of schools and two academics seeking to tackle issues of character or ethical education across the pyramid from elementary to high schools. Because the schools become daily more multi-cultural, the challenge for teacher–parent relationships are greater. Many immigrant cultures presume an *in loco parentis* role, related of course to the specific culture's norms and values. The anomic character of high schools in particular tests the cultural values of the home and, more clearly, the school's and the teacher's capacity to cope with such cultural diversity.

Yet however splendidly the schools in the partnership face up to such issues as prejudice and community, each continually returns to the issue of parent relationships and how families can be supported in good relations with schools. Each school ethos team is confronting the challenge in different and creative ways, defying the public caricature of the teacher. For the most part, teachers are deeply concerned at their difficulty in building relations with immigrant parents who seek success for their children and,

shape it. The comparative differences between family relationships in *Lea*
it to Beaver and *Roseanne* are indicative of how distinctive these shifts ar
Authority has not been lost by parents to the schools (Timpane, 1975).
has dissipated, with some gains by children, and a vacuum of guidance ar
support has developed. Legislatively children have become more protecte
from their parents. Socially children have asserted rights, and the develo
ments in the youth culture have accelerated this process with successiv
generations (Freeman, 1983; Schrag, 1978). The *de jure* authority of tl
parent over the child has often ceased to be *de facto* by the time the ch
dren are out of ninth grade. Forty percent of children are not raised l
their natural parents, frequently leaving a vacuum of authority and stab
ity (Hodgkinson, 1991). The term *parent*, therefore, has become as much
description of a caretaking role as of a biological relationship.

It is difficult to understate the impact of these changes on society ar
the forbidding character of the political challenge it creates. For soci
cohesion has been effected by the family unit, irrespective of its virtu
and vices. Presently, it seems, schools are left in a moral vacuum. Tra
tional family life may be difficult to promote as virtuous in schools for fe
of upsetting children not so placed socially or in the context of social,
not political, uncertainty about its value. Politically, the volatile charact
of some issues (e.g., abortion) compared with the apathetic attitude to equa
significant family issues (e.g., poverty and homelessness) makes it almc
impossible to address in the political forum what many would regard
one of the major tragedies of the twentieth century—the collapse of the fam
and the disappearance of childhood (Postman, 1984).

The relationship with a parent is potentially the most complex respc
sibility in a teacher's role in public education. Parents are legally compell
to surrender a child to the influence of adults whom they may or may n
know, to expose that child to formal evaluations, to invidious comparisor
and to the influence of other children whom, again, they do not kno
Parents have also been students themselves and thus approach the schc
and the teacher with a mix of deference, hostility, respect, and uncertain
As in their student experience, parents in dispute with teachers will rar
find any overt support from the building administrator. Moreover, fam
styles rarely match that of a school—compare the functionally specific ru
governed school with a functionally diffuse, indulgent, impulsive, lovir
and hating family.

Teachers often regard parents with grave suspicion. Do they suppc
the school's values? Are they interested or just interfering? Why do th
keep the child away "ill" when he or she should be in detention? Why t
they not realize there are 30 children in this class? Lightfoot (1978) st
gests that teachers and mothers may often be in conflict in elementa

following the tradition of immigrants to this country, work unusually hard to make ends meet, which provides an initial obstacle in promoting relationships. The teacher in this context takes risks with due process to establish some kind of trust. Teachers are nervous about due process, but they try to create a new kind of role for themselves in the face of overwhelming need. Like Jessica Seigel, what else can they do?

The demands on their professional relationships with parents place a heavy premium on every professional virtue, particularly such qualities as caring, honesty, and certainly courage. Teachers need great clarity on education and its ideals, and they must face up to ways in which these can be communicated to parents. This may not be possible in the turbulent context of the public school, particularly at secondary level, because the organizational structure and bureaucratic management systems make it very difficult. Escalante had a child whose father insisted she leave school to work in his restaurant. The math teacher cajoled and argued with the father, putting courage into his student to fight an insensitive parent for her future. Keating found himself supporting a boy who wanted to become an actor. Disagreements between son and father about the boy's ambitions were profound and tragic, but Keating could not behave as a simple mouthpiece of the parent without betraying the boy. Jessica Seigel literally was acting as a parent, chauffeuring children to college interviews and doing much else.

Parental Choice of School

Could these parent–teacher problems be ameliorated if parents chose the school? Parental choice of school is a notional solution to problems in the institutional infrastructure of education (Boyd & Walberg, 1990; Chubb & Moe, 1990). It is intended to ensure that parents are empowered. Choice advocates are often unsophisticated in their model of the parent as consumer, for parents' motivations and interests in schools are much more subtle. It is being cited as something of a panacea for changing the parent-school, or parent–teacher, relationships. Those who advocate choice often have a market analogy, and they talk of incentives for both parties. Some talk of taking control of the schools back from educrats (Finn, 1991), and there is also talk of destroying bureaucracies—a goal with which we all may have some sympathy.

Parents who choose schools are not homogeneous in attitude, motive, wants, or perceptions. At least three notional types of parent are visible: (1) the consumer, (2) the replicator of privilege, and (3) the spiritual sponsor.

The parent-as-consumer is the parental type most favored by those who want to break up the educational establishment and its bureaucracies and let the consumer and market forces take control. Such parents are often first-generation private school users, aggressively upwardly mobile, who shop around to sustain for their children the mobility they have achieved. Only a detailed empirical survey could spell out distinctions much more clearly within this group. Contract for services delivered characterizes the parent–school relationship within this model.

The parent-as-replicator-of-privilege sends children into private schools to continue a family tradition, usually to replicate the upper-middle-class values for which these parents usually stand, but crucially for the child to grow up with children of his or her class, and often to replicate the parent's education (Johnson, 1987; Tyack & Hansot, 1982). Understood conventions and trust characterize this relationship, as it does in the third type.

Here the parent-as-spiritual-sponsor sends children to a school of denominational or specialist (e.g., military, progressive) choice, where the spiritual values of both school and family are generally perceived as at least as important in the child's education as academic attainment, if not more so. A parent who sponsors a child for a religious or military upbringing may even be determinedly providing a vocational education for the child. Such a parental type may be more common among the relatively less well off who, if given the opportunity, would choose a denominational religious school to access a free public education unconstrained by the private (religious)–public (secular) divide.

Of course, actual parents do not neatly fall into one or other part of this typology. Motives are very mixed and certainly not as simplistic as "consumer." A parent-as-replicator may not need to be an active consumer because the quality of the school he or she supports is so excellent and, for him or her, family tradition is far more important. He or she sends children to school X, like he or she always uses Cartier as the jewelry store. Other replicator-minded parents may decide to shop around (unlike their own parents) because "their" school policy has changed, say on co-education, and they do not like it. The parent-as-spiritual-sponsor may often be a replicator, too, but it would be a travesty of the intimacy of the relationship among church, school, and family ever to regard such a parent as a consumer.

What does this oversimple typology illustrate about parent–teacher relationships as viewed through the fact of their choosing a school?

First, it is simply misleading for any school to assume that all parents would behave like consumers in a mall, as if that relationship provides a palpably correct contractual model for what ought to be the case in public education.

Second, it is also misleading to assume that parents will take a more proactive role in their children's education if they choose the child's school. For the spiritual sponsor and replicator parent, there is no such contingent connection at all. Indeed, many replicator (and some consumer) parents send their children to residential schools, glad in the knowledge that they will not have to be much involved in their child's education but also trusting that the child will turn out to have the same value system or class attitudes as their own. For the spiritual sponsor in particular, it is not the act of choice that brings the parent into a close relationship with the school, but the spiritual foundation of the church–family relationship, where teachers are understood to be in loco parentis.

Third, there are fewer potential difficulties in the teacher–parent relationship with some of these types of parents—for different reasons. Private schools often have huge resource advantages, so that children may get better individual treatment in much smaller classes. Or even if they have no particular resource advantage, they may be much less bureaucratic. Either way, once the choice of a school is made, private schools for the most part expect teachers to exercise much more care and responsibility for a child. Teachers are put in the in loco parentis role, a fact that reflects not choice but the character of the school. The shared traditions, the common religious bias, the similar social-class background, the commitment to a view of education, or the developing identities of goal between parent and teacher create and become the basis of trust (Hill, Foster, & Gendler, 1989). All teachers are indeed accountable, but that does not mean they have to be regulated and controlled (see Chapter 6). They do not have to be hemmed in by threats of litigation or volumes of rules and regulations, any more than a mother who needs a regular baby-sitter draws up a contract with her own mother when Grandma babysits. The moral contract of trust can be restored to replace the litigiousness of due process.

Fourth, the paradox of parental choice is that where it works it can become selection of parents, not selection of school. Where a school is successful and popular (for whatever reason), the competition is then a consumer battle among parents for precious places. Parental choice becomes a bizarre lottery. It may even mean a few nights camping out on a sidewalk; or, as has often happened in England, parents register a child for entry to a school at 13 years of age on the night of the child's birth! For privileged schools or "spiritual" schools, the school will search for parents with the "right" background and the "right" values, something not possible for the public school, which has to take all-comers.

Parental roles in a private school: An example. Parental choice clearly alters the parent–school relationship as the crude typology demonstrates. Francis W. Parker School in Chicago is a good example of a private progressive school that has established, honored traditions. Founded at the end of the nineteenth century, the school consistently attracts replicator, con-

sumer, and spiritual-sponsor parents. Parker parents have to commit themselves to intimate involvement in the school's governance, and they support a broad conception of education and experience (e.g., all children
participate in drama productions). All parents are also told that the balanced attitude toward academic achievement is not likely to yield annual
crops of National Merit Scholars or Ivy League entries. They are expected
to attend school functions, to work on school committees, and to support
classroom teachers. Wealthy parents are expected to contribute substantial
funds beyond their children's fees, which the school uses to broaden the
social spectrum of the intake. Entry to the school is immensely competitive. The school selects.

The relationship of teacher to parent is therefore dramatically different from that presently possible in public education. The intimacy of
understanding makes an *in loco parentis* role natural for Parker teachers,
acknowledging that the wealth and social status of parents plays a major
part in the continuing success of this school. For some children (and some
parents) this does not work out, and children are asked to move or are moved
elsewhere by their parents. None of this absolves the teacher from accountability, but the weight of children's and parents' concern for quality teachers is mediated not through tests but through the intimacy of the school as
a community. The school's mission is strongly focused.

It would be as much of an earthquake in the social matrix of that
school for parents to resort to due process as it would be for teachers to
ignore bad behavior by Parker children outside the school campus. A teacher
can act as a parent would on issues defined within a range of explicit and
implicit understandings, mediated by tradition, class attitudes, religion,
progressive political commitments, and so on. This is notionally possible
in all communities, and a basis of shared cultural assumptions can even
last through fundamental disagreements. Parker teachers are *in loco parentis*,
but that does not mean that the teacher is legally a substitute for the parent. It is a definition of a teacher's privileges and moral responsibilities as
a professional teacher—to offer to the child what a "wise" parent would offer.
It is possible because goals are clear and shared, and teachers are trusted
to execute them with parental support. So if a Parker teacher saw children
misbehaving on the street, a failure to act "as a good parent would" would
itself be reprehensible in the eyes of the Parker community.

Choice and the professional teacher's role.   Do such private schools as
Parker act as models for replication of parent–school relations across public education, as advocates of choice might suggest? Not directly. Public education has never been able to compete with private education in resource
terms because it is responsible to an electorate. Nor has public education

found a way to cut the Gordian knot and reconcile private wants for all with public needs in the framework of compulsory attendance at *designated* schools. Nor, since the body of parents in any one school can be a rainbow of educational attitudes, has it been able to offer anything more than academic achievements, those arcane mental competitions of different kinds, as positional goods or educational benefits (Hollis, 1982). Nor in recent years have many public schools been able to match private education offering any benefit of great importance, parallel to academic prowess (e.g., a religious atmosphere, or an honored tradition).

Our discussion of Mrs. Simpson and Louise pointed to a role in which the child's best welfare is central with a level of care and concern like that of a parent coming from the teacher. To repeat, the description of this role as *in loco parentis* is not a literal one, that is, a demand that a teacher behave like the actual parent, but a description of parent-like attitudes, motives, and commitments.

Does this discussion of parental choice add anything to a conception of an ideal role? First, neither a teacher (nor a parent) can or should be an expert across all roles, given the social contexts of schools. We can recognize that through the lives of Escalante and Seigel. Second, choice of school seems to give parents, whatever their type, a much more substantial basis of trust, perhaps because an implicit moral contract is part of making a choice. Educational systems are inadequate if they fail to embody mutual trust. Third, the Parker example indicates how that trusting relationship can be sustained by the sort of intensive parental involvement that provides support for teachers acting *in loco parentis*.

Professional and Moral Integrity

Suppose Tom to be a Quaker pacifist. He is aware that in teaching history he will be teaching students who may be gung-ho patriots, or interested in such issues as a just war, or lovers of violence and war stories, and just occasionally a would-be pacifist like himself. He has a continuing problem of resolving his commitment to teaching with his beliefs as a Quaker, because while he does his best to get students to develop a critical stance on all things and to see war as a moral issue, he has to pretend he does not believe what he says when he raises the topic of pacifism. Yet teaching is vocationally fitting for him, and his personal ideals mesh with those necessary in the profession. How can he (morally) put up with a workplace context in which his beliefs have to be constantly suppressed, beliefs that are part of his real self?

This more general problem is how a teacher retains his or her integrity, and it is widely applicable to all kinds of teachers. In present conventions, we could deal with this issue quickly as we dealt summarily with Mrs. Simpson. If Tom as a Quaker chooses to teach history, then he has to put up with social restrictions and expectations or go teach in a Quaker school. Yet the problem with Tom is the way in which we (as the public and as the parents) cut out of his distinguished professional life something of great importance to him, about him, and of direct relevance to students and the general task of education. We deny his students the opportunities of discussing the issues openly with him, and we force him to dissemble. In the classroom he is not himself.

To say that a person has integrity usually conveys that we think he or she is honest, a good moral sort. One particular form of moral integrity is of great importance in teaching. It is where we speak of a person having a coherence, a wholeness, about everything that he or she does or believes. The role of teaching makes particular kinds of demands on men and women, and they can be faced with all manner of dissonances and conflicts between what the role demands and what they believe.

Integrity is the relationship between a person and his or her acts (Winch, 1968). A person becomes attached to one, perhaps several forms of life. It is as if he or she is heir to particular traditions. These are not mere lifestyles, in the sense that Bellah and colleagues (1985) define, but ways of living filled with moral and other norms. We retain our integrity by having different parts of our life in harmony. Sometimes, perhaps often, there are conflicts between such traditions, or we are unfaithful to them, or we are not true to ourselves. We let our commitments and ideals slip away. We lose our altruism. We then have to face up to the question—am I the sort of person who would do this? Each of us has to face the question of who we are.

In Tom's case the clash is between a personal belief and a role. It is not a clash that will make any sense to someone outside a moral tradition of some kind. So this issue of moral integrity will not make much sense to teachers who do not see their own moral agency as significant in their lives or in their profession, teachers who regard themselves as just pushed around by the law and social convention and unable to act in an *in loco parentis* role. The dilemma of integrity is raised whenever a person finds him- or herself doing things of importance in the role of teacher that are in conflict with his or her private beliefs. Tom's case originates in his religious beliefs—and there are all manner of examples of that in teaching. There are those who are intolerant of the nonreligious world, and they may find themselves impossibly constrained by the challenge of promoting a nonreligious view of the world in classrooms. There are also religious teachers—Muslims, for example—whose religious beliefs include attitudes toward sex, gender, and the family that are not widespread outside the major countries of Islam; but if they become teachers in public schools, they have to accept secular laws that do not embody those religious or cultural beliefs. Issues of integrity arise in many secular contexts, too, for example, in a teacher's sexual orientation and lifestyle. Does it compromise the integrity of a gay person that he or she may be obliged not to model that lifestyle in school situations where the heterosexual norm predominates? These dramatic cases cover what is, I suspect, the most common dilemma of integrity for the teacher—the extent to which he or she compromises his or her educational beliefs and ideals.

Institutions, as much as individuals, may themselves lack integrity, especially if members do not invest them with their own ideals and values and fight for what they believe in. But institutional integrity is not like institutional central heating. It is the sum of, and the interplay between, the ideals and commitments of the actors within it. An institution will lack integrity if it has flawed actors or if it has individuals within it whose sense of self-interest defines their view of their institution. The most visible test of that integrity is the extent to which institutions trust their members, are loyal and committed to them, and receive in return loyalty and commitment to the institution's ideals and mission. To ensure that starry-eyed state, consistent opportunity for debate on ideals and their effect on policy must be built into the institutional fabric. In universities in particular the need for constant negotiation and discussion about the institution's character is critical for its intellectual integrity if there is to be any reconciliation between radical and conservative perspectives.

Institutions can be especially let down by individuals who get accustomed to pragmatic accommodation rather than putting their ideals into practical form. This is true particularly of educational managers who see themselves as powerbrokers, not transformational moral leaders. This sounds excessively high-minded, or simply moralistic, for there are often good reasons for not pursuing an ideal right now—the mortgage, the kids, the spouse, even that I will live to fight another day. Moreover, institutions each have political realities that are sometimes very harsh. We all must judge between what would be best or ideal to achieve and what, as a matter of pragmatic fact, is actually achievable. We must do so in a living political context. In Ibsen's play *The Wild Duck*, Gregers, a moral purist *par excellence*, destroys a family out of an excessive commitment to having people face the truth about themselves. Such moral fanatics can be excessively dangerous.

Yet pragmatic accommodation becomes an easy habit. It is not necessarily the way to preserve one's integrity or to advance one's personal and professional ideals. It may be pernicious. Such accommodation is expressed in Reinhold Neibuhr's prayer, "God grant me the serenity to accept the things I cannot change, the courage to change the things I can, and the wisdom to know the difference," the popularity of which may be due more

to its cadences than its content. Secularized out of the context of the religious belief within which it is located—as many a plaque exemplifies—this
nostrum has gained enough popularity for it to be worth examination as a
piece of advice, as it is a statement of what a person's integrity is.

How does it look? First, we most often do not know what is possible
to change until we try. The difference between what is and what is not
changeable is never clear. A small group of people gathered in a square in
Leipzig in 1990 to protest the government. Within a month, a well-established political regime of 45 years standing collapsed in ruins. Second, the
advice is socially conservative, contrasting with the fervor of such radicals
as Gandhi, Jesus of Nazareth, or Karl Marx, for whom this kind of serenity was just the problem—that people of goodwill can and do allow great
wrong to continue. Third, it offers a rationale, or at least an excuse, for
doing nothing. The fatalism of accepting things I cannot change brings a
strange kind of serenity. I cannot today prevent children in American
cities from bringing guns into school and killing one another but, even if
I am smug, complacent, or self-satisfied, I cannot be serene about that. I
ought to be angry and be doing something, not simply accepting no change.

The prayer is also strikingly individualist, even self-centered, in that it
roots the individual as private (and with a contract with God), not in the
thrall of moral imperatives, principles, virtues, or ideals. It goes for com-
fort, not challenge. Taking it as a guide to life, Tom could "serenely" accept
that he had no authority or moral right to have his students examine the
pacifist viewpoint. Mrs. Simpson could "serenely" accept that Louise would
continue to be distressed by her parents' beliefs. This prayer translates
issues of potentially deep moral conflict into matters of judgment as to their
changeability. If we cannot change something then we can just accept it,
confident that we have been wise in making the judgment about what is or
is not changeable. At bottom what Neibuhr offers to the secular mind is a
lowest common denominator of moral integrity, because the possible range
of our acts need make no moral demands on us. It is also, of course, an
excellent motto for political appeasement.

The problem with pragmatic accommodation to the powers that be
in any context is its cumulative effect, as Goodlad (1990) has pointed out
in the context of transactional leadership of colleges of education. To stand
up for what one believes, even to state one's views, can be a daunting pros-
pect when one arrives in a new workplace, and the less often one contributes in this way, the more difficult it becomes. Hierarchical management
of institutions, poverty-stricken in-service programs, workloads that prevent
thought are among the institutional factors that impede both the articulation and the development and sophistication of the educational beliefs of
individual teachers.

What any teacher role requires as an ideal is people who are able and willing to stand up for their beliefs, since educational values and respect for learners and learning are not acknowledged as universal goods. If personal integrity is made impossible—that is, if a person cannot as a teacher reconcile personal with professional values—it is difficult to see how we can get a cogent sense of a moral role. *In loco parentis* as a conception locates that broad responsibility and can be seen thereby as an ideal role for the teacher.

In Loco Parentis

The responsibilities of the teacher have been implicit throughout this book. Professionalism has been defined as quality expressed in a complex moral role. In this chapter on the broad function of ideals in the development of a profession, I have concentrated on one of these ideals, namely what is the ideal role for the teacher. I have used three issues—teacher–student relations, parents and choice, and individual integrity—to show how wide-ranging are the considerations influencing our conversations on ideals.

Specifically, we are left with the determination of a role in which (1) a teacher is bound to act morally as a person with the interests of the whole child at heart without being expert on all specialist matters, (2) that broad role is constructed through a depth of trust between teacher, child, and parent, (3) the teacher has complete integrity in the fit between personal and professional values to fulfill this role, and (4) the teacher and the institution create institutional frameworks for the exercise of that role. These characteristics of a teacher's role cannot be pursued through a framework of due process, which is an implicit recognition of a lack of trust. An *in loco parentis* role is not therefore literal. It describes attitudes, motivations, and commitments that would constitute an ideal role for the teacher.

It is unlikely that my discussion of this view of the ideal role of the teacher through the three areas in which I have located the issues will be convincing. On reading this, teachers will seize on some issues as highly disputable and others as less so. *That is precisely what conversations about ideals embody.* They are continuously debatable. They can function in a person's life as a guide or a sustenance. They can be learned and debated as we learn to practice our role, and they form a conversation around the bedrock of the social practice of teaching. Discussing ideals is, I believe, an important form of moral conversation with a quite distinct place in our moral language. We need to recapture that kind of conversation, even though we may find it rather embarrassing at first to engage in such controversial and personal issues. But we will soon get used to it.

CHAPTER 8

Transforming Education through Teacher Professionalism

I have presented a broad vision of teacher professionalism that links the professional role of the generic teacher, the men and women who occupy it, the moral demands it makes, and the practical arts of teaching to the institution of education. My focus on the quality of practice has provided the conceptual and moral apparatus for this endeavor. In this concluding chapter, I describe ways in which this account of professionalism fits into the transformation of public education.

I have criticized many of our present practical arrangements in educational institutions as inadequate, among which are the split profession, the absence of a career conception, modes of teacher education dependent on outmoded circumstances, the lack of serious attention to the preeminence of the moral, a system that demands industrialized forms of accountability, and the absence of a professional conversation about ultimate purposes. I am, however, even more profoundly disenchanted with the inertia of educational institutions in dealing with overwhelming problems, even though in Boston (Greer, 1990) and Chicago (Hess, 1990) there are different responses and initiatives. We are, I believe, at the end of an era in the adventure of public education. It will disappear if we do not alter it drastically (Finn, 1991; Kearns, 1988; National Commission on Excellence in Education, 1983).

SOCIAL AND EDUCATIONAL CHANGES

Attendance and access has so far been delivered for all children (Graham, 1991), and the development of the world's economy, inventions, and discoveries in this century would have been impossible without the ingenuity of the educated. The success of the United States has, however, left a legacy of problems, constituting challenges to public education and the political and social order.

Decreasing Wealth

P. Kennedy (1987) has described the United States as suffering from the attempt to maintain military preeminence in order to protect its economic power and influence while simultaneously undermining its economic preeminence by that very commitment. The political will to maintain such preeminence relies, in a democratic society, on a politically passive educational system. When, as with Vietnam, educational institutions become active, the political will can be severely tested. The changes that follow such loss of economic power for a society are invariably harsh. Industry and commerce, used to affluence, are forced to undertake structural reforms, such as downsizing or relocating factories in countries where labor is much cheaper. Educational crises are then intensified in the need to find job-related education for the unemployed poor—as well as for the middle class, for whom current models provide no relevant employment either (National Center on Education and the Economy, 1990).

A Crisis of Identity

Adjustment to loss of international strength often means a loss of national purpose and identity. Victory in the Cold War may make Americans proud, but it may also make them poorer. Such national crises of identity have followed the eclipse of all major imperial powers, and they often induce political volatility. Political assertion of "world power" rings increasingly hollow in the face of constrained domestic economic circumstances, and people and parties are split between the realistic and the nostalgic. In this context, education for responsible citizenship is a necessity, but it demands hard-nosed appraisal of political and economic realities, which is very difficult for an education system gone intellectually and politically soft. It also becomes necessary to accept interdependence as politically and economically desirable, which presents to educators the challenge of giving young Americans a sense of their global citizenship.

National and Global Changes

The rise in the economic power of the Pacific Rim countries, with their apparently stable family patterns, contrasts markedly with the economic position of the United States, with its complexity of multicultural and ethnically diverse patterns. Many industrial societies are also experiencing a period of major social change in living circumstances (Elkind, 1984), in the family, in familiar problems in inner cities (Kozol, 1991), and in the gradual but steady rise of poverty (Hodgkinson, 1991), but these are particularly marked in the United States, which has continued to absorb ethnically diverse immigrant populations even in an economic recession. The educator faces intractable problems of multiculturalism and multilingualism. The social context makes it almost impossible for the society to view such multilingualism as a huge resource and opportunity both to train Americans to speak a second language and to enable them to take advantage of the global marketplace.

The Premium on Knowledge

Advanced economies of the world are well into the process of an industrial revolution in which human knowledge and ingenuity have replaced human labor as the primary commodity needed for wealth, manufacturing, or even service. We face the explosion of what is called a knowledge-driven society. High-tech industry is fast replacing traditional, mass-production, smokestack industry. Increasingly, sophisticated and complex knowledge is required from everyone in a democratic society if they are to contribute to social well-being through productive employment.

Decreasing wealth exacerbates the problems of relevant vocational education. The crisis of national identity heightens the need for realistic education in responsible citizenship. National and global changes seem to leave us with a sense of the multicultural society as a source of further problems of poverty rather than as a rich educational opportunity. The acceleration of knowledge makes our educational institutions increasingly weak agencies to provide individuals with access to positional goods. Public education is inevitably enmeshed with each challenge and is thereby part of the problem, not the solution, primarily because its institutions are insufficiently dynamic. That is not to blame teachers, schools, school boards, superintendents, or parents, but to recognize that we share it as a national responsibility. We need to recognize the challenge of the future and define it properly. While our schools and colleges may be doing better than ever (Bracey, 1991), that is simply not enough.

THE CHALLENGE OF EDUCATIONAL TRANSFORMATION

To meet these challenges, nothing less than the total transformation of public education is needed. We need a radical reshaping of our public and private attitudes, beliefs, and commitments, and that change must be rooted in the perceptions and practices of teachers. A comparison across the previous centuries makes the central point. In the nineteenth century, public schools were the institutions assigned the responsibility for socializing and for custodial purposes. In the twentieth century, knowledge has exploded and the diversity of social breakdown has become intense—poverty, the inner cities, family disruption. In the twenty-first century, facing contemporary global economy and the problems inherited from the previous century, the knowledge children require cannot be delivered by schools *alone*.

Transformation therefore demands the construction of new forms of mass public education through new partnerships—structurally integrated to ensure multidimensional approaches—between schools and other public and private institutions, with new roles for adults, new approaches to the problems, new systems, new conceptions of the products of learning, and drastically new educational experiences for children (Institute for Educational Transformation, 1992).

Transformation is the *process* of developing these structurally integrated partnerships between schools and other public and private institutions for the delivery of public education. It demands a shift of focus from institutions to individuals—whether they be adult teachers (as has been suggested in this book), children, undergraduates, or the many other categories of learner. Transformation presages the development of new institutions to replace the concept of school, its buildings, habits, and images. This process may take two or more decades, and it cannot be established within our current social institutions.

This represents a huge agenda, and I can here elaborate only on one part of it. What happens to the teacher as moral professional in an age of transformation?

The Conceptual Transformation

The pervasiveness of the moral in our thought and practice about education heralds a conceptual transformation whereby moral language will become the language of teaching. That may initially de-skill us—to use that quaint psychological phrase—because we have an undeveloped moral vocabulary in teaching because we have not used it. Elizabeth Beck, for example, will begin to write in detail about the problems of classroom order in terms of how children respect one another and to understand her own thinking about them, and her relationship with Mrs. Old, as a complex moral relationship. If we are serious about the centrality of moral discourse in teaching, then we have to realize the profound character of that as a transformative task and not be deflected by psychological talk (e.g., about how the brain works) as a basis for strategy.

A person is morally responsible for what he or she does. We will see that installed within teaching, giving us a role with autonomy and responsibility. It will apply to how we see ourselves, as individuals with a professional life and career, and the transformation will have a major effect on our present frameworks, specifically in teacher education. Mrs. Simpson will come to see herself as empowered or emancipated, not as a pawn of the bureaucracy. However, no longer can Mrs. Simpson stand alone in her classroom. The huge complexity of contemporary education means that partnership, collegiality, and team work will be essential to the work of public education.

Perhaps the most dramatic conceptual transformation will appear in the concept of the teacher. It may be necessary to redefine the role of teacher-as-partner—in perhaps the same way as the word *wife* conceptually implies a partnership. *The teacher-isolate will be rejected as identifying the concept of the teacher.* The conceptual transformation needed thus means a switch to moral discourse as the primary language of teaching—as has been argued for in this book—and within it, that the concept of the teacher become that of an autonomous and responsible agent working in partnership with others.

Transformation and Reflective Practice

Part of the teacher's intellectual task is to understand forms of systematic inquiry—teacher-research—because that is the primary way to continuously improve practice (Hollingsworth & Sockett, in press). The composition of a career does not rest in officially sponsored professional development programs for the individual teacher. Each teacher therefore will work as a reflective practitioner, with partners and within a team in order to develop and enhance the skills of sophisticated reflection. Activities that exemplify that process, often in partnership, will include:

1. The search for the continuous improvement of our practical wisdom within a developed conception of professional expertise, as modeled by Elizabeth Beck
2. The development of the skills and insights of moral dialogue, as Mrs. Simpson has perfected with her young children
3. Determined mutual reflection on the moral character of our practice, for example, how we distribute time and attention, how we encourage and discourage children, how we handle problems of honesty and deceit, how we work with individuals with care
4. Reflection on our professional ideals, for example, the extent to which we are rigorous, imaginative, and creative, as is apparent in the work of Elizabeth Beck and—unsystematically—Tom Stevenson

5. The establishment, development, and testing of morally innovative pedagogical stances, for example, what it means to work as a coach (Schön,
   1983) or a neutral chairperson (Stenhouse, 1970)
6. A systematic and continuing examintion of the actions and responsibilities of being moral or ethical models for students (Ryan, 1987)
7. Responsiveness to "quality of practice" assessment, which will deliver
   individual and team accountability while demonstrating professional
   expertise

Elizabeth Beck was being trained in reflective practice and in the systematic examination of her own classroom. Tom and Mrs. Simpson are intelligent, thoughtful teachers, but they do not undertake the kind of rigorous self-inquiry manifest by Elizabeth. *Reflective practice* is a paradigm for educational transformation. It produces knowledge of practice. It identifies strength and weakness and is therefore central to improvement. It requires moral commitment and intellectual rigor. It creates a culture of learning in institutions. It undermines the routinization tendencies in teaching. It supports professional autonomy. It cannot be taught by those who do not do it. It can change the relationships with students if it is made a self-conscious exercise. Above all, if it is systematic, it is a form of moral self-education that will enhance the person.

Collegial Partnerships and Teams

Although the word *team* has strong overtones of games, it is this partnership of autonomous individuals that will define our work in institutions. For teachers, student teachers, and leaders across the profession, a transformed system will make new moral demands. These demands will be made, not on the individual per se, but on individuals in teams and in groups. Partnership and collaboration will cover every aspect of our individual and institutional endeavors—with our colleagues, with other educational institutions, and with business and the community as yet outside the education network (Bracey, 1990; Parish, Underwood, & Eubanks, 1986–87; Pine & Keane, 1990).

There are many familiar ways of breaking down professional isolation in classrooms or seminar rooms—by developing collaborative habits in novices, by installing mentorships in teaching on a one-to-one basis, and by collaborative projects such as are promoted in teacher-research. Joint appointments and joint activities will be promoted across institutions, for example, in professional development schools and in university-supported, in-service, school-based programs. Extensive frameworks for reflective discussion, which draw individuals from diverse professional roles, easily create professional dialogue and conversation. These examples show that we can create a unified profession, but what follows for the professional practitioner as a team member?

Professional teams of teachers are likely to offer very different strengths and educational styles, philosophies, and patterns linked to other professions (and to communities and parents). I have indicated the need for a professional community (see Chapter 2), but we need to look at what should distinguish a collegial team of professional teachers. The character of collegiality is dependent on the institution. It takes different forms in a law practice, a convent, or an officers' club.

It is also different in a corporation and a republic. Emphasis on hierarchy in schools (as in a stereotypical corporation) seems to have alienated the professionals, developed a sense of dependence on administrators, undermined autonomy, and restricted initiative. Emphasis on self-government by committee in universities (as in a model republic) has produced coalitions of self-interest and elaborate structures for the defense of private interests masquerading as the defense of academic freedom, as well as institutional conservatism and paralysis in the face of needed change. Emphasis on structured teamwork is not institutionally rare, nor is it a commonplace in either of these institutional types. It can be found, for example, in a research team in a university, in a school department, or in a grade-level group. However, a team is minimally marked by shared goals, shared decision-making, and mutual respect. Its character is specific to the institution. Neither the stereotypical corporation nor the republic are effective engines of transformative change.

Team collegiality in an educational institution—the school, the university, or the college—is appropriate because, transformed, it is a place where *everybody* defines themselves as a learner. Such an institutional framework and culture are needed to promote an enriched professional role. The necessity for such a team derives from the nature of knowledge and the epistemology of practice I have described (see Chapter 5). Organizational features needed include time built in for reflective discussions, extensive mutual examinations of the work students do, and collaborative teaching.

New understandings will be developed—of nonhierarchical leadership, of how teams can be constructed and consistently reinvigorated, and of how administration can be constructed as a force for enabling and supporting professionals congruent with efficiency and commitment. Collegiality within the community will also be redefined, using such enterprises as the professional development school (academic–practitioner partnerships) and site-based management (practitioner–administrator partnerships) to construct new models. In particular, different learning formats for professionals will provide more sophisticated forms of course evaluation, unlike current university programs, which see evaluation not as a learning process but as a mere report.

In particular we will develop a transformed system through legitimizing different kinds of teams. For example, teachers may work formally as partners, contracting themselves out for hire by the public, much as a legal firm might do. Such a team might also expand to include a range of tutors from business or the community. A high school department, a middle school team, or a grade-level team in an elementary school is such a team—with two outstanding differences. Members do not usually choose the other members of the team, and they do not function as a corporation, making their own full decisions. Rather, they are treated simply as employees. Both of those differences can be removed. If we begin to view teachers as morally and professionally autonomous, that will invite new forms of employment and new legal forms of organization. Whatever the internal relations to a school, however, interinstitutional partnerships are essential to a transformed system.

Interinstitutional Partnerships

Marriage is a classic example of institutionalized partnership. For it to work, people at least have to subject themselves to purposes held in common with another, because partnership demands radically changing one's own activities for a common purpose in the light of appropriate analysis and evaluation. The goal of working with business and the professions has emerged in education not just because of concern about children's measured learning achievements, but also because of this recognition that the complexity of social life and the knowledge explosion have made it impossible for schools to deliver what the public requires of its schools. (See Chapter 2 for a discussion of Sirotnik's advocacy of a fusion between university and school.) Partnership requires not just token representation on a board that has an executive core, but also practical activity of mutual benefit. In education the character of partnership can be captured as being at four levels:

1. *General-marginal*: Business supports general activities that are marginal to the school's mission, for example, the "adopt-a-school" activity.
2. *Specific-marginal*: Business funds or supports activities that are jointly run and curricular, but still marginal. For example, vocational education students build a house with their teachers and with business participation, then sell it.

3. *Mainstream-central*: Business supports a jointly run, mainstream activity. For example, scientists and engineers join teachers in the reconstruction and teaching of a physics curriculum.
4. *Transformative-central*: A level of transformation of partners is brought about through the partnership. For instance, when a business itself seeks the partnership of education in its activities as a learning corporation, it is also transformed by its educational responsibilities through supporting school teachers and running a program on its time and on its premises for its workers who are parents.

One could, I suppose, evaluate marriages on these criteria. Certainly the same category levels apply to the relationship between schools and universities, including colleges of education. The teaching of student teachers, for example, has for years been a level-2 activity—specific-marginal for a school. Professional development schools are certainly at level 3 (mainstream-central). Whether they will reach level 4 and transform the college or university, as well as the school, remains to be seen. The proposal for a school-based master's degree (see Chapter 3) will emerge as Level 4, changing both school and university, particularly through the characteristics of team recruitment and partnership evaluation. A similar kind of analysis could be made of businesses and university schools of business, or of hospitals and volunteer organizations. Self-conscious examination of the transformation through partnership requires this kind of analytic frame for examining the problem.

Transforming the Individual's Relations with the System

Why do school districts so naturally appear as hierarchies, not partnerships? We have seen the development in recent years of a grossly adversarial relationship between educational government and educational institutions, built on accountability systems long since out of fashion in industry and commerce. It would seem natural, especially where a school district is coincidental with a genuine community, for the educational enterprise to be communitarian and cooperative. Teachers' unions and school boards, with politicians of all colors, have made governance as significant a problem as test scores, if less publicly visible.

In a transformed system, however, institutions will be built for individuals, not the other way round. The primary individual, of course, is the client or the consumer—the child for whom the enterprise is designed. However, within such institutions, understanding the careers and lives of teachers, as well as the educational needs of the clients, will also contribute to the construction of the institutions needed. Putting to one side matters of how to create the kind of community fabric necessary for governance reform, a teacher composing a career in such a transformed system should expect the following:

1. A system (including individual schools, professional organizations, and universities) will have a coherent conception of a career upon which it will make practically sensible decisions about teacher growth and development and provide programs for them. The career conception will be built through an extensive partnership with relevant groups and individuals, particularly with a sense of such issues as gender (Hollingsworth, 1992; Laird, 1988)
2. Each novice and each practicing teacher in a university, college, or school will have the opportunity and the guidance to frame the development of his or her own career with such a model and will be helped to realize his or her ability to compose it.
3. The system will provide each professional with a mentor—not a supervisor—whose task will be to assist in the individual's relationship to one or more elements of this career framework *as a permanent feature of employment.* Individuals will choose their own mentors.
4. Individuals will negotiate their own career development, using such ideas as "creativity contracts" (Boyer, 1990), which combine contractual commitment with monitoring of one's own professional growth. Much greater individual autonomy and responsibility, as well as a continuing sense of profoundly important purpose, will be valued and expected. Jaime Escalante, as we have seen, fought for and got that kind of autonomy and responsibility.
5. Individuals will accept responsibility for a system's program and evaluate it against a career framework (see the model suggested in Chapter 2), for the professional development of all of us is our responsibility as much as that of our employers. Careers that demand specialization—for example, content (special education), administration (principal, superintendent, dean), or research (research faculty)—will be seen as branches out from that career framework that individuals can be encouraged to try.

No coherent blueprint can be developed for a system of governance. Different systems need to be constructed that reconcile the public's need for accountability with the professional's autonomy.

The Task of Transformational Educational Leadership

Questions in the ethics of educational leadership speak to the moral character of such leaders, the moral ethos they create or sustain in an institution, the moral quality of their leadership, and the moral efficacy of the means they use to realize or to achieve the educational ends in view. Goodlad (1990) distinguishes a transformational from a transactional leader. The transactional leader is a "pragmatic power broker who seeks to convince workers that their needs will be met if and when the organization's needs are met" (p. 138). The transformational leader, however, draws out and improves on the best in his or her followers, creating a "relationship of mutual stimulation and education that converts followers into leaders and might convert leaders into moral agents" (p. 139). However, in the modern university, we have an ethos that is neither hierarchically bureaucratic (the case in most schools) nor transformationally democratic.

Goodlad believes transformative leadership can succeeed because, as with Lortie's (1975) account of schoolteachers, he finds deep commitment among teacher-education faculty to the cause of improving schools, even though that commitment seems at odds with the rhetoric and the official culture of many of the institutions. For realization of the promise in this data, he concludes, what is needed are "unusually charismatic, transforming leaders capable of sensing the nature of the moral imperatives stemming from responsibilities outside of the university and reducing ambiguity, increasing predictability and providing direction on the inside" (Goodlad, 1990, p. 142). These are people of moral virtue, undoubted courage, and the ability to live and work within a continuously moral frame of reference.

The increasing interest of business and businesspeople in education is benevolent, concerned, and appropriately partly self-interested. Educators have much to learn from innovative management and leadership practices in business. One such philosophy is variously labeled "total quality management" or "continuous process of improvement." It has several proponents, the most distinguished of whom is W. Edwards Deming, and a range of educational exponents (M. Walton, 1991). This management practice contains an ethically significant strategy for would-be transformative leadership that reveals moral imperatives in defining the ethical responsibilities of the transformative leader. As Marchese (1991) describes Deming's fourteen points, they are less a set of management tools framed in a new orthodoxy and more a call to leadership for the reform of American enterprise. Its five salient features are critically relevant to educational leadership:

1. A total focus on quality, not just in rhetoric or mission statements but pervading the organization as a mindset and built into strategic planning
2. A determination to be customer-driven, that is, explicit identification of the customers and their needs and a profound commitment to meeting those needs

intellectual resistance to that influence imposes a particular responsibility on teachers for making tough-minded demands on children, as well as for the right ordering of the beliefs they express as professionals (Quinton, 1987). Tom, Escalante, and John Keating manifest this, but its wider importance to a democracy is obvious. Freedom and being a free person depend on challenging what is received and being dogged in the pursuit of truth (Peters, 1979b). The instrumental importance of rigor in a knowledge-driven society is, of course, essential, if the knowledge is to be worth anything.

To achieve this capacity for rigor, students will continuously practice it. They will be helped to challenge received wisdom by teachers rather than search for what works or for the A grade. They will experience stimulation, intellectual provocation, and challenge. The demeaning notion that students should "feel good about themselves" will disappear, for there is nothing to feel good about if you have an educational experience that develops in you a mind like Donald Duck's, a body like Humpty Dumpty's, and a character like Bugs Bunny's. The pursuit of rigor and the determination to struggle with difficulty is an important way to get self-respect and a critical mind able to confront educational and social challenge. If student teachers do not become adults with critical minds, they can never provide an example to those they teach. They will also never become the free people on which democracy depends (White, 1986) and for which, as teachers, they carry a special responsibility.

Caring and connectedness. Yet the transformed system will find ways to create caring, not custodial, educational institutions. Thus the dialogues student teachers have with one another and with their clients especially parents or care-givers will be framed within a ethic of caring and connectedness. The danger to be avoided is that of seeing such dialogues as akin to exercises in salesmanship, where trust is manipulated into existence, not built up into a sensitive mutual awareness of wants and concerns. These skills are valuable only as techniques within a wider moral purpose—that of helping parents or others reach an accommodation with the school on what is best for the child (see Chapter 4)—if they can communicate the affective side of caring without sentiment.

Gender and race. Gender and race will be pervasive and primary topics in teacher education, primarily because we gain our individual identity in part through our gender and our race and because our society is going to become increasingly multiethnic. Students intending to teach should mutually come to terms with other races and the other gender, for our moral personhood is not an abstraction. It can only be coherently understood

3. A commitment to continuous improvement that entails a finely tuned focus on every aspect of the organization, but specifically the service or the product, disciplined by data and by detailed, up-to-date, relevant (often statistical) information
4. Across all activities and levels, shared responsibility through teamwork, which implies driving out fear from the organization and empowering individuals, especially through massive and continuous retraining and education as a corporate priority
5. Leadership that provides vision, listens, enables people-driven improvement, and is avid but patient for long-term ends

Quality is embedded in everything in the institution—the relationships, the destruction of built-in biases (of gender or race), the commitment, the productivity, the time taken to develop innovations, the planning, and so forth. The ethical responsibility of the transformative leader is to nurture a sense of quality and to accept nothing but the best, among which is a sense of social conscience. Transformative leaders also have to develop a sense of the institutions' customers. In education, defining our customer—the individual child—demands asking ourselves how children appear in the fabric of our institutions, how institutional judgments are seriously influenced by children, and how responsive teacher-educators are to students (also partly customers) such that they will conceive their responsibilities to colleagues and children in morally sensitive ways. An additional task for the transformative leader is how to install a culture of improvement, not merely continue a culture in which repetition of existing standards is seen as good enough. To do this effectively means accepting that failure is a norm to be attended to and that continuous improvement as an educational practice could wreak havoc with our stilted forms of evaluation.

This notion of leadership is not a matter of manipulative skill. It translates as the following moral imperatives, to which virtuous transformative leaders will adhere:

1. Promote a sense of commitment to top quality as a moral mindset and a moral attitude.
2. Create a framework and a substance wherein continuous improvement is a goal and an obligation, and ensure that the process is driven by information, not prejudice.
3. Develop a sense of mutual obligation, trust, and care through teamwork, and foster an accepted responsibility for the well-being of the institution.

Such terms as *quality, improvement, obligation, trust, care* and *teamwork* within a moral frame reflect the depth of the conceptual transformation into moral understanding of the work of individuals.

Transformation in Teacher Education

If the transformed system were to be effective in abandoning teaching framed entirely through the constructs and concepts of psychology, the task for teacher education would become considerable—specifically in respect to the development of moral commitment and motivation to teach, the moral climate, the intellectual climate, caring and connectedness, and issues of gender and race.

Commitment, motivation, and moral climate.   Where will teacher-education students get a professional moral education (Ryan, 1987; Beyer, 1991)? The following broad principles seem central:

1. Pre-service students will be given consistent opportunities to face self-consciously their motivation for teaching—in the privacy of tutorial rooms and in the public arena of the seminar.
2. Students will not be judged exclusively on classroom performance as the initial part of the professional warrant.
3. Students will examine themselves in terms of their openness to their own classes, their ability to discuss frankly the conduct and direction of their teaching, their style expressed in particular lessons, and their wish to spend their professional lives in the company of young people.
4. Young teachers will be helped to see their professional career as one demanding continual and consistent advice, support, and critical appraisal from others; in particular, they will be helped to value that critique.

Express concern with moral issues in moral language will be central. Student teachers should develop the sense of the importance of collegial support but also of being someone who can create a sense of trust. That may be through force of personality, but it is also manifest in behavioral traits such as consistency in carrying out what is expressly said, punctuality, patience, and much more. A student keeps his or her word, not simply where a promise is made to a class, but in the minutiae of commitments, for on that basis of classroom and professional habit, the other elements of fidelity, care, and friendliness may be built. Experience in sharing self-critique is an endeavor that creates trust and fidelity. Without developing such professional sensibilities, as opposed to competencies, they will not acquire the initial professional motivational requirement.

This is the motivational side of an ethical matter. The problem, as indicated by Lortie (1975), is that "socialization into teaching is largely self-

socialization: one's personal predispositions are not only relevant, b fact, stand at the core of becoming a teacher" (p. 79). Individual idiosyr has to be examined. The wisdom of an individual's choice of a profe as well as the fit between the demands of the job and a person's di tion, (Williams, 1987), temperament, personality, and competence, r considered judgments of what individuals want, what they are capal and what is *worth* wanting (see Chapter 7). Teacher education in effect contexts that highlight the moral cast of the person beneath the s act. As Kogan (1986) puts it, "a teacher develops standards of appro behavior and of teaching performance as a product of both innate propensities and through education and socialization which are ex forms of influence" (p. 31). But can teacher education programs p us with knowledge of what an Elizabeth Beck will be like as a colleag her "innate moral propensities"? As things stand, probably not. In the moral context of a reshaped teacher education, perhaps.

For the practicing teacher, the context of teacher education is pr nantly within the workplace. For the pre-service teacher, both scho university are the locus for learning to teach. The moral climate of institutions, which is shaped by curriculum and the example offe teacher-educators, is important in respect to professional tasks and r sibilities.

The intellectual climate of teacher education.   The emphasis on the throughout this book may be misinterpreted as an emphasis on h feel about one another. While our emotions are of immense importa our moral behavior (Peters, 1979b), we must have the intellectual ness for moral argument if we are to be morally educated. American schools (and teacher education) seem anti-intellectual to some (Fi Ravitch, 1987). Children of all ages do not seem to be engaged in tling with ideas. Far too much is mediated through the textbook (T 1988). "Rigor" approaches dangerously close to the rigor of a game of Pursuit, and the anti-intellectual character of many tests, rooted as tl in psychological constructs, may be the cause (Madaus, 1988). Som it seems as if people believe that a concert consists of a violinist d strating his skill rather than actually playing music, or that the musicianship lies in the ability to play scales.

Intellectual rigor demands the pursuit of ideas for their own s; a way of life. A teacher and a student can pursue the truth of the r rather than simply receive it. However, such elements as tests, the climate, the school's expectations, and much else can combine to n easy for a teacher to tolerate lack of rigor. The combination of insti alized power a teacher has together with the students' lack of resour

within the physical reality of our gender and our race, which can give us a moral equilibrium in respect of ourselves. Detailed analysis of and engagement with these matters demand moral understanding, for both genders and all races. Given the pervasive character of sexism and racism in our society, the development of morally appropriate relationships with colleagues, students, parents, and the community is integral to a teacher's own self-development as a morally autonomous and unprejudiced individual, even though we know that our upbringing, whatever our ethnic identity, will leave us with vestigial and real prejudices. *Our present arrangements for the moral education of teachers seem to assume the absence of prejudice rather than its pervasiveness, and we lack a moral pedagogy that will enable us to deal with it.* One great advantage of a self-acknowledged feminist pedagogy (Hollingsworth, 1992) is that it liberates all students and teachers to discuss gender.

CONCLUSION

The goal of transformation, then, is a root and branch change in our professionalism and in ourselves. I am engaged, with many others, in continuous experiment to improve teacher professionalism by seeking to develop for educators new roles, new products, new systems, new approaches, and new experiences.

I seem to work in two modes. One may be described as a kind of institutional entrepreneurship, where I spend time working with business-people or administrators about how we build partnerships by creating networks for all kinds of different relationships. My focus in this part of my life is on such questions as:

1. How can politicians and bureaucrats be persuaded to break up the constraints impeding teacher creativity?
2. What kinds of self-interest for noneducational organizations are legitimate in the promotion of partnerships?
3. What systems of community governance of schools would promote education?

The other is a reflective but practical teaching and writing mode, where I seek to frame the context and its predicament for myself. For example, I have become concerned with these problems:

1. How can we restore the *in loco parentis* conception?
2. What changes would make the custodial institution where I teach a properly caring institution?

3. How can we face up to our own race and gender prejudices, beginning in our own workplaces?

These two parts of my professional life work, I think, in unison, although I am daunted by what I see as the challenges to our professionalism in public education. But it is crucial that we do not allow ourselves to be defeated by them. That means that individual educators must take urgent action to discard many of our traditions; to open up ourselves and our institutions to authentic partnerships, and to define ourselves—whatever our status—as part of a common professional enterprise. As we do this, we will find four primary themes at the core of our discussions: what our community is, what our expertise is, what the nature of our accountability is, and what the ultimate purposes that govern us are. These are the foundation themes for the moral professional. Our serious engagement with them cannot wait.

References

American Psychological Association. (1983). *Ethical guidelines for the teaching of psychology in the secondary school*. Washington, DC: Author.

American Sociological Association. (1984). *Code of ethics*. Washington, DC: Author.

Arnstine, B. (1990). Rational and caring teachers: Reconstructing teacher preparation. *Teachers College Record*, 92(2), 230–248.

Bailey, C. H. (1984). *Beyond the present and the particular: A theory of liberal education*. London: Routledge & Kegan Paul.

Barrow, R. (1982). *Injustice, inequality and ethics*. Brighton, England: Wheatsheaf.

Barry, B. (1965). *The liberal theory of justice*. Oxford, England: Oxford University Press.

Barry, B. (1973). *Political argument*. London: Routledge & Kegan Paul.

Barth, R. (1988). School: A community of leaders. In A. Lieberman (Ed.), *Building a professional culture in schools* (pp. 129–148). New York: Teachers College Press.

Bateson, C. M. (1989). *Composing a life*. New York: Plume.

Becher, R. A., Eraut, M. J., & Knight, J. (1979). *Policies for educational accountability*. London: Heinemann.

Belenky, M. F., Clinchy, B. M., Goldberger, N. R., & Tarule, J. M. (1986). *Women's ways of knowing*. New York: Basic Books.

Bell, D. (1973). *The coming of the post-industrial society*. New York: Basic Books.

Bellah, R. N., Madsen, R., Sullivan, W. M., Swidler, A., & Tipton, S. M. (1985). *Habits of the heart*. New York: Harper & Row.

Bennett, J. (1964). *Rationality*. London: Routledge & Kegan Paul.

Bettelheim, B. (1977). *The uses of enchantment*. New York: Vintage.

Beyer, L. E. (1991). Schooling, moral commitment and the preparation of teachers. *Journal of Teacher Education*, 42(3), 205–215.

Bloom, A. (1987). *The closing of the American mind*. New York: Simon & Schuster.

Bloom, B. S. (1971). Mastery learning and its implications for curriculum development. In E. Eisner (Ed.), *Confronting curriculum reform* (pp. 17–49). Boston: Little, Brown.

Bok, D. (1982). *Beyond the ivory tower: Social responsibilities of the modern university*. Cambridge, MA: Harvard University Press.

Bok, S. (1978). *Lying: Moral choice in public and private life*. New York: Pantheon.

Boyd, W. L., & Walberg, H. J. (Eds.). (1990). *Choice in education: Potential and problems*. Berkeley: McCutchan.

Boyer, E. L. (1983). *High school*. New York: Harper & Row.

Boyer, E. L. (1990). *Scholarship reconsidered: Priorities of the professoriate*. Princeton, NJ: Carnegie Foundation for the Advancement of Teaching.

Boyer, E. L. (1991). *Ready to learn: A mandate for the nation*. Princeton, NJ: Carnegie Foundation for the Advancement of Teaching.

Bracey, G. W. (1989). Why so much education research is irrelevant, imitative and ignored. *American School Board Journal, 70*(7), 20–22.

Bracey, G. W. (1990). Rethinking school and university roles. *Educational Leadership, 47*(8), 65–66.

Bracey, G. W. (1991). Why can't they be like we were? *Phi Delta Kappan, 73*(2), 104–118.

Brandon, E. P. (1987). *Do teachers care about truth?* London: Allen & Unwin.

Bruner, J. (1974). *The process of education*. New York: Vintage.

Buchmann, M. (1990). Beyond the lonely, choosing will: Professional development in teacher thinking. *Teachers College Record, 91*(4), 481–508.

Calfee, R. (Ed.). (1987). *The study of Stanford and the schools: Part II: The research*. Stanford University: School of Education.

Carnegie Forum on Education and the Economy. (1986). *A nation prepared: Teachers for the twenty-first century*. Hyattsville, MD: Carnegie Foundation.

Carr, W. (1986). Theories of theory and practice. *Journal of Philosophy of Education, 20*(2), 176–186.

Carr-Saunders, A. M., & Wilson, P. A. (1964). *The professions*. London: Cass.

Choppin, B. (1982). Is education getting any better? *British Educational Research Journal, 7*(1), 3–17.

Chubb, J. E., & Moe, T. M. (1990). *Politics, markets and America's schools*. Washington, DC: Brookings Institute.

Clandinin, J., & Hogan, P. (1991). *Collaboration as improvisatory art guided by an ethic of caring*. Unpublished manuscript.

Clark, C. M., & Peterson, P. L. (1986). Teachers' thought processes. In M. C. Wittrock (Ed.), *Handbook of research on teaching* (pp. 255–296). New York: Macmillan.

Clark, R. M. (1983). *Family life and school achievement: Why poor black children succeed or fail*. Chicago: University of Chicago Press.

Clark, R. W. (1988). School–university relationships: An interpretive view. In K. A. Sirotnik & J. I. Goodlad (Eds.), *School–university partnerships: Concepts, cases and concerns* (pp. 32–67). New York: Teachers College Press.

Clifford, G., & Guthrie, J. W. (1990). *Ed school*. Berkeley: University of California Press.

Coleman, J. S., & Husen, T. (1985). *Becoming adult in a changing society*. Paris: Center for Educational Research and Innovation, Organization for Economic Cooperation and Development.

College Board, Educational Equality Project. (1983). *Academic preparation for college: What students need to know and be able to do*. New York: Author.

Corey, S. (1953). *Action research to improve school practices*. New York: Teachers College Bureau of Publications.

Corwin, R. G. (1965). Teachers as professional employees: Role conflicts in the public schools. In R. G. Corwin (Ed.), *A sociology of education* (pp. 217–264). New York: Appleton-Century-Crofts.

Cremin, L. (1989). *Popular education and its discontents*. New York: Harper & Row.

Cusick, P. (1983). *The egalitarian school and the American high school*. New York: Longman.

Cusick, P., & Wheeler, C. W. (1988). Educational morality and organizational reform. *American Journal of Education, 96*(2), 231–255.

Darling-Hammond, L. (1988). Policy and professionalism. In Ann Leiberman (Ed.), *Building a professional culture in schools* (pp. 55–78). New York: Teachers College Press.

Darling-Hammond, L. (1990). Accountability for professional practice. *Teachers College Record, 91*(1), 59–80.

Darling-Hammond, L., & Berry, B. (1988). *The evolution of teacher policy*. Washington, DC: Rand Corporation.

Davies, H. M., & Aquino, J. T. (1975). Collaboration in continuing professional development. *Journal of Teacher Education, 26*, 274–277.

Dearden, R. F., Hirst, P. H., & Peters, R. S. (Eds.). (1973). *Education and the development of reason*. London: Routledge & Kegan Paul.

Derber, C. (1982). *Professionals as workers: Mental labor in advanced capitalism*. Boston: Hall.

Downie, R. S. (1990). Professions and professionalism. *Journal of Philosophy of Education, 24*(2), 147–161.

Downie, R. S., Telfer, E., & Loudfoot, E. (1974). *Education and personal relationships*. London: Methuen.

Dray, W. H. (1964). *Philosophy of history*. Englewood Cliffs, NJ: Prentice-Hall.

Dunn, J. (1980). *Western democratic theory in the face of the future*. Cambridge, England: Cambridge University Press.

Durkheim, E. (1951). *Suicide*. Glencoe, IL: Free Press (Original work published 1897).

Eames, S. M. (1970). Dewey's theory of valuation. In J. A. Boydston (Ed.), *Guide to works of John Dewey* (pp. 183–200). Carbondale, IL: Southern Illinois Press.

Education Commission of the States. (1983). *Task Force on Education for Economic Growth*. Denver: Education Commission of the States.

Egan, K. (1986). *Individual development and the curriculum*. London: Hutchinson.

Ehrenreich, B., & Ehrenreich, J. (1979). The professional-managerial class war. In P. Walker (Ed.), *Between labor and capital* (pp. 173–192). Boston: South End.

Eisner, E. (Ed.). (1985). *Eighty-fourth yearbook of the National Society for the Study of Education. Part II: Learning and teaching the ways of knowing*. Chicago: University of Chicago Press.

Elkind, D. (1984). *All grown up and nowhere to go*. Reading, MA: Addison-Wesley.

Elliott, J. (1991). *Action research and educational change*. Buckingham, England: Open University Press.

Elliott, J., & Adelman, C. (1974). *The Ford Teaching Project*. Norwich, England: Center for Applied Research in Education, University of East Anglia.

Elliott, J., & Adelman, C. (1983). Reflecting where the action is. *Education for Teaching*, 92, 8–20.

Elliott, J., Bridges, D., Ebbutt, D., Gibson, R., & Nias, J. (1975). *School accountability*. London: Grant McIntyre.

Emmett, D. (1958). *Function, purpose and powers*. London: Macmillan.

England, H. (1986). *Social work as art*. London: Allen & Unwin.

Feiman-Nemser, S., & Floden, R. E. (1986). The cultures of teaching. In M. C. Wittrock (Ed.), *Handbook of research on teaching* (pp. 505–527). New York: Macmillan.

Fenstermacher, G. D. (1986). Philosophy of research on teaching: Three aspects. In M. C. Wittrock (Ed.), *Handbook of research on teaching* (pp. 37–50). New York: Macmillan.

Finn, C. E. (1991). *We must take charge: Our schools and our future*. Glencoe, IL: Free Press.

Finn, C. E., & Ravitch, D. (1987). *What do our 17-year-olds know?* New York: Harper & Row.

Fox, J. (1990). *The impact of research on education policy* (OR 980-522). Washington, DC: Office of Educational Research and Innovation, US Department of Education.

Frankena, W. K. (1963). *Ethics*. Englewood Cliffs, NJ: Prentice-Hall.

Freedman, S. (1990). *Small victories: The real world of a teacher, her students and their high school*. New York: Harper & Row.

Freeman, M. D. A. (1983). *The rights and wrongs of children*. Dover, NH: Pinter.

Friedman, M. (1972). *Capitalism and freedom*. Chicago: University of Chicago Press.

Gilligan, C. (1979). Woman's place in man's life cycle. *Harvard Educational Review*, 49(1), 431–446.

Gilligan, C. (1982). *In a different voice: Psychological theory and women's development*. Cambridge, MA: Harvard University Press.

Gilligan, C., & Attanucci, J. (1988). Two moral orientations: Gender differences and similarities. *Merrill-Palmer Quarterly*, 34(3), 223–237.

Gilligan, C., Lyons, N. P., & Hammer, T. (1990). *Making connections: The relational world of adolescents at Emma Willard School*. Cambridge, MA: Harvard University Press.

Gitlin, A. (1990). Understanding teaching dialogically. *Teachers College Record*, 91(4), 537–561.

Goldman, A. H. (1980). *The moral foundations of professional ethics*. Totowa, NJ: Rowman & Littlefield.

Good, T. L., & Brophy, J. E. (1986). School effects. In M. C. Wittrock (Ed.), *Handbook of research on teaching* (pp. 570–605). New York: Macmillan.

Goodlad, J. I. (1984). *A place called school: Prospects for the future*. New York: McGraw-Hill.

Goodlad, J. I. (1990). *Teachers for our nation's schools*. San Francisco: Jossey-Bass.

Goodlad, J. I., & Sirotnik, K. A. (1988). The future of school-university partnerships. In K. A. Sirotnik & J. I. Goodlad (Eds.), *School-university partnerships: Concepts, cases and concerns* (pp. 205-224). New York: Teachers College Press.

Gouldner, A. (1978). The new class project. *Theory and Society, 6*(2), 89-99.

Gowin, D. B. (1981). *Educating.* Ithaca, NY: Cornell University Press.

Graham, P. A. (1983). An exciting and challenging year. *Harvard Graduate School of Education Association Bulletin, 28*(1), 2-3.

Graham, P. A. (1991). What America has expected of its schools over the past century. Address to Benton Center Conference on Democracy and Education, University of Chicago.

Grant, G. E. (1988). *The world we created at Hamilton High.* Cambridge, MA: Harvard University Press.

Grant, G. E. (1991). Ways of constructing classroom meaning. *Journal of Curriculum Studies, 23*(5), 397-409.

Graves, R. (1966). *Goodbye to all that.* Harmondsworth: Penguin.

Greene, M. (1986). Philosophy and teaching. In M. C. Wittrock (Ed.), *Handbook of research on teaching* (pp. 479-505). New York: Macmillan.

Greer, P. (1990). *The Boston University-Chelsea Public Schools first annual report.* Boston: Boston University.

Griffin, G. R. (1986). Clinical teacher education. In J. V. Hoffman & S. A. Edwards (Eds.), *Reality and reform in clinical teacher education.* New York: Random House.

Gudmundsdottir, S. (1991). Ways of seeing are ways of knowing. The pedagogical content knowledge of an expert English teacher. *Journal of Curriculum Studies, 23*(5), 409-423.

Guttmann, A. (1987). *Democratic education.* Princeton, NJ: Princeton University Press.

Halberstam, D. (1990). *The next century.* New York: Morrow.

Hall, S., & Clark, C. M. (1991). Real lessons from imaginary teachers. *Journal of Curriculum Studies, 23*(5), 429-435.

Hall, S., & Grant, G. E. (1991). On what is known and seen: A conversation with a research participant. *Journal of Curriculum Studies, 23*(5), 423-429.

Hamlyn, D. W. (1970). *The theory of knowledge.* London: Macmillan.

Hare, R. M. (1962). *The language of morals.* Oxford, England: Clarendon.

Hargreaves, A., & Dawe, R. (1989). *Coaching as unreflective practice: Contrived collegiality or collaborative culture.* Unpublished manuscript, American Educational Research Association, San Francisco.

Harre, R. (1983). *Personal being.* Oxford, England: Blackwell.

Harre, R., & Secord, P. F. (1972). *The explanation of social behavior.* Oxford, England: Blackwell.

Hart, H. L. A. (1961). *The concept of law.* Oxford, England: Oxford University Press.

Haydon, G. (Ed.). (1987). *Education and values.* London: University of London Press.

Hess, G. A. (1990). *Chicago school reform: What it is and how it came to be.* Chicago: Chicago Panel on Public School Policy and Finance.

Hill, P. T., & Bonan, J. (1991). *Decentralization and accountability in public education.* Santa Monica, CA: Rand Corporation.

Hill, P. T., Foster, G. E., & Gendler, T. (1989). *High schools with character.* Santa Monica, CA: Rand Corporation.

Hirsch, F. (1977). *The social limits to growth.* London: Routledge & Kegan Paul.

Hirst, P. H. (1972). *Knowledge and the curriculum.* London: Routledge & Kegan Paul.

Hodgkinson, H. (1991). Reform versus reality. *Phi Delta Kappan, 73*(1), 8–17.

Hollingsworth, S. (1989). Prior beliefs and cognitive change in learning to teach. *American Educational Research Journal, 26*(2), 160–189.

Hollingsworth, S. (1990). Teachers as researchers: Writing to learn about ourselves—and others. *Quarterly of the National Writing Project and the Center for the Study of Writing, 12*(4), 10–18.

Hollingsworth, S. (1992). Learning to teach through collaborative conversation: A feminist approach. *American Educational Research Journal, 29*(2), 373–405.

Hollingsworth, S., & Sockett, H. T. (in press). *Teacher research and educational reform.* Chicago: National Society for the Study of Education.

Hollis, M. (1975). My role and its duties. In R. S. Peters (Ed.), *Nature and conduct* (pp. 89–107). London: Routledge & Kegan Paul.

Hollis, M. (1977). *Models of man: Philosophical thoughts on social action.* Cambridge, England: Cambridge University Press.

Hollis, M. (1982). Education as a positional good. *Journal of Philosophy of Education, 16*(2), 235–244.

Holmes, M. (1988). The fortress monastery: The future of the common core. In A. C. Purves & I. Westbury (Eds.), *Eighty-seventh yearbook of the National Society for the Study of Education: Cultural literacy and the idea of general education* (pp. 231–259). Chicago: University of Chicago Press.

Holmes Group. (1986). *Tomorrow's teachers.* East Lansing, MI: Author.

Holmes Group. (1989). *Tomorrow's schools.* East Lansing, MI: Author.

Hoyle, E. (1980). Professionalization and deprofessionalization in education. In E. Hoyle & J. E. Meggary (Eds.), *The professional development of teachers* (pp. 42–57). London: Kogan Page.

Huberman, M. (1988). Teacher careers and school improvement. *Journal of Curriculum Studies, 20*(2), 119–133.

Huberman, M. (1989). The professional life cycle of teachers. *Teachers College Record, 91*(1), 31–58.

Illich, I. (1977). *Disabling professions.* London: Boyars.

Institute for Educational Transformation. (1992). *Prototypes for America 2000* (Proposal to the New American Schools Development Corporation). Fairfax, VI: Author.

Jackson, J. A. (1970). *Professions and professionalization.* Cambridge, England: Cambridge University Press.

Jackson, P. W. (1968). *Life in classrooms.* New York: Holt, Rinehart & Winston.

Jackson, P. W. (1986). *The practice of teaching.* New York: Teachers College Press.

Jackson, P. W. (1987). Facing our ignorance. *Teachers College Record, 88*(3), 388.

James, W. (1972). *Teacher education and training.* London: Her Majesty's Stationery Office.

Johnson, H. C. (1987). Society, culture and character development. In K. Ryan & G. F. McLean (Eds.), *Character development in schools and beyond* (pp. 59–97). Westport, CT: Praeger.

Kean, T. H. (1986). Who will teach? *Phi Delta Kappan, 68*(4), 205–207.

Kearns, D. (1988). An educational recovery plan for America. *Phi Delta Kappan, 71*(2), 107–112.

Keating, P. J., & Clark, R. W. (1988). Accent on leadership. In K. A. Sirotnik & J. I. Goodlad (Eds.), *School–university partnerships: Concepts, cases and concerns* (pp. 148–169). New York: Teachers College Press.

Kennedy, J. F. (1956). *Profiles in courage.* New York: Harper & Row.

Kennedy, P. (1987). *The rise and fall of the great powers: Military and economic conflict from 1500–2000.* New York: Random House.

Kirst, M. W. (1984). *Who controls our schools? American values in conflict.* New York: Freeman.

Kirst, M. W. (1991). *Accountability: Implications for state and local policy-makers* (IS 90-982). Washington, DC: Office of Educational Research and Innovation.

Kleibard, H. M. (1988). Fads, fashions and rituals: The instability of curriculum change. In L. N. Tanner (Ed.), *Critical issues in curriculum* (pp. 16–34). Chicago: National Society for the Study of Education.

Kleinig, J. (1981). Compulsory schooling. *Journal of Philosophy of Education, 15*(2), 191–205.

Kogan, M. (1986). *Educational accountability: An analytic overview.* London: Hutchinson.

Kogan, M. (1990). Accountability and teacher professionalism. In W. Carr (Ed.), *Quality in teaching: Arguments for a reflective profession* (pp. 135–144). London: Falmer.

Kohlberg, L. (1981). *Essays on moral development, Volume One: The philosophy of moral development.* San Francisco: Harper & Row.

Kohlberg, L. (1984). *Essays on moral development, Volume Two: The psychology of moral development.* San Francisco: Harper & Row.

Kohn, A. (1991). Teaching children to care. *Phi Delta Kappan, 72*(7), 496–507.

Kottkampf, R. B., Provenzo, E. F., & Cohn, M. M. (1986). Stability and change in a profession: Two decades of teacher attitudes, 1964–1984. *Phi Delta Kappan, 559–567.*

Kozol, J. (1991). *Savage inequalities: Children in America's schools.* New York: Crown.

Krimmermann, L. I. (1978). Compulsory education: A moral critique. In K. A. Strike & K. Egan (Eds.), *Ethics and educational policy* (pp. 79–105). London: Routledge & Kegan Paul.

Kubey, R., & Csikszentimihalyi, M. (1990). *Television and the quality of life: How viewing shapes everyday experience.* Hillsdale, NJ: Erlbaum.

Labbett, B. (1989). Skillful neglect. In J. F. Schostak (Ed.), *Breaking into the curriculum* (pp. 89–105). London: Methuen.

Laird, S. (1988). Reforming "women's true profession": A case for feminist peda-gogy in teacher education? *Harvard Educational Review, 58*(4), 449-464.

Langford, G. (1978). *Teaching as a profession.* Manchester, England: Manchester University Press.

Lanier, J. E., & Little, J. W. (1986). Research on teacher education. In M. C. Wittrock (Ed.), *Handbook of research on teaching* (pp. 527-550). New York: Macmillan.

Lessinger, L. M., & Tyler, R. W. (1971). (Eds.). *Accountability in education.* Worth-ington, OH: Charles A. Jones.

Levin, K. (1946). Action research and minority problems. *Journal of Social Issues, 2,* 24-46.

Lieberman, A. (1988). *Building a professional culture in schools.* New York: Teachers College Press.

Lieberman, A., & Miller, L. (1990). Teacher development in professional practice schools. *Teachers College Record, 91*(1), 105-122.

Lightfoot, S. L. (1978). *Worlds apart.* New York: Basic Books.

Lightfoot, S. L. (1983). *The good high school.* New York: Basic Books.

Little, J. W. (1987). Teachers as colleagues. In V. Richardson-Koehler (Ed.), *The educator's handbook: Research into practice* (pp. 491-519). New York: Longman.

Little, J. W. (1990). The persistence of privacy: Autonomy and initiative in teach-ers professional relations. *Teachers College Record, 91*(4), 509-536.

Lortie, D. C. (1975). *Schoolteacher.* Chicago: University of Chicago Press.

Lovass, O. I. (1967). A behavioral therapy approach to the treatment of childhood schizophrenia. In J. Hill (Ed.), *Symposia on child development* (pp. 108-159). Minneapolis: University of Minnesota Press.

Lyons, N. (1990). Dilemmas of knowing: Ethical and epistemological dimensions of teachers' works and development. *Harvard Educational Review, 60*(2), 159-181.

Lytle, S., & Cochran-Smith, M. (1990a). Learning from teacher research: A work-ing typology. *Teachers College Record, 92*(1), 83-103.

Lytle, S., & Cochran-Smith, M. (1990b). Research on teaching and teacher research: The issues that divide. *Educational Researcher, 19*(2), 2-11.

Macdonald, B. (1977). Hard times: Educational accountability in England. *Educa-tional Analysis, 1*(1), 18-28.

Macdonald, J. P. (1988). The emergence of the teacher's voice: Implications for the new reform. *Teachers College Record, 89*(4), 82-90.

MacIntyre, A. (1984). *After Virtue* (2nd ed.). Notre Dame, IN: University of Notre Dame Press.

MacIntyre, A. (1988). *Whose justice? whose rationality?* Notre Dame, IN: Univer-sity of Notre Dame Press.

Madaus, G. (1988). The influence of testing on the curriculum. In L. N. Tanner (Ed.), *Critical issues in curriculum* (pp. 83-122). Chicago: University of Chicago Press.

Malan, R. (1990). *A traitor's gate.* New York: Atlantic Monthly.

Marchese, T. (1991, November). TQM reaches the academy. *American Association of Higher Education Bulletin,* pp. 3-13.

McKernan, J. (1988). The countenance of curriculum action research: Traditional, collaborative and emancipatory-critical conceptions. *Journal of Curriculum and Supervision, 3*(3), 179.

McLaughlin, M. W., & Lee, S. M. (1988). School as a place to have a career. In A. Lieberman (Ed.), *Building a professional culture in schools* (pp. 23-45). New York: Teachers College Press.

Mill, J. S. (1950). On the logic of the moral sciences. In E. Nagel (Ed.), *Mill's philosophy on scientific method.* New York: Hafner. (Original work published 1843).

Mischel, T. (Ed.). (1969). *Human action.* New York: Academic.

Mischel, T. (Ed.). (1971). *Cognitive development and epistemology.* New York: Academic.

Mischel, T. (Ed.). (1974). *Understanding other persons.* Oxford, England: Blackwell.

Mohr, M. M., & MacLean, M. S. (1987). *Working together: A guide for teacher researchers.* Urbana, IL: National Council of Teachers of English.

Murdoch, I. (1970). *The sovereignty of good.* London: Routledge & Kegan Paul.

National Board for Professional Teaching Standards. (1989). *Towards high and rigorous standards for the teaching profession.* Detroit: Author.

National Center on Education and the Economy. (1990). *America's choice: High skills or low wages!* New York: Author.

National Commission for Excellence in Teacher Education. (1985). *A call for change in teacher education.* Washington, DC: American Association of Colleges of Teacher Education.

National Commission on Children. (1991). *Beyond rhetoric: A new American agenda for children and families.* National Commission on Children, Washington, DC.

National Commission on Excellence in Education. (1983). *A nation at risk.* Washington, DC: U.S. Government Printing Office.

National Governors Association. (1986). *Time for results: The governors' 1991 report on education.* Washington, DC: Author.

Nias, J. (1975). The nature of trust. In J. Elliott, D. Bridges, D. Ebbutt, R. Gibson, & J. Nias (Eds.), *School accountability* (pp. 211-224). London: Grant McIntyre.

Noddings, N. (1984). *Caring: A feminine approach to ethics and moral education.* Berkeley: University of California Press.

Noddings, N. (1988). An ethic of caring and its implications for instructional arrangements. *American Journal of Education, 96*(2), 215-231.

Oakeshott, M. (1967). *Rationalism in politics and other essays.* London: Methuen.

Oja, S. N., & Smulyan, L. (1989). *Collaborative action research: A developmental approach.* London: Falmer.

Olson, J. (1991). The concept of the expert and its limitations for practice. Unpublished manuscript, Canadian Society for the Study of Education, Kingston, Ontario.

Paley, V. (1984). *Boys and girls: Superheroes in the doll corner.* Chicago: University of Chicago Press.

Parish, R., Underwood, E., & Eubanks, E. E. (1986-87). We do not make change: School-university collaboration. *Metropolitan Education, 5,* 44-55.

Patterson, R. W. K. (1979). *Values, education and the adult.* London: Routledge & Kegan Paul.

Peters, R. S. (1966). *Ethics and education.* London: Allen and Unwin.

Peters, R. S. (1979a). Michael Oakeshott's philosophy of education. In R. S. Peters (Ed.), *Psychology and ethical development* (pp. 433–457). London: Allen & Unwin.

Peters, R. S. (1979b). *Psychology and ethical development.* London: Routledge & Kegan Paul.

Phenix, P. H. (1964). *Realms of meaning.* New York: McGraw-Hill.

Piaget, J. (1968). *Play, dreams and imitation in childhood.* London: Routledge & Kegan Paul.

Pincoffs, E. L. (Ed.). (1975). *The concept of academic freedom.* Austin: University of Texas Press.

Pine, G. J., & Keane, W. G. (1990). School–university partnerships: Lessons learned. *Record in Educational Administration and Supervision, 11*(1), 19.

Polanyi, M. (1960). *Personal knowledge.* Oxford, England: Oxford University Press.

Postman, N. (1984). *The disappearance of childhood.* New York: Dell Publishing Co.

Power, C., Higgins, A., & Kohlberg, L. (1989). The habit of the common life: Building character through democratic community schools. In L. P. Nucci (Ed.), *Moral development and character education: A dialogue* (pp. 125–145). Berkeley: McCutchan.

Price, C. W. (1922). Ethics of the mechanical engineer. *Annals of the American Association of Political and Social Science, 101*(73), 71–84.

Pring, R. A. (1972). Bloom's taxonomy: A philosophical critique II. *Cambridge Journal of Education, 2,* 1–11.

Quinton, A. (1987). On the ethics of belief. In G. Haydon (Ed.), *Education and values* (pp. 37–55). London: University of London Press.

Rawls, J. (1963). A sense of justice. *The Philosophical Review, 62,* 281–305.

Rawls, J. (1972). *A theory of justice.* Oxford, England: Oxford University Press.

Reeves, T. C. (1991). *A question of character: A life of John F. Kennedy.* Glencoe, IL: Free Press.

Reynolds, M. C. (Ed.). (1989). *Knowledge base for the beginning teacher.* New York: Pergamon.

Richardson-Koehler, V. (1988). What works and what doesn't. *Journal of Curriculum Studies, 20*(1), 71–79.

Rogers, D., & Webb, J. (1991). The ethics of caring in teacher education. *Journal of Teacher Education, 42*(3), 173–181.

Rorty, R. (1989). *Contingency, irony, and solidarity.* Cambridge, England: Cambridge University Press.

Rosenshine, B. V. (1971). *Teaching behaviors and student achievement.* Slough, England: National Foundation for Educational Research.

Rudduck, J. (1991). *Innovation and change.* Buckingham, England: Open University Press.

Ryan, K. (1987). The moral education of teachers. In K. Ryan & G. F. McLean (Eds.), *Character development in schools and beyond* (pp. 358-380). Westport, CT: Praeger.

Ryle, G. (1963). *The concept of mind.* Harmondsworth, England: Penguin.

Ryle, G. (1973). Can virtue be taught? In R. F. Dearden, P. H. Hirst, & R. S. Peters (Eds.), *Education and the development of reason* (pp. 434-447). London: Routledge & Kegan Paul.

Sadker, M., Sadker, D., & Klein, S. (1991). The issue of gender in elementary and secondary education. In G. Grant (Ed.), *Review of research in Education 17* (pp. 269-335). Washington, DC: American Education Research Association.

Sanger, J. (1989). *Awakening a stream of consciousness: The role of the critical group in action-research.* Unpublished manuscript, Norwich City College, England.

Schlechty, P. C., & Whitford, B. L. (1988). Shared problems and shared vision: Organic collaboration. In K. A. Sirotnik & J. I. Goodlad (Eds.), *School-university partnerships: Concepts, cases and concerns* (pp. 191-205). New York: Teachers College Press.

Schön, D. A. (1983). *The reflective practitioner.* London: Temple Smith.

Schön, D. A. (1989). *Educating the reflective practitioner.* San Francisco: Jossey-Bass.

Schrag, F. (1978). From childhood to adulthood: Assigning rights and responsibilities. In K. A. Strike & K. Egan (Eds.), *Ethics and educational policy* (pp. 61-79). London: Routledge & Kegan Paul.

Schrag, F. (1989). Values in educational inquiry. *American Journal of Education, 97*(2), 171-184.

Shulman, L. S. (1986a). Paradigms and research programs in the study of teaching. In M. C. Wittrock (Ed.), *Handbook of research on teaching* (pp. 3-37). New York: Macmillan.

Shulman, L. S. (1986b). Those who understand: Knowledge growth in teaching. *Educational Researcher, 15*(2), 4-14.

Shulman, L. S. (1987). Knowledge and teaching: Foundations of the new reform. *Harvard Educational Review, 57*(1), 1-22.

Shulman, L. S. (1988). The wisdom of practice. In D. C. Berliner & B. V. Rosenshine (Eds.), *Talks to teachers: A festschrift for N. L. Gage* (pp. 369-386). New York: Random House.

Shulman, L. S. (1989). Sounding the alarm: A reply to Sockett. *Harvard Educational Review, 57*(4), 473-481.

Shulman, L. S. (1990). Aristotle had it right: On knowledge and pedagogy (*Occasional Paper No. 4).* East Lansing, MI: Holmes Group.

Silber, J. (1983). *Straight shooting: what's wrong with America and how to fix it.* New York: Harper & Row.

Sirotnik, K. A. (1988). The meaning and conduct of inquiry in school-university partnerships. In K. A. Sirotnik & J. I. Goodlad (Eds.), *School-university partnerships: Concepts, cases and concerns* (pp. 169-191). New York: Teachers College Press.

Sirotnik, K. A., & Goodlad, J. I. (Eds.). (1988). *School-university partnerships: Concepts, cases and concerns.* New York: Teachers College Press.

Sizer, N. F., & Sizer, T. R. (Eds.). (1970). *Moral education.* Cambridge, MA: Harvard University Press.

Sizer, T. R. (1984). *Horace's compromise: The dilemma of the American high school.* Boston: Houghton Mifflin.

Skinner, B. F. (1975). *Beyond freedom and dignity.* New York: Knopf.

Smith, P. (1990). *Killing the spirit: Higher Education in America.* New York: Viking/Penguin.

Sockett, H. T. (1971). Bloom's taxonomy: A philosophical critique I. *Cambridge Journal of Education, 1*(1), 1–12.

Sockett, H. T. (1980). Educational research and the challenge of continuing education. *Aspects of Education, 24,* 46–53.

Sockett, H. T. (1987). Has Shulman got the strategy right? *Harvard Educational Review, 57*(2), 208–21.

Sockett, H. T. (1988). Education and will: Aspects of personal capability. *American Journal of Education, 92*(2), 195–214.

Sockett, H. T. (1989a). A moral epistemology of practice. *Cambridge Journal of Education, 19*(1), 33–41.

Sockett, H. T. (1989b). Practical professionalism. In W. Carr (Ed.), *Quality in teaching: Arguments for a reflective profession* (pp. 115–135). London: Falmer.

Sockett, H. T. (1989c). Research, practice and professionalism. *Journal of Curriculum Studies, 2*(1), 97–113.

Sockett, H. T. (1990). Accountability, trust and ethical codes of practice. In J. I. Goodlad, R. Soder, & K. A. Sirotnik (Eds.), *The moral dimensions of teaching* (pp. 224–251). San Francisco: Jossey-Bass.

Sockett, H. T. (1992). The moral aspects of the curriculum. In P. W. Jackson (Ed.), *Handbook of research on curriculum* (pp. 543–569). New York: Macmillan.

Steifels, P. (1979). *The neoconservatives.* New York: Simon & Schuster.

Stenhouse, L. (1970). *The humanities project: An introduction.* London: Heinemann.

Stenhouse, L. (1975). *An introduction to curriculum research and development.* London: Heinemann.

Stenhouse, L. (1982). *Teaching about race relations.* London: Routledge & Kegan Paul.

Stenhouse, L. (1983). *Authority, education and emancipation.* London: Heinemann.

Stout, J. (1988). *Ethics after Babel: The languages of morals and their discontents.* Boston: Beacon.

Strike, K. A. (1991). The moral role of schooling in a liberal democratic society. In G. A. Grant (Ed.), *Review of research in education 17* (pp. 413–477). Washington, DC: American Educational Research Association.

Strike, K. A., & Soltis, J. F. (1985). *The ethics of teaching.* New York: Teachers College Press.

Sykes, C. J. (1988). *Profscam: Professors and the demise of higher education.* New York: St. Martins Press.

Tanner, D. (1988). The textbook controversies. In L. N. Tanner (Ed.), *Critical issues in curriculum* (pp. 122–148). Chicago: University of Chicago Press.

Taylor, D. M. (1970). *Explanation and meaning.* Cambridge, England: Cambridge University Press.

Tibble, J. W. (Ed.). (1966). *The study of education*. London: Routledge & Kegan Paul.

Timpane, M. (1975). *Youth policy in transition*. Santa Monica, CA: Rand Corporation.

Tom, A. (1984). *Teaching as a moral craft*. New York: Longman.

Tyack, D. B., & Hansot, E. (1982). *Managers of virtue*. New York: Basic Books.

Urmson, J. O. (1969). Saints and heroes. In J. Feinberg (Ed.), *Moral concepts* (pp. 60–74). Oxford, England: Oxford University Press.

U.S. Department of Education. (1986). *What works: Research about teaching and learning*. Washington, DC: Author.

U.S. Department of Education. (1991). *America 2000: An education strategy*. Washington, DC: Author.

Walker, D. F. (1990). *Fundamentals of curriculum*. New York: Harcourt Brace, Jovanovich.

Walton, D. N. (1982). *Courage: A philosophical investigation*. Berkeley: University of California Press.

Walton, M. (1991). *Deming management at work*. New York: Putnam.

White, P. A. (1986). Self-respect, self-esteem and the school: A democratic perspective on authority. *Teachers College Record, 88*, 95–107.

Wilavsky, B. (1992, Winter). Can you not teach morality in public school? *The Responsive Community*, pp. 46–54.

Williams, B. (1981). *Moral luck*. Cambridge, England: Cambridge University Press.

Williams, B. (1987). The primacy of dispositions. In G. Haydon (Ed.). *Education and values* (pp. 56–65). London: University of London Press.

Winch, P. (1968). *Moral integrity*. Oxford, England: Blackwell.

Wittgenstein, L. (1963). *Philosophical investigations* (E. Anscombe, Trans.). Oxford, England: Blackwell.

Zahorik, J. A. (1987). Teachers' collegial interaction: An exploratory study. *The Elementary School Journal, 87*(4), 384–396.

Zeichner, K. (1991). Contradictions and tensions in the professionalization of teaching and the democratization of schools. *Teachers College Record, 92*(3), 363–380.

Index

About the Author

Hugh Sockett graduated from the University of Oxford in 1959 and taught history in an inner-London comprehensive school for five years. He worked at colleges and universities in London, Cambridge, Northern Ireland, and Norwich from 1964 to 1987 and was dean of the School of Education at the University of East Anglia before coming to George Mason University as Director of the Center for Applied Research and Development in Education. He founded the Institute for Educational Transformation in 1990 and is now its president. He holds master's degrees from the universities of Oxford, London, and Cambridge and a Ph.D. in philosophy of education from the University of London. He has published two books and more than 30 articles.